T0383510

THE
FAR EASTERN
FELLS

WALKERS EDITIONS

Published *2015*		*First published*	*First revision*
Book One:	The Eastern Fells	1955	2005
Book Two:	The Far Eastern Fells	1957	2005

Published *2016*		*First published*	*First revision*
Book Three:	The Central Fells	1958	2006

Published *2017*		*First published*	*First revision*
Book Four:	The Southern Fells	1960	2007

Published *2018*		*First published*	*First revision*
Book Five:	The Northern Fells	1962	2008

Published *2019*		*First published*	*First revision*
Book Six:	The North-Western Fells	1964	2008

Published *2020*		*First published*	*First revision*
Book Seven:	The Western Fells	1966	2009

PUBLISHER'S NOTE

Fellwalking can be dangerous, especially
in wet, windy, foggy or icy conditions.
Please be sure to take sensible precautions
when out on the fells. As A. Wainwright himself
frequently wrote: use your common sense
and watch where you are putting your feet.

A PICTORIAL GUIDE
TO THE
LAKELAND FELLS
WALKERS EDITION
REVISED BY CLIVE HUTCHBY

being an illustrated account
of a study and exploration
of the mountains in the
English Lake District
by

AWainwright

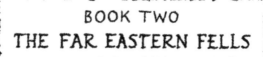

BOOK TWO
THE FAR EASTERN FELLS

Frances Lincoln Publishing
74–77 White Lion Street
Islington
London N1 9PF
www.QuartoKnows.com

First published by Henry Marshall, Kentmere, 1957
First published by Frances Lincoln 2003
Second (revised) edition published by Frances Lincoln, 2005
Reprinted with minor corrections 2007
Walkers (revised) edition published by Frances Lincoln, 2015

Printed and bound in the United Kingdom.

A CIP catalogue for this book
is available from the British Library

ISBN 978 0 7112 3655 4

2 4 6 8 8 9 7 5 3 1

THIS REVISED AND UPDATED EDITION PUBLISHED BY
FRANCES LINCOLN, LONDON

THE FAR EASTERN FELLS

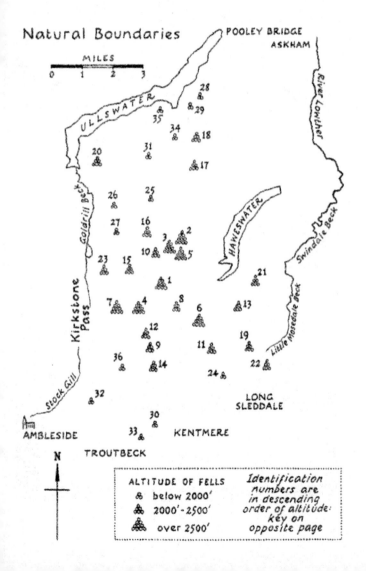

Natural Boundaries

POOLEY BRIDGE
ASKHAM

MILES
0   1   2   3

ULLSWATER

River Lowther

28
29
35
34   18
31   17
20
HAWESWATER
26
25
27   16
Swindale Beck
23   15   3   2
10   5
21
1
7   4   8
6   13
Little Mosedale Beck
12
9   11   19
36   14   22
24

LONG
SLEDDALE

32
30
33   KENTMERE
AMBLESIDE
TROUTBECK
N

Goldrill Beck
Kirkstone Pass
Stock Gill

ALTITUDE OF FELLS
& below 2000'
& 2000'-2500'
& over 2500'

Identification
numbers are
in descending
order of altitude:
key on
opposite page

THE FAR EASTERN FELLS

Each fell is the subject
of a separate chapter

INTRODUCTION
TO THE
WALKERS EDITION
BY CLIVE HUTCHBY

When I finished work on *The Wainwright Companion* in April 2012 I never expected that, less than two years later, I would be following literally in the footsteps of AW on his beloved Lakeland fells. And those of Chris Jesty, as well, whose Second Edition revision of the guidebooks spurred me, at the end of 2010, to purchase the complete set for the umpteenth time — oh, how must the publishers have loved me down the years.

The full extent of Chris Jesty's revisions might surprise many people, but to revise books that were half a century old really was a monumental task. A lot had happened in the previous fifty years, and almost as much has followed in the ten years since. Typical changes in that period have been stiles being replaced by gates, new footbridges, paths being repaired — and even re-aligned — by Fix The Fells, the construction of fences and planting of trees, as well as all the usual things that happen when thousands of people tramp the fells: some paths fall out of fashion and others spring up from nowhere.

I have largely succeeded in checking all the recommended routes without paths in the Far Eastern Fells, despite some annoying snow that kept refusing to melt. As I found when researching in the Eastern Fells, some routes that I expected to now be popular are still without any trace of humans having been that way before, while other routes have now become well used. Since the last revision, two paths in particular have changed considerably: much of the route from Garburn Pass to Yoke (up to the intake wall) has been re-surfaced by Fix The Fells, making it a kind of high-level 'super highway'; similarly, the path from Boredale Hause to just below Round How on Place Fell has been given the same treatment. This is perfectly understandable, as both routes are subject to a lot of foot traffic, Garburn to Yoke because it is a part of the hugely popular Kentmere Horseshoe ridge walk, and Place Fell because it is an easily accessible fell (right on Patterdale's doorstep) in one of the most beautiful corners of Lakeland.

Likewise, the tourist path up Wansfell from Stock Ghyll, has now been paved for a considerable part of its length because constant use was causing erosion. The irony is that this route, in my view, is a poor second from Ambleside in terms of beauty, interest and views: that accolade has to go to the ascent *via* Kelsick Scar and the fell's sublime western flank, a route that has not featured in this guidebook until now. On *Wansfell Pike 6* you will find a new ascent diagram, created entirely using Adobe Photoshop software. The Pictorial Guides truly have arrived in the 21st century!

INTRODUCTION TO THE WALKERS EDITION

AW said that he hoped people would use his guidebooks as a basis for their own notes; that is what I have tried to achieve with the changes made in this revision, plus, where space has allowed, I have added information that might be of interest. As in the Second Edition, paths remain in red, but this time a brighter tone and with bolder lines to make them stand out more. Also, I have used three criteria for the paths (formerly they were just *'clear'* and *'intermittent'*); now they are *'clear'*, *'intermittent or thin'* and *'sketchy'*. Of course, if you would like to use AW's original guidebooks as the basis for your own notes, you can still do so, as the original hardback editions remain in print. I'll always have a set in my bookcase.

The Far Eastern Fells are much more well known among fellwalkers than they were in AW's day, but they are still an area where it is possible — *probable* on many fells — to go a whole day without seeing a fellow fellwalker. To walkers who only know Place Fell, Angletarn Pikes, Hallin Fell, Wansfell, High Street and the Kentmere Horseshoe (the most popular parts of the area), I would say: explore! Fells such as Mardale Ill Bell, Caudale Moor and Bonscale Pike offer so much more than you might expect. Even well known fells can offer something new when approached from a different direction. On one memorable early morning I set off past Martindale Old Church into the shy valley of Bannerdale (you can follow the route on *Angletarn Pikes 6*); the scree slope below Heck Crag was a foot deep in crisp white snow that became gold-tinted when the first rays of sunshine appeared above the valley. Crampons on, I climbed to a sudden and astonishing view across a bejewelled Angle Tarn looking to snow covered peaks from Red Screes around to Catstycam. The return, along the lovely ridge of Beda Fell, was just as good.

I would like to thank the following for their help and support in revising Book Two: Maggie Allan (who very kindly researched a number of paths on Loadpot Hill, Wether Hill, Arthur's Pike, Grey Crag and High Raise), Margy Ogg, Chris Jesty, Sean McMahon, Chris Stanbury, Stan Hawrylak, Lesley Ritchie, Andy Beck, Derek Cockell, Jane King and Annie Sellar (from the Wainwright Estate), and (from publishers Frances Lincoln) John Nicoll, Andrew Dunn and Michael Brunström.

Clive Hutchby
Ambleside, September 2015

BOOK TWO

is dedicated to
the memory of

THE MEN WHO BUILT THE STONE WALLS,

which have endured
the storms of centuries
and remain to this day as monuments to
enterprise, perseverance and hard work

INTRODUCTION
BY
AWainwright

INTRODUCTION

Surely there is no other place in this whole wonderful world quite like Lakeland ... no other so exquisitely lovely, no other so charming, no other that calls so insistently across a gulf of distance. All who truly love Lakeland are exiles when away from it.

Here, in small space, is the wonderland of childhood's dreams, lingering far beyond childhood through the span of a man's life: its enchantment grows with passing years and quiet eventide is enriched by the haunting sweetness of dear memories, memories that remain evergreen through the flight of time, that refresh and sustain in the darker days. How many, these memories .... *the moment of wakening, and the sudden joyful realisation that this is to be another day of freedom on the hills ...... the dawn chorus of bird song ...... the delicate lacework of birches against the sky .... morning sun drawing aside the veils of mist; black-stockinged lambs, in springtime, amongst the daffodils .... silver cascades dancing and leaping down bracken steeps ..... autumn colours .... a red fox running over snow .... the silence of lonely hills ...... storm and tempest in the high places, and the unexpected glimpses of valleys dappled in sunlight far beneath the swirling clouds .... rain, and the intimate shelter of lichened walls ....fierce winds on the heights and soft breezes that are no more than gentle caresses .... a sheepdog watching its master ...... the snow and ice and freezing stillnesses of*

midwinter: a white world, rosy-pink as the sun goes down ...... the supreme moment when the top cairn comes into sight at last, only minutes away, after the long climb .... the small ragged sheep that brave the blizzards ...... the symphonies of murmuring streams, unending, with never a discord .... curling smoke from the chimneys of the farm down below amongst the trees, where the day shall end ...... oil lamps in flagged kitchens, huge fires in huge fireplaces, huge suppers .... glittering moonlight on placid waters ...... stars above dark peaks ..... the tranquillity that comes before sleep, when thoughts are of the day that is gone and the day that is to come .... All these memories, and so many more, breathing anew the rare quality and magical atmosphere of Lakeland .... memories that belong to Lakeland, and could not belong in the same way to any other place .... memories that enslave the mind forever.

Many are they who have fallen under the spell of Lakeland, and many are they who have been moved to tell of their affection, in story and verse and picture and song.

This book is one man's way of expressing his devotion to Lakeland's friendly hills. It was conceived, and is born, after many years of inarticulate worshipping at their shrines.

It is, in very truth, a love letter.

Classification and Definition

Any division of the Lakeland fells into geographical districts must necessarily be arbitrary, just as the location of the outer boundaries of Lakeland must always be a matter of opinion. Any attempt to define internal or external boundaries is certain to invite criticism, and he who takes it upon himself to say where Lakeland starts and finishes, or, for example, where the Central Fells merge into the Southern Fells and *which* fells *are* the Central Fells and which the Southern and *why* they need be so classified, must not expect his pronouncements to be generally accepted.

Yet for present purposes some plan of classification and definition must be used. County and parochial boundaries are no help, nor is the recently defined area of the Lakeland National Park, for this book is concerned only with the high ground.

First, the external boundaries. Straight lines linking the extremities of the outlying lakes enclose all the higher fells very conveniently. There are a few fells of lesser height to the north and east, however, that are typically Lakeland in character and cannot properly be omitted: these are brought in, somewhat untidily, by extending the lines in those areas. Thus:

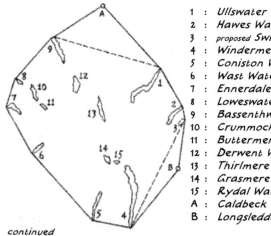

1 : *Ullswater*
2 : *Hawes Water*
3 : proposed *Swindale Resr.*
4 : *Windermere*
5 : *Coniston Water*
6 : *Wast Water*
7 : *Ennerdale Water*
8 : *Loweswater*
9 : *Bassenthwaite Lake*
10 : *Crummock Water*
11 : *Buttermere*
12 : *Derwent Water*
13 : *Thirlmere*
14 : *Grasmere*
15 : *Rydal Water*
A : *Caldbeck*
B : *Longsleddale* (church)

continued

Classification and Definition

continued
The complete Guide includes all the fells in the area enclosed by the straight lines of the diagram. This is an undertaking quite beyond the compass of a single volume, and it is necessary, therefore, to divide the area into convenient sections, making the fullest use of natural boundaries (lakes, valleys and low passes) so that each district is, as far as possible, self-contained and independent of the rest.

This division gives seven areas, each with a well defined group of fells, and each area is the subject of a separate volume

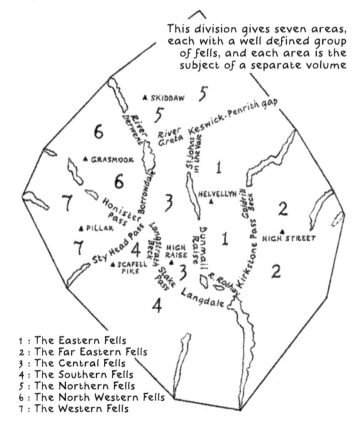

1 : The Eastern Fells
2 : The Far Eastern Fells
3 : The Central Fells
4 : The Southern Fells
5 : The Northern Fells
6 : The North Western Fells
7 : The Western Fells

INTRODUCTION

Notes on the Illustrations

THE MAPS .... Many excellent books have been written about
Lakeland, but the best literature of all for the walker is that
published by the Director General of Ordnance Survey, the 1″ map
for companionship and guidance on expeditions, the 2½″ map for
exploration both on the fells and by the fireside. These admirable
maps are remarkably accurate topographically but there is a
crying need for a revision of the paths on the hills: several
walkers' tracks that have come into use during the past few
decades, some of them now broad highways, are not shown at
all; other paths still shown on the maps have fallen into neglect
and can no longer be traced on the ground.

The popular Bartholomew 1″ map is a
beautiful picture, fit for a frame, but this
too is unreliable for paths; indeed here
the defect is much more serious, for
routes are indicated where no paths
ever existed, nor ever could — the
cartographer has preferred to take
precipices in his stride rather than
deflect his graceful curves over easy
ground.

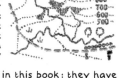

Hence the justification for the maps in this book: they have
the one merit (of importance to walkers) of being dependable as
regards delineation of *paths*. They are intended as supplements
to the Ordnance Survey maps, certainly not as substitutes.

THE VIEWS .... Various devices have
been used to illustrate the views from
the summits of the fells. The full
panorama in the form of an outline
drawing is most satisfactory generally,
and this method has been adopted for
the main viewpoints.

THE DIAGRAMS OF ASCENTS .... The routes of ascent of the
higher fells are depicted by diagrams that do not pretend to
strict accuracy: they are neither plans
nor elevations; in fact there is deliberate
distortion in order to show detail clearly:
usually they are represented as viewed
from imaginary 'space stations'. But it is
hoped they will be useful and interesting.

THE DRAWINGS .... The drawings at least are honest attempts
to reproduce what the eye sees: they illustrate features of
interest and also serve the dual purpose of breaking up the
text and balancing the layout of the pages, and of filling up
awkward blank spaces, like this:

THE
FAR EASTERN
FELLS

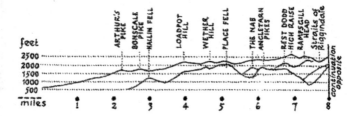

The Far Eastern Fells rise to the east of Kirkstone Pass and the Patterdale valley, which together form a natural western boundary to the group. To north and south these fells run down to low country, and it is on the east side that difficulty arises in fixing a demarcation line, for here high ground continues, to merge ultimately into the Pennines. Nevertheless, it is possible to adopt a satisfactory boundary, not so much by a selection of obvious natural features as by observation of the characteristics of the fells in this area. Lakeland's fells have a charm that is unique: they are romantic in atmosphere, dramatic in appearance, colourful, craggy, with swift-running sparkling streams and tumbled lichened boulders — and the walker along this eastern fringe constantly finds himself passing from the exciting beauty that is typically Lakeland to the quieter and more sombre attractiveness that is typically Pennine. Broadly, this 'aesthetic' boundary runs along the eastern watersheds of Longsleddale, Mosedale and Swindale.

The group has a main spine running through it, due north and south, that keeps consistently above 2000' over a distance of eight miles and culminates midway in the greatest of these fells, High Street. From this central point there is a general decline in altitude

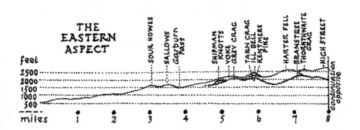

THE EASTERN ASPECT

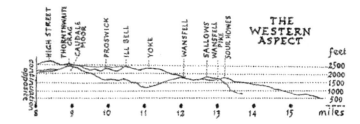

THE
WESTERN
ASPECT

feet
2500
2000
1500
1000
500
miles

towards the boundaries of the group in all directions
but it is not to be inferred that all ridges radiate from
High Street: on the contrary, it is the pivot of a
complicated system of parallel and lateral ridges
separated by deep valleys that contributes greatly to
the attractiveness of these fells east of Kirkstone.

The relative inaccessibility of many of the heights
(due to a decided lack of tourist accommodation in the
valleys) can be the only reason why they remain
lonely and unfrequented by visitors, for in the high
quality of the scenery and the excellence of the walks
they rank with the best. In one respect, indeed, they
are supreme, for their extensive and uplifting views
across to the distant Pennines are a delight not to be
found elsewhere in the district. Solitary walkers will
enjoy the area immensely, but they must tread
circumspectly and avoid accident. Mountain camps
and bivouacs offer the best means of exploration; for
the walker who prefers a bed, Mardale Head used to be
the best centre but now has no hospitality nearer than
the Haweswater Hotel (which is badly sited for
travellers on foot) and the Patterdale valley is most
convenient as a base. The area will be appreciated
best, however, if occasional nights can be arranged
at Howtown, Haweswater, Kentmere and Troutbeck.

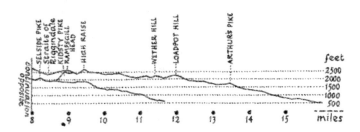

feet
2500
2000
1500
1000
500
miles

Angletarn Pikes 1857'

OS grid ref: NY413148

Howtown •

▲ PLACE FELL
• Patterdale
▲ ANGLETARN
PIKES

• Hartsop

HIGH STREET ▲

MILES
0   1   2   3   4

from Brothers Water

NATURAL FEATURES

The distinctive double summit of Angletarn Pikes is a familiar feature high above the Patterdale valley: the two sharp peaks arrest attention from a distance and are no less imposing on close acquaintance, being attainable only by rock-scrambling, easy or difficult according to choice of route. The western flank of the fell drops steeply in slopes of bracken to the pleasant strath of the Goldrill Beck; on this side Dubhow Crag and Fall Crag are prominent. More precipitous is the eastern face overlooking the quiet deer sanctuary of Bannerdale, where the great bastion of Heck Crag is a formidable object rarely seen by walkers. The fell is a part of a broad curving ridge that comes down from the High Street watershed and continues to Boredale Hause, beyond which Place Fell terminates it abruptly.

The crowning glory of the Pikes, however, is the tarn from which they are named, cradled in a hollow just below the summit. Its indented shore and islets are features unusual in mountain tarns, and it has for long, and deservedly, been a special attraction for visitors to Patterdale. The charms of Angle Tarn, at all seasons of the year, are manifold: in scenic values it ranks amongst the best of Lakeland tarns.

1 : The summit
2 : The summit of Brock Crags
3 : Boredale Hause
4 : Ridge continuing to Beda Fell
5 : Ridge continuing to Rest Dodd
6 : Heck Crag
7 : Fall Crag
8 : Dubhow Crag
9 : Bannerdale
10 : Angle Tarn
11 : Dubhow Beck
12 : Angletarn Beck
13 : Goldrill Beck
14 : Brothers Water
15 : Hayeswater Gill

looking north

Red Screes and Brothers Water from the top of Dubhow Beck

Heck Crag from the Patterdale–Martindale path

MAP

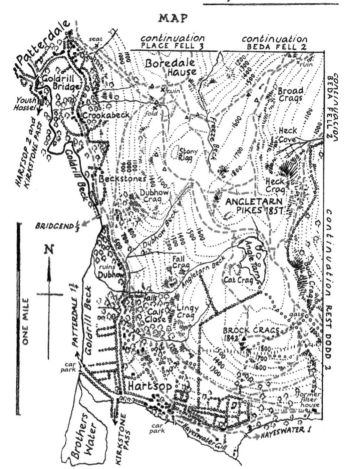

continuation
PLACE FELL 3

continuation
BEDA FELL 2

Patterdale

Goldrill Bridge

Youth Hostel

Crookabeck

Boredale Hause

x ruin

fold

Broad Crags

Heck Cove

Stony Rigg

Beckstones

Dubhow Crag

Heck Crag

ANGLETARN PIKES 1857'

CONTINUATION BEDA FELL 2

BRIDGEND ⅔

N

ONE MILE

Dubhow Beck

Angletarn Beck

Fall Crag

Angle Tarn

Cat Crag

ruins Dubhow

Calf Close

falls

Lingy Crag

BROCK CRAGS 1842'

continuation REST DODD 2

Brock Crag

gate

HARTSOP 2 and KIRKSTONE PASS

PATTERDALE 1¼

Goldrill Beck

car park

Hartsop

former filter house

Brothers Water

KIRKSTONE PASS

car park

Hayeswater Gill

→ HAYESWATER 1

Boredale Hause

For more details about the maze of paths at this busy walkers' crossroads see *Place Fell 4.*

Angle Tarn

Angle Tarn

Angle Tarn is situated at a height of 1571' and is one of the most distinctive of Lakeland tarns, with its five bays, two islands and a narrow peninsula. It measures 420 yards by 285 yards and has a maximum depth 30'.

ASCENT FROM PATTERDALE
1400 feet of ascent : 1¾ miles

Note that this is the initial part of the route to High Street

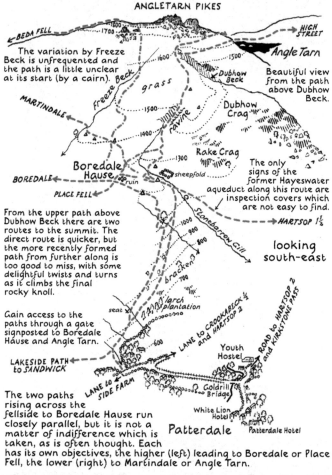

ANGLETARN PIKES

← BEDA FELL

HIGH STREET →

Angle Tarn

The variation by Freeze Beck is unfrequented and the path is a little unclear at its start (by a cairn).

Freeze Beck

grass

Dubhow Beck

Beautiful view from the path above Dubhow Beck.

MARTINDALE →

ravine

Dubhow Crag

Rake Crag

Boredale Hause

ruin

sheepfold

The only signs of the former Hayeswater aqueduct along this route are inspection covers which are not easy to find.

BOREDALE ←

PLACE FELL ←

HARTSOP 1½ →

From the upper path above Dubhow Beck there are two routes to the summit. The direct route is quicker, but the more recently formed path from further along is too good to miss, with some delightful twists and turns as it climbs the final rocky knoll.

Stonebarrow Gill

looking south-east

bracken

Gain access to the paths through a gate signposted to Boredale Hause and Angle Tarn.

seat

larch plantation

LANE to CROOKABECK ¼ and HARTSOP 2

Youth Hostel

ROAD to HARTSOP 2 and KIRKSTONE PASS

LAKESIDE PATH to SANDWICK

LANE to SIDE FARM

Goldrill Bridge

White Lion Hotel

Patterdale

Patterdale Hotel

The two paths rising across the fellside to Boredale Hause run closely parallel, but it is not a matter of indifference which is taken, as is often thought. Each has its own objectives, the higher (left) leading to Boredale or Place Fell, the lower (right) to Martindale or Angle Tarn.

This delightful walk should be in the itinerary of all who stay at Patterdale; the climb is pleasant and the views excellent. Combined with a detour to Angle Tarn, it is an easy half-day's excursion.

ASCENT FROM MARTINDALE
1300 feet of ascent : 3½ miles from Martindale Old Church

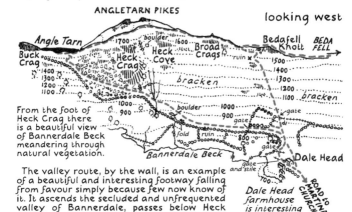

ANGLETARN PIKES

looking west

From the foot of Heck Crag there is a beautiful view of Bannerdale Beck meandering through natural vegetation.

Dale Head farmhouse is interesting architecturally.

The valley route, by the wall, is an example of a beautiful and interesting footway falling from favour simply because few now know of it. It ascends the secluded and unfrequented valley of Bannerdale, passes below Heck Crag by a sporting path on steep scree and crosses a low saddle to Angle Tarn, which comes into view suddenly and dramatically: the highlight of the walk. An easy climb on a good path to the right leads to the top.

The more direct way makes use of the path to Patterdale, but turns left when the ridge is gained and keeps to the Bannerdale edge until the summit is close on the right.

Two routes are illustrated; both are good. If the return is to be made to Martindale, use the valley route below Heck Crag for the ascent (because of the sudden revelation of Angle Tarn, a surprise worth planning) and the ridge route for descent.

THE SUMMIT

The north (main) summit

Angle Tarn from the south summit

Twin upthrusts of rock, 200 yards apart, give individuality to this unusual summit; the northerly is the higher. Otherwise the top is generally grassy, with an extensive peat bog in a depression.

DESCENTS : Routes of ascent may be reversed. (Note that, to find the Bannerdale path that goes below Heck Crag, it is necessary first to descend to Angle Tarn and there turn left at a low saddle and follow the thin but clear path on grass). *In mist*, there is comfort in knowing that the path for Patterdale is only 100 yards distant down the west slope.

THE VIEW

Although the view is largely confined by surrounding heights to a five-mile radius it is full of interest. The abrupt summit gives splendid depth and fall to the prospect south-west, where there is a beautiful picture of Brothers Water and Kirkstonefoot. Deepdale, directly below, is especially well seen.

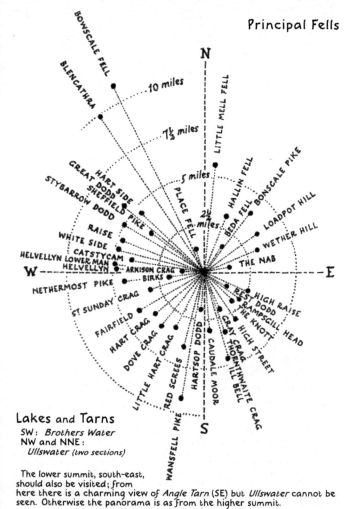

Principal Fells

Lakes and Tarns

SW: *Brothers Water*
NW and NNE:
   Ullswater (two sections)

The lower summit, south-east,
should also be visited; from
here there is a charming view of *Angle Tarn* (SE) but *Ullswater* cannot be seen. Otherwise the panorama is as from the higher summit.

RIDGE ROUTES

BEDA FELL ▲ (BEDA HEAD)

To BEDA FELL, 1670' : 2 miles
NE, then N and NE
*Main depression at 1450'
and several minor depressions*
300 feet of ascent

*An easy walk, the latter part being dull.
Aim for the high knoll north-east, where
an interesting path leads down a narrowing
shoulder (good views of Bannerdale and
Heck Crag here). Beyond the Patterdale-
Martindale path the walk becomes
uninteresting. In mist, Beda Fell
needs care, having precipitous
crags on the eastern
flank. The path must be
adhered to at all times.*

The
Patterdale—
Martindale path
is an easy way
of escape in bad
weather; there
is a cairn where
the paths cross.

Bedafell Knott
ruin
Broad Crags
MARTINDALE

N
ONE MILE
PATTERDALE
Heck Cove
Heck Crag
ANGLETARN PIKES

To REST DODD, 2283'
1¾ miles · SE, then E
Depression at 1600'
700 feet of ascent

*An easy climb;
route confusing in mist.*
Descend to Angle Tarn and
there join the path for High
Street, leaving it at Satura
Crag in favour of a shoulder
that rises to the final dome
*but in mist keep to the fence
and wall from Satura Crag.*

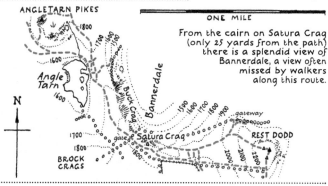

ANGLETARN PIKES

ONE MILE

From the cairn on Satura Crag
(only 25 yards from the path)
there is a splendid view of
Bannerdale, a view often
missed by walkers
along this route.

Angle Tarn
Buck Crag
Bannerdale
gateway
gate
Satura Crag
REST DODD
N
BROCK CRAGS

To PLACE FELL, 2154'
1¾ miles : NW then N : *Depression at 1309' : 875 feet of ascent*
The route *via* Boredale Hause is easy to follow all the way. *Refer to
the maps on Angletarn Pikes 4 and Place Fell 3.*

Arthur's Pike

1747'

OS grid ref: NY460207

- Pooley Bridge
- Askham

▲ ARTHUR'S PIKE

- Howtown

▲ LOADPOT HILL

MILES

0 1 2 3 4

from the Howtown road

NATURAL FEATURES

Arthur's Pike is the northerly termination of the long High Street range, and, like the northerly termination of the parallel Helvellyn range at Clough Head, it contrasts with the usual Lakeland fell structure by exhibiting its crags generally westwards to the afternoon sun; the eastern slopes, which are commonly roughest, are without rock. The steep flank falling to Ullswater has several faces of crag below the summit rim, and, especially around the vicinity of the ravine of Swarthbeck Gill, which forms the southern boundary of the fell, acres of tumbled boulders testify to the roughness of the impending cliffs and the power of the beck in flood. Above the crags, there is little to excite, and the summit merges without much change in elevation into the broad expanses of Loadpot Hill. The gradual, crag-free north-eastern slope is partly clothed with heather.

Note that the scale of the map below is smaller than commonly used in this book (in order to include the full Howtown route).

MAP

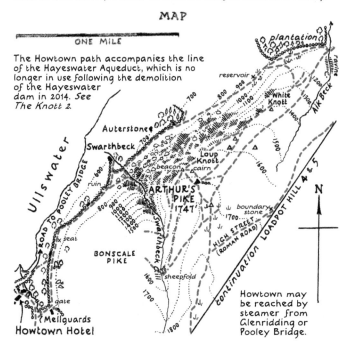

The Howtown path accompanies the line of the Hayeswater Aqueduct, which is no longer in use following the demolition of the Hayeswater dam in 2014. *See The Knott 2.*

Howtown may be reached by steamer from Glenridding or Pooley Bridge.

Ullswater, from the Howtown path

ASCENT FROM HOWTOWN
1450 feet of ascent : 3½ miles

Arthur's Pike looks particularly forbidding from the Howtown path, by which it is usually climbed, and the timid walker who doubts the wisdom of proceeding will be reassured to discover that the ascent is not only not intimidating but surprisingly easy and everywhere pleasant if the route shown on the map on the previous page (*via* the reservoir and White Knott) is followed.

The obvious and direct alternative by the Swarthbeck Gill ravine is anything but obvious and direct when attempted, and nervous pedestrians should keep away from it; it could lead to dangerous situations. *See page 6.*

For the approaches from Helton, and from Askham and Pooley Bridge *via* Moor Divock, *see Loadpot Hill 10.*

THE SUMMIT

Above the edge of the steep Ullswater flank, grassy undulations culminate in a conical knoll crowned by a large cairn; nearby is a short stretch of broken wall. There are distinct paths on the top, with a cairned track skirting the precipice, on the brink of which is a well made beacon; and on the eastern side is a good path that is continuous from Moor Divock to Loadpot Hill. The beacon cannot be seen from the summit cairn; it stands 250 yards distant in the direction of Blencathra.

THE VIEW

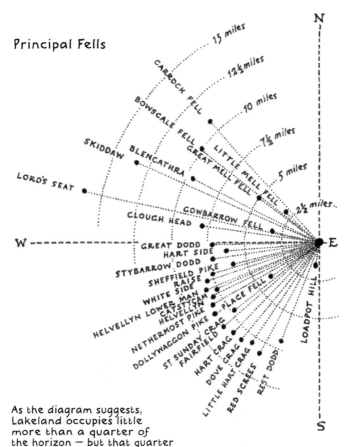

Principal Fells

As the diagram suggests, Lakeland occupies little more than a quarter of the horizon — but that quarter is magnificent, especially on a day of sunshine and shadows, the full Helvellyn and Fairfield ranges presenting their finest aspects above the deep trench of Ullswater. Eastwards, there is an uninterrupted view of the northern Pennines beyond the Eden valley.

Lakes and Tarns

W to N: *Ullswater (two sections: middle and lower reaches)*
Ullswater is better seen from the beacon: an impressive sight.

RIDGE ROUTES

To LOADPOT HILL, 2201': 2¼ miles
S. then SSW, SSE and finally N
Minor depressions: 500 feet of ascent

*A dull, easy walk which is
not recommended in mist.*
Follow the path to the south
from the summit. In 200
yards this joins a clearer
path going the same way.
When the path bears right
at Lambert Lad, keep
straight on to Loadpot Hill.
Alternatively, stay on the
main path to the remains of
Lowther House, where turn
north to the summit cairn
and Ordnance Survey column.
*This is not a walk for a
wet day, and the whole
of this moorland is a
nightmare in mist.*

To BONSCALE PIKE, 1718'
1 mile: S. then SSW and NW
*Depression at 1575'
150 feet of ascent*

*A simple walk which should
not be attempted in mist.*
Follow the path to the south
from the summit and bear
right to a sheepfold in the
depression between the two Pikes.
If starting from the beacon, a thin
path to the west can be followed to
a lower crossing point with a new path to the summit. *On no
account should a direct route be attempted between the two
summits; Swarthbeck Gill is dangerous below the fold.*

Ullswater, from the beacon

Swarthbeck Gill

Swarthbeck Gill, if it were but more accessible, would be one of the showplaces of the district. Here, between towering rockwalls, are beautiful cataracts, but, alas, they are out of the reach of the average explorer. The ferny, tree-clad lower gorge, however, may (and should) be visited. The prudent venture no further!

Beda Fell

1670'

summit named Beda Head

OS grid ref: NY429172

from Hallin Fell

Beda Fell is the long north-east ridge of Angletarn Pikes, narrowing as it descends; but midway it asserts itself, broadens considerably and rises to a definite summit, known as Beda Head, which is the geographical centre of the quiet, enchanting, exquisitely beautiful area known affectionately as 'Martind'l.' Beyond this top the descent continues over the rocky spine of Winter Crag to valley level at Sandwick on Ullswater. The fell, although mainly grassy, with bracken, has a most impressive east face, broken into three great tiers of crag. It is bounded by deep valleys, Boredale, Bannerdale and Howe Grain, whose combined waters meet at its northern tip.

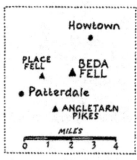

MAP

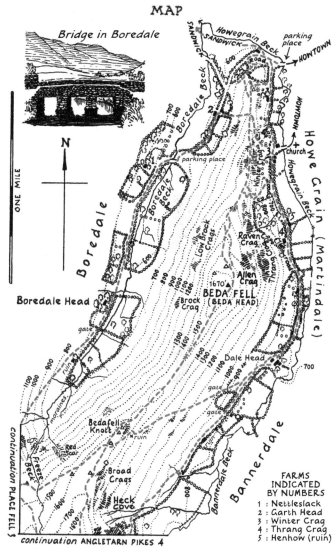

Bridge in Boredale

N

ONE MILE

SANDWICK

Howegrain Beck

parking place

HONTOWN

Boredale Beck

700 800

parking place

Boredale Beck

church

Howegrain Beck

Howe Grain (Martindale)

600

700

600

Low Brock Crags

Raven Crag

800

900

1000 1100 1200

Allen Crag

1670 ▲ **BEDA FELL** (BEDA HEAD)

Thrang Crag

Brock Crag

Boredale Head

Boredale

gate

800

900

1000

ruin

1100

1300

1400 1500

1600

Dale Head

1400

1300

1200

1100

1000 900

700

gate

gate

moraines

ruin

Bannerdale Beck

Bedafell Knott

ruin

Red Scar

Broad Crags

Heck Cove

Freeze Beck

continuation PLACE FELL 3

1500

1600

1700

1800

continuation ANGLETARN PIKES 4

800

Bannerdale

FARMS INDICATED BY NUMBERS

1 : Nettleslack
2 : Garth Head
3 : Winter Crag
4 : Thrang Crag
5 : Henhow (ruin)

Traces of aircraft wreckage can be found on the steep Boredale flank, the result of a Second World War tragedy when, on 10 November 1942, an RAF Lockheed Hudson twin-engined light bomber crashed.

ASCENTS FROM MARTINDALE AND BOREDALE
1100 feet of ascent : 1¾ miles

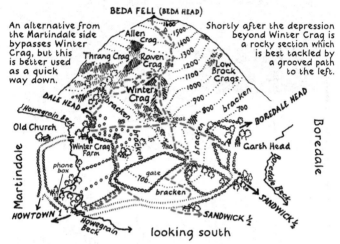

An alternative from the Martindale side bypasses Winter Crag, but this is better used as a quick way down.

Shortly after the depression beyond Winter Crag is a rocky section which is best tackled by a grooved path to the left.

looking south

The ridge may be gained directly at its extremity from the unenclosed road curving round its tip (in high summer, this route involves a tussle with bracken) or by the short paths from Winter Crag Farm and Garth Head.

The fell is best climbed along its north ridge, over the serrated crest of Winter Crag which is very enjoyable. However, the final slope is dreary, although it may be improved by keeping well to the left to look down the crags into Martindale, *but should be avoided in mist.*

THE SUMMIT

The highest point, Beda Head, is an uninteresting mound set upon undulating grassy slopes. Infinitely more exciting and attractive is the rocky top of Winter Crag along the ridge.
DESCENTS : Use the routes of ascent for returning, unless an extension of the walk is desired, in which case the ridge may be continued south-west as far as the Patterdale—Martindale path and a descent made along it.

In mist, exceeding care is necessary to avoid getting entangled among the crags on the east (Martindale) flank, Allen Crag especially being dangerous. In such conditions, it is advisable to descend from the lower cairn, 150 yards north-west, keeping always to the ridge.

THE VIEW

Principal Fells

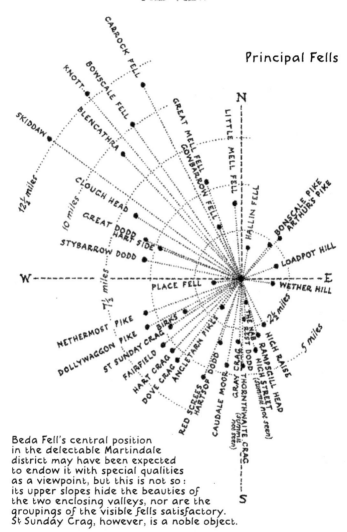

N

CARROCK FELL
KNOTT
BOWSCALE FELL
SKIDDAW
BLENCATHRA
GREAT MELL FELL
COWBARROW FELL
LITTLE MELL FELL
12½ miles
CLOUGH HEAD
10 miles
GREAT DODD
HART SIDE
HALLIN FELL
BONSCALE PIKE
ARTHURS PIKE
STYBARROW DODD
LOADPOT HILL
7½ miles
W
E
PLACE FELL
WETHER HILL
NETHERMOST PIKE
BIRKS
2½ miles
DOLLYWAGGON PIKE
ST SUNDAY CRAG
5 miles
FAIRFIELD
HART CRAG
DOVE CRAG
ANGLETARN PIKES
THE NAB
THE REST DODD
HIGH RAISE
RAMPSGILL HEAD
HIGH STREET (summit not seen)
RED SCREES
HARTSOP DODD
CAUDALE MOOR
GRAY CRAG
THORNTHWAITE CRAG (summit not seen)

S

Beda Fell's central position
in the delectable Martindale
district may have been expected
to endow it with special qualities
as a viewpoint, but this is not so :
its upper slopes hide the beauties of
the two enclosing valleys, nor are the
groupings of the visible fells satisfactory.
St Sunday Crag, however, is a noble object.

Lakes and Tarns

N to NE : *Ullswater (two sections, divided by Hallin Fell)*

RIDGE ROUTE

To ANGLETARN PIKES, 1857'
2 miles : SW, then S and SW
*Main depression at 1450'
and several minor depressions*

An easy walk on grass, increasing in interest.

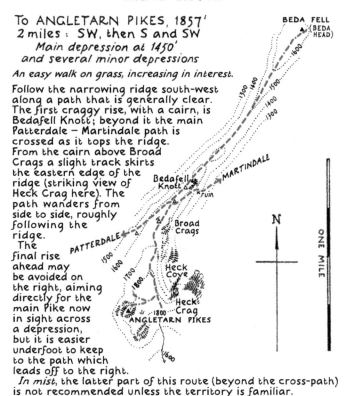

Follow the narrowing ridge south-west
along a path that is generally clear.
The first craggy rise, with a cairn, is
Bedafell Knott; beyond it the main
Patterdale — Martindale path is
crossed as it tops the ridge.
From the cairn above Broad
Crags a slight track skirts
the eastern edge of the
ridge (striking view of
Heck Crag here). The
path wanders from
side to side, roughly
following the
ridge.
  The
final rise
ahead may
be avoided on
the right, aiming
directly for the
main Pike now
in sight across
a depression,
but it is easier
underfoot to keep
to the path which
leads off to the right.

  *In mist, the latter part of this route (beyond the cross-path)
is not recommended unless the territory is familiar.*

The ridge south from the cairn
above Broad Crags; on the right
the main Angletarn Pike.

Beda Fell
from
Martindale Old Church

Bonscale Pike

1718'

OS grid ref: NY453201

from Hallin Fell

• Pooley Bridge

▲ ARTHUR'S PIKE
▲ BONSCALE PIKE
• Howtown
♦ LOADPOT HILL

MILES

0 1 2 3 4

  Rising steeply behind the little hamlet of Howtown is a broad buttress of the High Street range, Swarth Fell, the turretted and castellated rim of which has the appearance, when seen from Ullswater far below, of the ruined battlements of a castle wall : this aspect is sufficiently arresting to earn for the rocky facade and the summit above it the separate and distinctive name of Bonscale Pike. This escarpment, however, is a sham, for it defends nothing other than a dreary plateau of grass; and indeed there is little else of interest on the fell — excepting Swarthbeck Gill, its northern boundary, which abounds in interest but is out of bounds for the walker because of its obvious dangers. Bonscale Pike presents a bold front, that overlooking the lake, but on all other sides it loses its identity in the high mass of land supporting the great dome of Loadpot Hill.

MAP

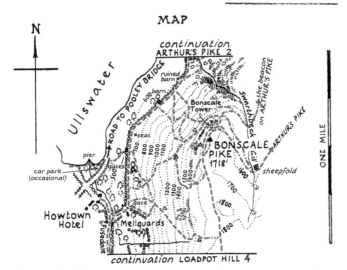

Bonscale Tower

Neither of the two stone pillars seen so prominently against the skyline from below marks the highest point. The lower and older of the pillars is known as Bonscale Tower; a cairn some 200 yards south of Bonscale Tower marks the site of where a third pillar once stood. The men who selected the sites for the three pillars surely had a good appreciation of drama! All four of the fells on the southern side of the lower and middle reaches of Ullswater have prominent beacons: *Arthur's Pike* ('the beacon'), *Bonscale Pike* (the two towers), *Hallin Fell* (summit) and *Place Fell* (Low Birk Fell).

The work of a craftsman
Bonscale Tower

The effort of amateurs
The higher pillar

ASCENT FROM HOWTOWN
1200 feet of ascent : 1¼ miles

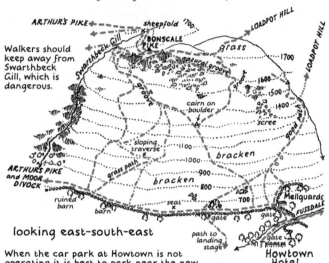

looking east-south-east

When the car park at Howtown is not operating it is best to park near the new church and use the pleasant path from there to Mellguards (see the map on *Steel Knotts 2*). A delightful alternative to the narrow road from Pooley Bridge is to arrive by boat: there are steamers to Howtown from Glenridding and Pooley Bridge.

via the Arthur's Pike path

Three paths ascend the steep flank, the first of which begins indistinctly at the foot of a shallow valley. The grass path starting from a dip beyond the barn is a delightful way up: it becomes a little indistinct as it nears the higher path. The most direct route begins at a rise 75 yards before a ruined barn. It, too, joins the higher path, from which there are intimate views of the two towers and the crags below the summit.

The path follows easy ground, but a direct route is possible.

via the Mellguards flank

The fellside above Mellguards is steep, and the pull up to the cairn is relentless. In summer the path is plagued by bracken. From the cairn (perched on a flat rock) the popular way is to the right, following an angled path which enters a groove and doubles back on itself before the slope eases on the grassy plateau. A thin path leads directly to the summit.

The grooved path to Loadpot Hill is a roundabout alternative – see map on page 2.

Starting from the pretty hamlet of Howtown, there are a surprising number of ways to ascend the fell of modest height that so dominates the settlement below.

THE SUMMIT

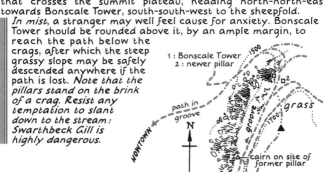

FAIRFIELD · ST SUNDAY CRAG · DOLLYWAGGON PIKE · NETHERMOST PIKE · HELVELLYN · CATSTYCAM · HELVELLYN LOWER MAN · WHITE SIDE · RAISE · STYBARROW DODD

PLACE FELL · SHEFFIELD PIKE · Ullswater · HALLIN FELL

The highest point of the fell lies behind Bonscale Tower on a grassy hummock with a small summit cairn. It is an unsatisfactory summit because higher ground rises immediately beyond it on the long undulating slope to Loadpot Hill; it does, however, indicate an excellent viewpoint, and also defines the limit of interest, which is centred in the broken wall of crag immediately below. Bonscale Pike, in fact, gives a display of rock scenery that would improve many a bigger fell. There is no doubting, however, that the major summit attraction is Bonscale Tower and to a lesser extent its higher colleague: the paths to and from here are distinct, whereas the path that visits the summit is thin and clearly less used.

DESCENTS: By walking 60 yards west from the summit cairn, a good path can be found. Another 20 yards on is the second path that crosses the summit plateau, heading north-north-east towards Bonscale Tower, south-south-west to the sheepfold.

In mist, a stranger may well feel cause for anxiety. Bonscale Tower should be rounded above it, by an ample margin, to reach the path below the crags, after which the steep grassy slope may be safely descended anywhere if the path is lost. *Note that the pillars stand on the brink of a crag. Resist any temptation to slant down to the stream: Swarthbeck Gill is highly dangerous.*

1 : Bonscale Tower
2 : newer pillar

path in groove

groove

grass

NEWTOWN

N

cairn on site of former pillar

Plan of the summit

100 yards

THE VIEW

Principal Fells

The distant fell peeping over the skyline, right of Arthur's Pike, is Cross Fell, the highest of the Pennines.

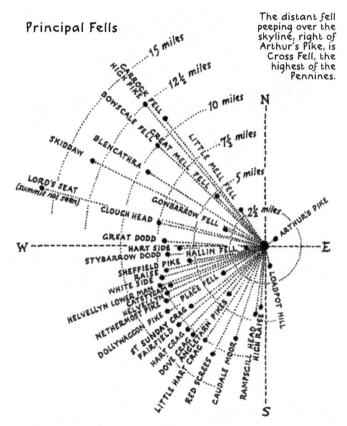

The prospect of the Helvellyn and Fairfield ranges, although crowded into a quarter-circle, is excellent, and the more distant northern fells are nicely grouped. In other directions there is little to be seen but the nearby dreary slopes falling from Loadpot Hill. The pillars are better viewpoints. The site of the (now gone) third pillar in particular offers a splendid view of Howtown Bay backed by Hallin Fell, Place Fell and the Helvellyn range.

Lakes and Tarns

W to N: *Ullswater (middle and lower reaches)* — better seen from either of the two pillars

RIDGE ROUTES

To ARTHUR'S PIKE, 1747': 1 mile
SE, then NNE and N
Depression at 1575'
200 feet of ascent

A simple walk, needing care in mist.

  Slant down a grass slope south-
east to the beck, crossing it above
a sheepfold and doubling back
along the opposite slope. A recent
alternative is a thin path to a
crossing further downstream; on
the far bank a path leads to the
beacon. Any other short cuts
across Swarthbeck Gill, *especially
in mist,* are dangerous.

To LOADPOT HILL, 2201': 1½ miles
S, then SSE and finally N
Minor depressions
550 feet of ascent

*An easy walk, not
recommended in mist.*

Cross the undulating plateau
southwards until the ground
steepens into the dome of Loadpot
Hill. A short climb brings the old High
Street (a grassy groove) underfoot:
it leads to the ruins of Lowther House,
where turn north to the handsome
cairn. The more direct route is a
steeper alternative.

ONE MILE

Ullswater:
the middle reach

Branstree

2339'

OS grid ref: NY478100

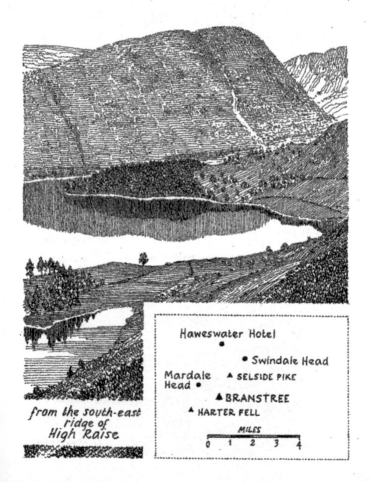

from the south-east ridge of High Raise

Haweswater Hotel
●

● Swindale Head

Mardale Head ● ▲ SELSIDE PIKE

▲ BRANSTREE

▲ HARTER FELL

MILES
0 1 2 3 4

NATURAL FEATURES

Branstree occupies a fine position at the head of three valleys, Mardale, Swindale and Longsleddale, and a fourth, Mosedale, runs along its southern base. This geographical attribute aside, the fell is dreary, and must disappoint all who climb it, for a good deal of perambulation is necessary across the flat and featureless top before these valleys can be brought sufficiently into view for full appreciation. All is grass, although there is a slight boulder slope below Artlecrag Pike (extravagantly hachured as a crag on most maps), and Woodfell Gill, a remarkable dry gully, the result of a landslide, cleaves the fellside on the Mardale flank from top to bottom. Eastwards there are some subsidiary summits, and a line of crags overlooking Swindale; there is an odd little hanging valley, and noble hidden waterfalls on this side. The Mosedale flank has been extensively quarried. Mosedale Beck is the principal stream : it runs into Swindale Beck. Manchester Corporation once coveted Swindale as the site of a proposed reservoir.

High Street
from the north ridge

Some 1300 feet below Branstree runs the pipeline carrying water from Haweswater towards its destination 90 miles away in Manchester. It continues below Tarn Crag and Grey Crag's subsidiary Great Howe before emerging into Longsleddale.

Branstree 3

MAP

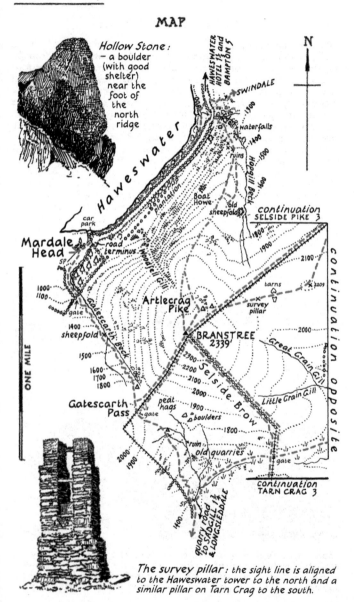

Hollow Stone:
– a boulder
(with good
shelter)
near the
foot of
the
north
ridge

N

HAWESWATER HOTEL 1¼ and BAMPTON 5

SWINDALE

1900

waterfalls

1800

Hop Gill Beck

ruins

1600

Haweswater

plantation

Boat Howe

old sheepfold

continuation SELSIDE PIKE 3

1800

1900

car park

Mardale Head

road terminus

SP

Wood Gill

2100

tarns

2109

survey pillar

continuation opposite

1000
1100

gate

Artlecrag Pike

1400 sheepfold

Gatescarth Beck

BRANSTREE 2339'

Selside Brow

2000

Great Grain Gill

Little Grain Gill

1500

1600
1700
1800

2300

2200

2100

2000

ONE MILE

Gatescarth Pass

gate

peat hags

boulders

1900

1800

gate

2000

1900

ruin

old quarries

continuation TARN CRAG 3

SP

1400

quarry road to SADGILL 1½ & LONGSLEDDALE

The survey pillar: the sight line is aligned
to the Haweswater tower to the north and a
similar pillar on Tarn Crag to the south.

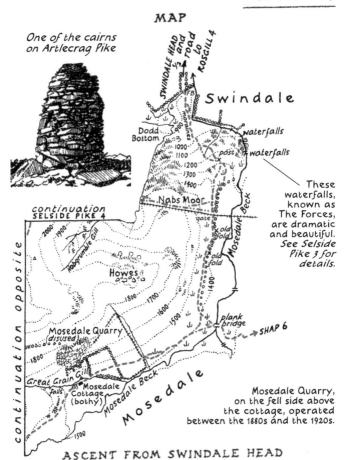

One of the cairns
on Artlecrag Pike

MAP

SWINDALE HEAD and road to ROSGILL 4

Swindale

FB

Dodd
Bottom

900
1000
1100
1200
1300
1400

post

waterfalls

waterfalls

These
waterfalls,
known as
The Forces,
are dramatic
and beautiful.
*See Selside
Pike 3 for
details.*

Nabs Moor

*continuation
SELSIDE PIKE 4*

2000
1900

Hobgrumble Gill

Howes

1800 1700

1600

gate

old
fold

old
fold

Mosedale Beck

1400

1500

plank
bridge

SHAP 6

1800

continuation opposite

Mosedale Quarry
(disused)

Great Grain Gill

falls

Mosedale
Cottage
(bothy)

Mosedale Beck

Mosedale

1500

Mosedale Quarry,
on the fell side above
the cottage, operated
between the 1880s and the 1920s.

ASCENT FROM SWINDALE HEAD

1700 feet of ascent : 4½ miles (via Mosedale)
NOTE : *6 miles from Swindale Foot (the last place to park)*

   This long walk is an excellent introduction to the beautiful head
of Swindale and the less attractive higher valley of Mosedale
('dreary valley'), which fully lives up to its name. The final climb
to Branstree *via* Selside Brow is dull as well. Highlights are the
interesting path that winds through moraines on the approach
to Swindale's valley head and the mountain bothy of Mosedale
Cottage. The approach entails a mile and a half of road walking:
there is no parking for non-residents beyond Swindale Foot
(states a sign). An alternative is first to ascend Selside Pike,
descending *via* Mosedale. *See Selside Pike 5 and 6 for details.*

ASCENT FROM MARDALE
1500 feet of ascent : 1½ miles from the road

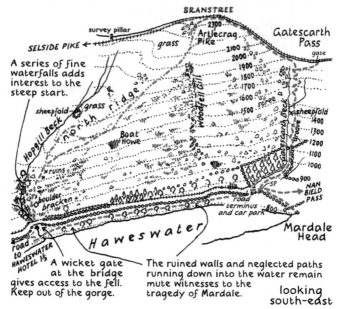

BRANSTREE

survey pillar

SELSIDE PIKE ←

grass

Artlecrag Pike

Gatescarth Pass

gate

2700

2100

2000

1900

1800

1700

1600

1500 scree

Woodhall Gill

A series of fine waterfalls adds interest to the steep start.

sheepfold

grass

north ridge

Boat Howe

Hopgill Beck

ruins

boulder

bracken

1400

1300

1200

1100

1000

900

sheepfold

Gatescarth Beck

raike

SP

NAN BIELD PASS

road

terminus and car park

800

Haweswater

Mardale Head

road to HAWESWATER HOTEL 1½

A wicket gate at the bridge gives access to the fell. Keep out of the gorge.

The ruined walls and neglected paths running down into the water remain mute witnesses to the tragedy of Mardale.

looking south-east

Above the ruins the path splits : the right-hand fork is clearer and more direct. Higher up, the path practically disappears.

The merit of the ascent by the north ridge lies in its intimate views of Mardale Head and Harter Fell, the climbing itself being dull after a promising start. The Gatescarth route is better used for the return.

ASCENT FROM LONGSLEDDALE
1750 feet of ascent
3½ miles from Sadgill

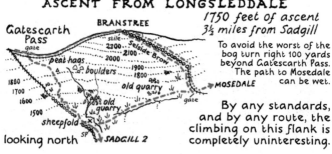

BRANSTREE

Gatescarth Pass

gate

stile

2200

2100

2000

Selside Brow

peat hags

boulders

1800

1900

1800

old quarry

1800

1700

1600

1500

old quarry

sheepfold

SP

SADGILL 2

looking north

gate

MOSEDALE

To avoid the worst of the bog turn right 100 yards beyond Gatescarth Pass. The path to Mosedale can be wet.

By any standards, and by any route, the climbing on this flank is completely uninteresting.

THE SUMMIT

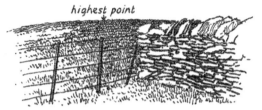

highest point

The 'official' watershed is about eighty yards north of the end of the wall; this is the highest point (2339').

The summit is grassy and flat-topped. The highest point is marked by a small cairn and an Ordnance Survey trigonometrical station, a circular structure about two feet across and two inches high with a small cone in the centre. A better place for a halt is Artlecrag Pike, nearby to the north-east; here there are two fine stone columns and some rock to relieve the drab surroundings.

DESCENTS: The quickest way off, and the safest in bad weather, is by the fence to Gatescarth Pass (keep to the right of the fence and watch for the gate that indicates the path for Longsleddale, left, and Mardale, right). The most attractive descent is that by the north ridge for Mardale, with good views of Haweswater.

RIDGE ROUTE

To TARN CRAG, 2176'
1¾ miles : SE, then S
Depression at 1650'
550 feet of ascent

Easy gradients; a dull walk.

Features of interest are lacking on this moorland trudge which can be boggy in places. Care is needed on Tarn Crag in mist.

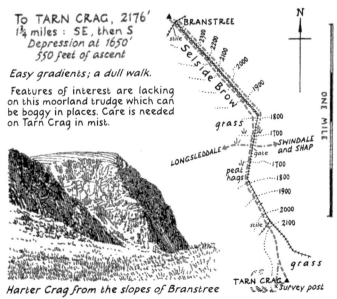

Harter Crag from the slopes of Branstree

RIDGE ROUTES

To HARTER FELL, 2552': 2 miles: SW then NW and SW
Depression at 1875' (Gatescarth Pass): 700 feet of ascent

An easy walk on grass. Safe in mist, with care.

Follow the right-hand side of the fence down to Gatescarth
Pass, then take the path that cuts off the corner. Where the
fence bends sharply left is the setting of the drawing that
was used to introduce the author's television programmes
in the 1980s (*see Harter Fell 10*).

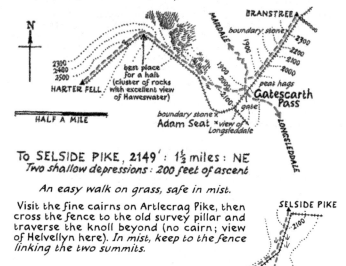

To SELSIDE PIKE, 2149': 1½ miles: NE
Two shallow depressions: 200 feet of ascent

An easy walk on grass, safe in mist.

Visit the fine cairns on Artlecrag Pike, then
cross the fence to the old survey pillar and
traverse the knoll beyond (no cairn; view
of Helvellyn here). *In mist, keep to the fence
linking the two summits.*

The survey pillar was built by Manchester Corporation during
the construction of the Haweswater Aqueduct. It does not
stand on the crest of the depression, as might have been
expected, but slightly below it; the top of the pillar, however,
overtops the crest and the next survey pillar, on Tarn Crag,
is visible from it (south).

THE VIEW

Despite Branstree's good geographical position, little is seen of Lakeland: the lofty skyline of the Mardale heights admits only two small vistas of distant fells. Compensation is found, however, in the wide prospect of the Pennines. An interesting feature is the glimpse of the Scafells with Mickledore – note that, of this group, only the Pike is in view from the wall end.

Principal Fells

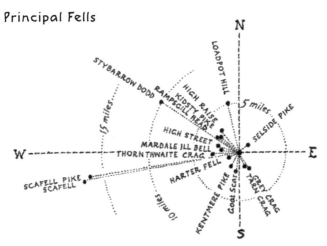

Lakes and Tarns

Branstree is one of the very few Lakeland fells that have no view of lakes or tarns from the highest point, but *Haweswater* is brought into view by walking a few paces north. The long strip of water in the distance southwards is the Kent estuary.

Mosedale Cottage – now maintained as a mountain bothy

Brock Crags

1842'

OS grid ref: NY417137

from Goldrill Beck

The unspoilt village of Hartsop has great charm and its environment is one of quiet loveliness, much of it contributed by the hanging woods of the steep fell that rises immediately behind. The fell, Brock Crags, is an offshoot of a ridge coming down to Ullswater from the main High Street watershed, and overlooks a meeting of many valleys: a feature in the view from the rocky top. Its slopes carry the old Hayeswater aqueduct, now no longer in use, and pipelaying operations there in the 1950s left an ugly scar along its fair breast. Nature is a great healer, however, and it has healed effectively here.

- Patterdale

ANGLETARN ▲ PIKES

BROCK ▲ CRAGS
- Hartsop

HIGH STREET ▲

MILES

0   1   2   3   4

MAP

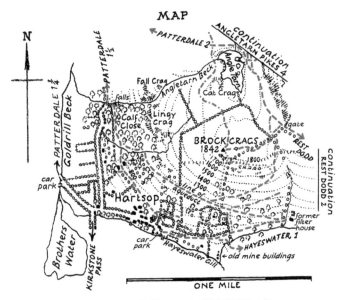

N

---PATTERDALE 2
continuation
ANGLETARN PIKES 4

PATTERDALE 1¾
PATTERDALE 1¼
Goldrill Beck

Fall Crag
falls
Angletarn Beck
Cat Crags
Calf
Close
Lingy
Crag
gate
REST DODD
BROCK CRAGS
1842
continuation
REST DODD 2

car park

Hartsop

aqueduct

former
filter
house

Brothers Water

car park
Hayeswater Gill
HAYESWATER 1

KIRKSTONE PASS
old mine buildings

ONE MILE

ASCENT FROM HARTSOP
1300 feet of ascent : 2 miles

From the car park at Hartsop follow the road up the valley to the former filter house, turning back above the old pipeline at a higher level, now an easy, grassy track. Ignore a thin path going right and continue on, following a wall on the left. A grooved path ascends right through a gap in an old wall, leading to the wall at 1800'. Follow the clear path, left, alongside the wall, which switches sides before the summit plateau is reached. The top is on a rocky knoll past some pools.

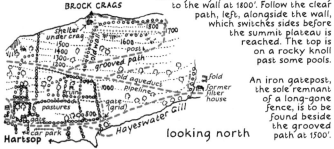

BROCK CRAGS

Shelter
under crag
1800
1700
1500
1600
1400
post
1300
1200
grooved path
old aqueduct
fold
former
filter
house
ruin
1000
Pipeline
pastures
800
gate
(grid)
gate
car park
Hayeswater Gill
Hartsop
looking north

An iron gatepost, the sole remnant of a long-gone fence, is to be found beside the grooved path at 1500'.

The two pathless routes from the grooved path are not recommended in bad weather. The steep short cut from the cattle grid cuts ten minutes off the walk but has no further merit.

An easy, safe walk to an interesting summit offering a beautiful and dramatic view of the upper Patterdale valley.

THE SUMMIT

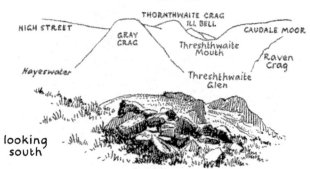

HIGH STREET

THORNTHWAITE CRAG
ILL BELL

GRAY CRAG

Threshthwaite Mouth

CAUDALE MOOR

Raven Crag

Hayeswater

Threshthwaite Glen

looking south

A series of rocky knolls, on the highest of which is a cairn, adds some interest to the rather drab surroundings. It is as a viewpoint that the summit merits most respect.

DESCENTS: A quick descent to Hartsop may be made by following the old wall that crosses the fellside 150 yards south-east; descents due west encounter rough ground and should not be attempted. For Patterdale, the Angle Tarn path may be joined near the Satura Crag gate by following the old wall eastwards. *In bad weather*, locate the wall and follow it down to the pastures of Hartsop.

RIDGE ROUTES

ANGLETARN PIKES

Angle Tarn

Cat Crag

BROCK CRAGS

gate

Brock Crags stands apart from the ridge that links Rest Dodd with Angletarn Pikes. To join the ridge, for either of these fells, follow the old wall eastwards to the gate on Satura Crag, where the connecting path will be found.

To ANGLETARN PIKES, 1851'
via Cat Crag : 1 mile : N
Depression at 1540' : 450 feet of ascent
An interesting walk on a new path.

via Angle Tarn : 1½ miles : E then NW
Depression at 1640' : 320 feet of ascent
Intimate views of the lovely Angle Tarn.

The direct route visits the impressive Cat Crag; *in mist* it should be avoided. The longer route to Angle Tarn is safe *in mist*. The final pull to the summit is on a narrow, zig-zagging path.

N

To REST DODD, 2283'
1½ miles : NE then E
Depression at 1750'
600 feet of ascent
Easy, but confusing in mist.

In mist, keep to the fence and wall past Satura Crag. Otherwise, this is an easy climb.

ONE MILE

BROCK CRAGS

gate

Satura Crag

REST DODD

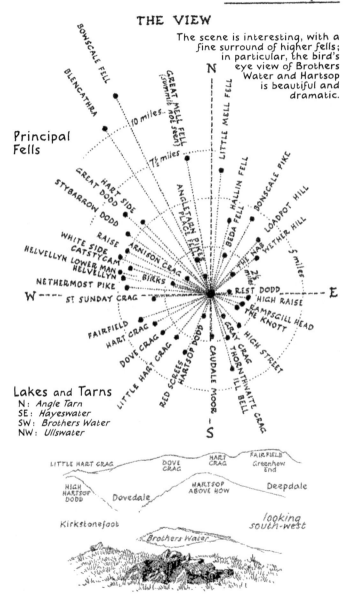

THE VIEW

The scene is interesting, with a fine surround of higher fells; in particular, the bird's eye view of Brothers Water and Hartsop is beautiful and dramatic.

Principal Fells

BOWSCALE FELL
BLENCATHRA
GREAT MELL FELL (summit not seen)
LITTLE MELL FELL
10 miles
7½ miles
GREAT DODD
HART SIDE
STYBARROW DODD
BEDA FELL
HALLIN FELL
BONSCALE PIKE
ANGLETARN PIKE
PLACE FELL
LOADPOT HILL
RAISE
WHITE SIDE
CATSTYCAM
HELVELLYN LOWER MAN
HELVELLYN
ARNISON CRAG
WETHER HILL
THE NAB
5 miles
NETHERMOST PIKE
BIRKS
2½
REST DODD
HIGH RAISE
W
ST SUNDAY CRAG
E
RAMPSGILL HEAD
THE KNOTT
FAIRFIELD
HART CRAG
DOVE CRAG
GRAY CRAG
HIGH STREET
LITTLE HART CRAG
HARTSOP DODD
THORNTHWAITE CRAG
ILL BELL
RED SCREES
CAUDALE MOOR

Lakes and Tarns
N: *Angle Tarn*
SE: *Hayeswater*
SW: *Brothers Water*
NW: *Ullswater*

S

LITTLE HART CRAG
DOVE CRAG
HART CRAG
FAIRFIELD
Greenhow End
HIGH HARTSOP DODD
HARTSOP ABOVE HOW
Dovedale
Deepdale
Kirkstonefoot
looking south-west
Brothers Water

Caudale Moor

2502'

OS grid ref: NY419100

often referred to as
  John Bell's Banner
summit named
  Stony Cove Pike

• Patterdale

• Hartsop

HIGH
STREET ▲
CAUDALE ▲ MOOR

▲ RED SCREES

• Ambleside

MILES
0   1   2   3   4

from Brothers Water

NATURAL FEATURES

Caudale Moor deserves far more respect than it usually gets. The long featureless slope flanking the Kirkstone Pass, well known to travellers, is not at all characteristic of the fell: its other aspects, less frequently seen, are considerably more imposing. There are, in fact, no fewer than six ridges leaving the summit in other directions, four of them of distinct merit and two of these rising to subsidiary summits, Wansfell and Hartsop Dodd, on their way to valley level. The craggy slopes bordering the upper Troutbeck valley are particularly varied and interesting: from this remote dalehead Caudale Moor looks really impressive, especially in snowy conditions. The best single feature, however, is the formidable wall of rock, Raven Crag, overlooking Pasture Beck. Of the streams draining the fell, those to the south join forces to form Trout Beck; all others go north to feed Ullswater.

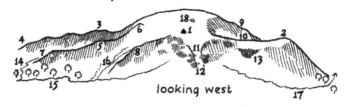

looking west

1 : The summit
    (Stony Cove Pike)
2 : Hartsop Dodd
3 : St Raven's Edge
4 : South (west) ridge
    continuing to Wansfell
5 : Hart Crag
6 : Pike How
7 : South (intermediate) ridge
8 : South (east) ridge

9 : North-west ridge
10 : North ridge
11 : East ridge
12 : Threshthwaite Mouth
13 : Raven Crag
14 : Woundale Beck
15 : Trout Beck
16 : Sad Gill
17 : Pasture Beck
18 : Caudale Head Tarn

The six ridges of Caudale Moor

1. The north-west ridge ridge is the route of the popular ascent from Caudale Bridge and Brothers Water;
2. The north ridge links to Hartsop Dodd;
3. The east ridge is the most rugged of the ridges, leading to the depression at Threshthwaite Mouth and Thornthwaite Crag;
4. The south (east) ridge leads to Sad Gill and Trout Beck;
5. The south (intermediate) ridge passes subsidiaries Pike How and Hart Crag on the way to the A592 Kirkstone road;
6. The south (west) ridge leads to the Kirkstone road. Midway, a popular path descends from St Raven's Edge to Kirkstone Pass.

Caudale Moor 3

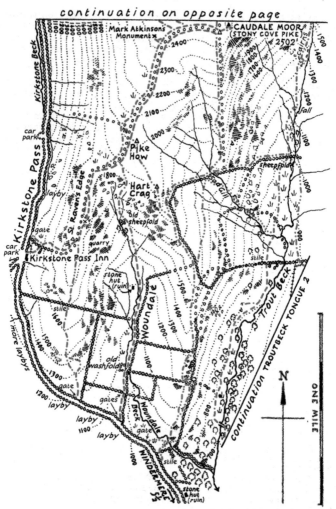

MAP

continuation on opposite page

For walkers looking to gain a foothold on Caudale Moor's sprawling southern flank, the A592 Kirkstone Pass road provides three laybys within barely half a mile where it is possible to leave a car. *For ascent details see page 8.*

MAP

There is some disagreement over what is called what on the summit plateau: Ordnance Survey maps name the main summit of the fell as *Stony Cove Pike*, the rise at the top of the north-west ridge as *Caudale Moor*, and the ridge descending to Sᵗ Raven's Edge as *John Bell's Banner*. The John Bell in question is thought to be the Revd. John Bell (1153-1620), curate and schoolmaster of Ambleside, who is said to have attempted to resolve a parish boundary dispute by placing a banner on the fell indicating the line of the boundary.

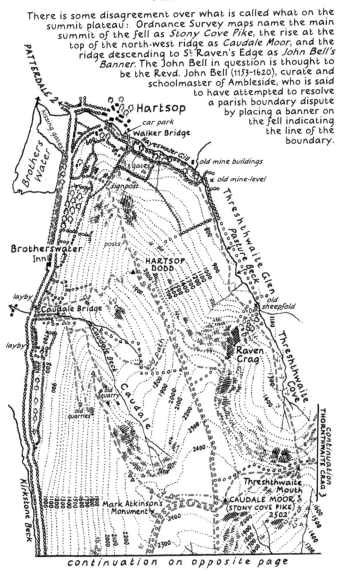

continuation on opposite page

ASCENT FROM BROTHERS WATER
2000 feet of ascent : 2½ miles from the Inn

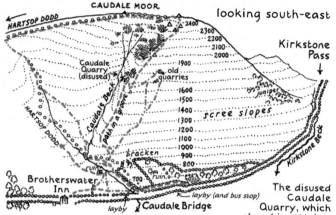

looking south-east

The route *via* the tongue to the left of Caudale Beck follows an old path to the ridge between Hartsop Dodd and Caudale Moor. It is longer and less steep than the main ridge; it offers a good alternative for the descent.

The disused Caudale Quarry, which closed in 1934, is a fascinating place, well worth visiting. The old quarries on the steep Kirkstone flank are less interesting, and the paths in their vicinity are sketchy in places and can be confusing.

The beautiful retrospect over Patterdale is justification for frequent halts during this continuously steep ascent. The route follows the well defined crest of the ridge. Of the many approaches to the summit, this is by far the best.

Caudale Head

Ullswater and Brothers Water
from Caudale Quarry

Red Screes and Middle Dodd
from the north-west ridge

ASCENT FROM KIRKSTONE PASS
1150 feet of ascent : 2¼ miles from the Inn

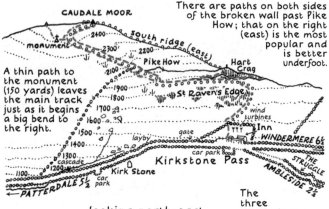

There are paths on both sides of the broken wall past Pike How; that on the right (east) is the most popular and is better underfoot.

CAUDALE MOOR

monument

2400

2300

2200

south ridge (east)

Pike How

Hart Crag

2100

St Raven's Edge

1900

wind turbines

A thin path to the monument (150 yards) leaves the main track just as it begins a big bend to the right.

1800

1700

1600

Inn

WINDERMERE 6¼

1500

layby

gate

1400

car park

THE STRUGGLE

1300

cascade

Kirkstone Pass

1200

AMBLESIDE 2¼

1100

Kirk Stone

car park

← PATTERDALE 5½

looking north-east

The summit cairn on St Raven's Crag is a popular destination for families with young children in particular: it is an easy, quick ascent. The view down to the inn and across the pass to the chaotic 1000' western flank of Red Screes — layers of crags, tumbled boulders and rivers of scree — is excellent, especially in view of the lack of effort required to see it.

The three small wind turbines behind the Kirkstone Pass Inn have a big advantage over many such structures elsewhere in the country — an almost constant supply of wind!

This route, with the advantage of a 1500' start, is one of the easiest ways up any of the higher fells, the only steep part being the short pull on to St Raven's Edge. It is also the dullest way up, and does not do justice to a fine hill that has much better than this to offer.

Mark Atkinson's Monument

The monument topped by a wooden cross commemorates Mark Atkinson, a farmer and licensee of the Kirkstone Pass Inn who died in 1930 and his son William Ion who died in 1987. Mr. Atkinson expressed the wish before he died that his ashes be laid to rest at a place on Caudale Moor overlooking the pass and the valley. The monument can be seen from the inn.

ASCENT FROM TROUTBECK
2200 (A) or 2350 (B) feet of ascent;
(A) 5 miles via Sad Gill; 5½ miles via Woundale (A)
(B) 6 miles via St Raven's Edge or Threshthwaite Mouth (B)

These distances can, by parking on the Kirkstone Pass road, be reduced to the following: via St Raven's Edge — 2¼ miles; via Woundale — 2½ miles; via Hart Crag — 3 miles; via the south (east) ridge, starting on the Hart Crag ridge and then switching at the final wall — 2¼ miles.

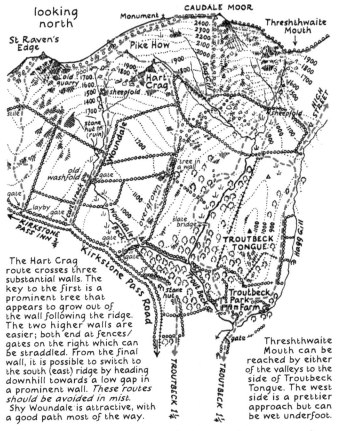

looking north

CAUDALE MOOR

Monument

Threshthwaite Mouth

St Raven's Edge

Pike How

Hart Crag

old quarry

sheepfold

stile

stone hut (ruin)

HIGH STREET

sheepfold

old washfold

gate

tree in a wall

gate

layby

gate

overgrown

slate bridge

TROUTBECK TONGUE

Hagg Gill

KIRKSTONE PASS INN

gate

Kirkstone Pass Road

Woundale Beck

Trout Beck

stone hut

Troutbeck Park Farm

TROUTBECK 1¼

TROUTBECK 1¼

gate

The Hart Crag route crosses three substantial walls. The key to the first is a prominent tree that appears to grow out of the wall following the ridge. The two higher walls are easier; both end at fences/gates on the right which can be straddled. From the final wall, it is possible to switch to the south (east) ridge by heading downhill towards a low gap in a prominent wall. *These routes should be avoided in mist.*
Shy Woundale is attractive, with a good path most of the way.

Threshthwaite Mouth can be reached by either of the valleys to the side of Troutbeck Tongue. The west side is a prettier approach but can be wet underfoot.

Illustrated are a number of interesting approaches, three of which join the path from Kirkstone *via* St Raven's Edge. The sprawling southern flank of this fine fell has many beautiful aspects.

Raven Crag

Threshthwaite Cove
from
Threshthwaite Mouth

THE SUMMIT

KENTMERE PIKE   FROSWICK   ILL BELL   YOKE

The summit is a dreary plateau of considerable extent, crossed by ruined walls, with grey rock outcropping in the wide expanse of grass. The highest point is not easy to locate on the flat top: it is indicated by a cairn about 120 yards east of the north-south wall, and bears the distinctive name of Stony Cove Pike.

Summit plan

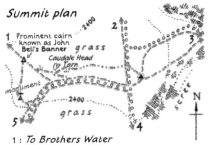

1: Prominent cairn known as John Bell's Banner
grass
Caudale Head Tarn
2400
monument
2400
grass
scree
N

1 : To Brothers Water
2 : To Hartsop
3 : To Threshthwaite Mouth
4 : To Troutbeck
5 : To Kirkstone Pass

YARDS
0   100   200   300

DESCENTS: All routes of ascent may be reversed in good weather. The paths on the top are fairly clear, and broken walls offer safe guides from the summit except along the north-west ridge.

In bad weather, note that the east face is everywhere craggy: it may be descended safely only by the broken wall going down to the col at Threshthwaite Mouth. The best way off the top in an emergency, whatever the destination, is alongside the broken wall running west — this continues all the way to the road near the Kirkstone Pass Inn.

Cairn on
Hart Crag
above Woundale

Cairn above the
north-west ridge

THE VIEW
(with distances in miles)

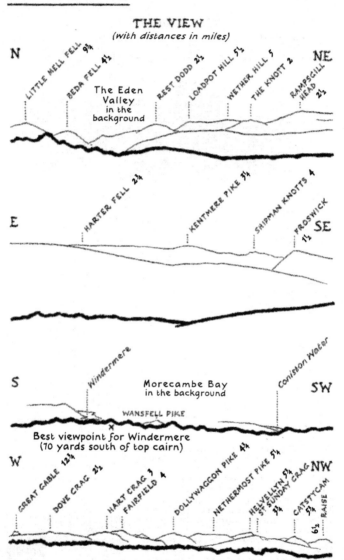

N — LITTLE MELL FELL 9¾ · BEDA FELL 4½ · The Eden Valley in the background · REST DODD 2½ · LOADPOT HILL 5½ · WETHER HILL 5 · THE KNOTT 2 · RAMPSGILL HEAD 2½ — NE

E — HARTER FELL 2¾ · KENTMERE PIKE 3¾ · SHIPMAN KNOTTS 4 · FROSWICK 1½ — SE

S — Windermere · Morecambe Bay in the background · WANSFELL PIKE · Coniston Water — SW

✗ Best viewpoint for Windermere
(70 yards south of top cairn)

W — GREAT GABLE 12¾ · DOVE CRAG 2½ · HART CRAG 3 · FAIRFIELD 4 · DOLLYWAGGON PIKE 4½ · NETHERMOST PIKE 5¼ · HELVELLYN 5½ · ST SUNDAY CRAG 3¼ · CATSTYCAM 5¼ · RAISE 6½ — NW

The view in this direction
is much better seen from
the western edge of the summit plateau

THE VIEW

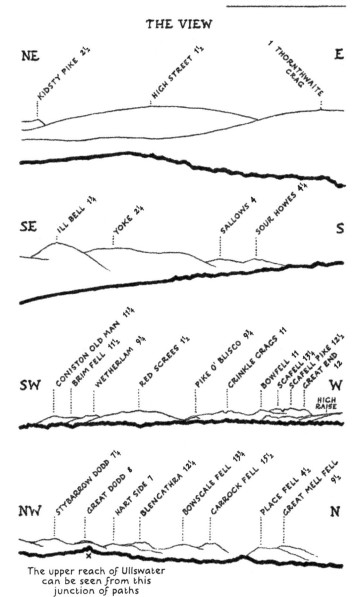

NE — KIDSTY PIKE 2½ — HIGH STREET 11½ — 1 THORNTHWAITE CRAG — E

SE — ILL BELL 1¾ — YOKE 2¼ — SALLOWS 4 — SOUR HOWES 4¼ — S

SW — CONISTON OLD MAN 11¾ — BRIM FELL 11½ — WETHERLAM 9¾ — RED SCREES 1½ — PIKE O' BLISCO 9¼ — CRINKLE CRAGS 11 — BOWFELL 11 — SCAFELL 13½ — SCAFELL PIKE 12½ — GREAT END 12 — HIGH RAISE — W

NW — STYBARROW DODD 7¼ — GREAT DODD 8 — HART SIDE 7 — BLENCATHRA 12¼ — BOWSCALE FELL 13¾ — CARROCK FELL 15½ — PLACE FELL 4½ — GREAT MELL FELL 9½ — N

The upper reach of Ullswater
can be seen from this
junction of paths

RIDGE ROUTE

To WANSFELL, 1597': 4½ miles : W, then SW and S
Depression at 1100': 500 feet of ascent

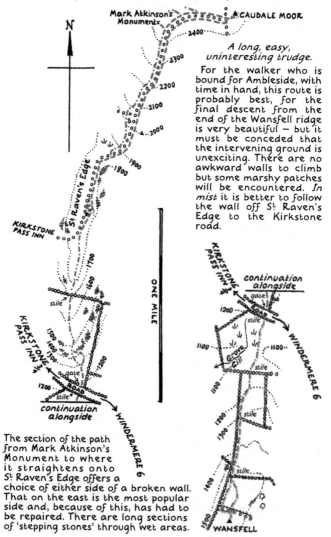

A long, easy, uninteresting trudge.

For the walker who is bound for Ambleside, with time in hand, this route is probably best, for the final descent from the end of the Wansfell ridge is very beautiful — but it must be conceded that the intervening ground is unexciting. There are no awkward walls to climb but some marshy patches will be encountered. *In mist it is better to follow the wall off St Raven's Edge to the Kirkstone road.*

The section of the path from Mark Atkinson's Monument to where it straightens onto St Raven's Edge offers a choice of either side of a broken wall. That on the east is the most popular side and, because of this, has had to be repaired. There are long sections of 'stepping stones' through wet areas.

RIDGE ROUTES

To THORNTHWAITE CRAG, 2569': 1 mile: ENE, then E and SE
Depression at 1950': 620 feet of ascent
A rough scramble, safe in mist.

This walk is not as simple as it looks, because the deep gap or col (Threshthwaite Mouth) between the two fells is unsuspected from the top of Caudale Moor. The descent to the gap is steep (if there is snow and ice it may be dangerous) and the climb from it is stony and loose. *In mist*, it is important to keep alongside the crumbled wall that links the two summits.

Caudale Moor from below Scot Rake

To HARTSOP DODD, 2028': 1½ miles: N, then NNW
Depression at 1900': 120 feet of ascent

An easy and straightforward walk by the wall. More interesting by the escarpment.

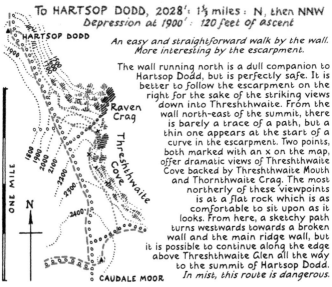

The wall running north is a dull companion to Hartsop Dodd, but is perfectly safe. It is better to follow the escarpment on the right for the sake of the striking views down into Threshthwaite. From the wall north-east of the summit, there is barely a trace of a path, but a thin one appears at the start of a curve in the escarpment. Two points, both marked with an x on the map, offer dramatic views of Threshthwaite Cove backed by Threshthwaite Mouth and Thornthwaite Crag. The most northerly of these viewpoints is at a flat rock which is as comfortable to sit upon as it looks. From here, a sketchy path turns westwards towards a broken wall and the main ridge wall, but it is possible to continue along the edge above Threshthwaite Glen all the way to the summit of Hartsop Dodd. *In mist, this route is dangerous.*

Froswick

2359'

OS grid ref: NY453085

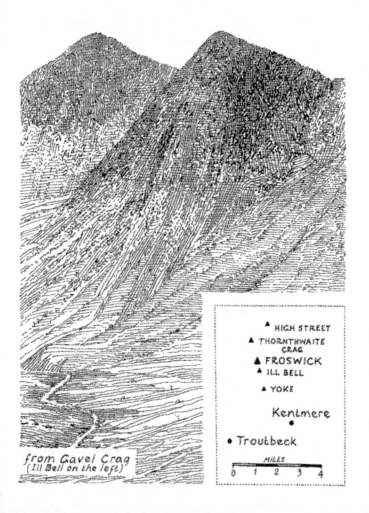

from Gavel Crag
(Ill Bell on the left)

▲ HIGH STREET

▲ THORNTHWAITE
    CRAG

▲ FROSWICK

▲ ILL BELL

▲ YOKE

Kentmere
●

● Troutbeck

MILES

0   1   2   3   4

NATURAL FEATURES

Sheltering in the shadow of Ill Bell on High Street's south ridge is the lesser height of Froswick. It takes its pattern from Ill Bell in remarkable degree, almost humorously seeming to ape its bigger neighbour. Both flanks are very steep, the Kentmere side especially being a rough tumble of scree: there are crags here facing up the valley. The grassy Troutbeck slope, west, is notable for Froswick's one touch of originality, for it is cleft by a tremendous scree gully, Blue Gill, that splits the fellside from top to bottom. Easy slopes link the summit with Thornthwaite Crag and Ill Bell; this is the finest part of the ridge.

MAP

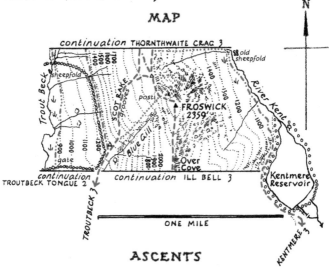

ASCENTS

FROM GARBURN PASS

Froswick is rarely climbed direct; invariably its summit is gained incidentally during the course of the Ill Bell ridge walk, starting at Garburn Pass. See *Ill Bell 4 and 10*.

FROM TROUTBECK

From Troutbeck its top may easily be visited on the way to Thornthwaite Crag or High Street by Scot Rake, or by the pathless shortcut alongside Blue Gill. See *Thornthwaite Crag 5*.

FROM KENTMERE

A direct ascent from Kentmere is not recommended, although the ridge north of the summit may be reached up a continuous steep tongue of grass from the old sheepfold.

THE SUMMIT

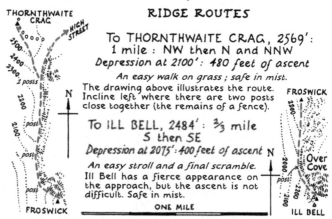

THORNTHWAITE CRAG

CAUDALE MOOR

Threshthwaite
Mouth

Froswick's peaked appearance from afar holds out the promise
of a small pointed summit. Small it is, and neat, with a tidy
cairn, but it will hardly satisfy the seeker of spires.
DESCENTS : The routes of ascent may be reversed. The
western flank is safe anywhere (but keep out of Blue Gill) ;
direct descents to Kentmere should not be attempted. *In mist,*
reach Kentmere by way of the ridge south to Garburn Pass.

RIDGE ROUTES

To THORNTHWAITE CRAG, 2569' :
1 mile : NW then N and NNW
Depression at 2100' : 480 feet of ascent

An easy walk on grass ; safe in mist.

The drawing above illustrates the route.
Incline left where there are two posts
close together (the remains of a fence).

To ILL BELL, 2484' : ⅔ mile
S then SE
Depression at 2075' : 400 feet of ascent

An easy stroll and a final scramble.
Ill Bell has a fierce appearance on
the approach, but the ascent is not
difficult. Safe in mist.

ONE MILE

NOTE : The route to Ill Bell is part of the western arm of the popular
Kentmere Horseshoe ; Thornthwaite Crag also is part of the ridge walk.

THE VIEW

Sandwiched between Thornthwaite Crag and Ill Bell, both higher, Froswick is an undistinguished viewpoint, the best feature being the serrated skyline of the Scafell and Langdale heights in the west.

Principal Fells

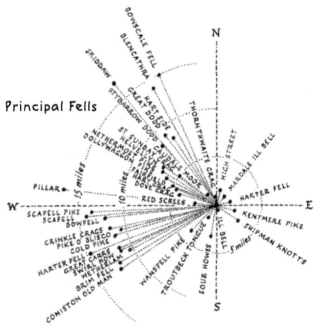

Lakes and Tarns
SE: *Kentmere Reservoir*
SSW: *Windermere*
NNW: *Ullswater*

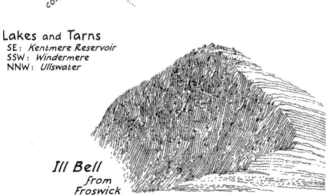

Ill Bell
from
Froswick

Gray Crag

2286'

OS grid ref: NY427119

● Hartsop

▲ GRAY CRAG

▲ HIGH
STREET

▲ THORNTHWAITE CRAG

MILES
0   1   2   3

from Hartsop

NATURAL FEATURES

A lofty ridge, bounded by exceedingly steep flanks, extends northwards from Thornthwaite Crag with a slight curve to the west, and culminates high above Hayeswater Gill in a level platform from which, on both sides, fall precipitous crags split by deep gullies. This is Gray Crag, a prominent object in the Hartsop landscape. Hayeswater forms its eastern base, while the stream issuing therefrom defines it to the north. The western boundary, below an impressive cliff of shattered rocks, is Pasture Beck.

MAP

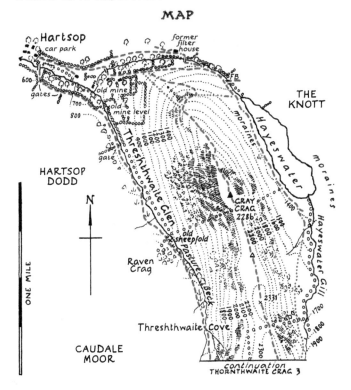

In the summer of 2014 the dam at Hayeswater was demolished, allowing the former reservoir to return to nature. This has affected a number of paths in the vicinity. For details about this major change to a corner of Lakeland, see *The Knott 2*.

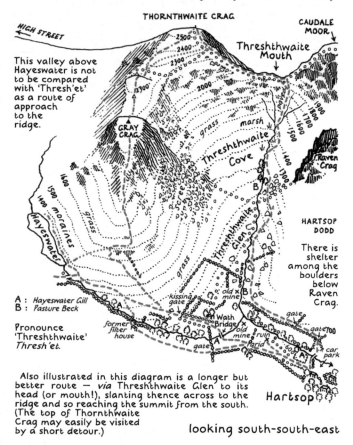

ASCENT FROM HARTSOP
1800 feet of ascent : 2 miles
(via Threshthwaite Mouth : 1950 feet of ascent : 4 miles)

THORNTHWAITE CRAG

CAUDALE MOOR

Threshthwaite Mouth

← HIGH STREET

This valley above Hayeswater is not to be compared with 'Thresh'et' as a route of approach to the ridge.

GRAY CRAG

Threshthwaite Cove

Raven Crag

HARTSOP DODD

There is shelter among the boulders below Raven Crag.

Threshthwaite Glen

Hayeswater

moraines

grass

A : Hayeswater Gill
B : Pasture Beck

Pronounce 'Threshthwaite' *Thresh'et.*

kissing gate

old mine

Wath Bridge

former filter house

gate

old mine

ruin

gate

gate

car park

Hartsop

Also illustrated in this diagram is a longer but better route — *via* Threshthwaite Glen to its head (or mouth!), slanting thence across to the ridge and so reaching the summit from the south. (The top of Thornthwaite Crag may easily be visited by a short detour.)

looking south-south-east

A more interesting alternative to the direct route is to continue first to Hayeswater and gain the ridge from there.

A new path climbs steeply to the ridge when free of the enclosing walls above Wath Bridge. It starts 30 yards after a prominent flat boulder and passes to the left of a band of crags before making a sharp right-hand turn to rejoin the apex of the ridge; this is better than the pathless direct route.

THE SUMMIT

The summit is a pleasant level plateau of grass between steep cliffs, which should be visited for their striking downwards views.
DESCENTS: The *only* practicable way off is by the descending north ridge. It is important to make sure the sharp right-hand turn is made before a band of crags.

In mist, take the path north from the summit keeping between the steep slopes (no rock has to be negotiated anywhere) for about half a mile. From here, it is simple and safe to descend the grassy slope eastwards to Hayeswater, where the path to Wath Bridge can be found.

RIDGE ROUTE

To THORNTHWAITE CRAG, 2569'
1¼ miles : slightly E of S
Two minor depressions : 350 feet of ascent

A simple stroll on grass; safe in mist.

A path may be followed for much of the way. The escarpments on both flanks of the ridge are steep enough to warn of danger in mist, when it is necessary to note that *the first two walls are crossed at right angles and the third followed.*

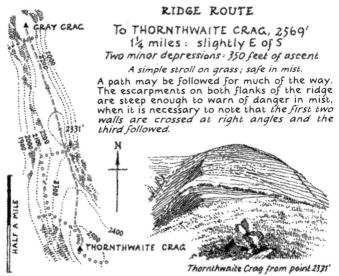

Thornthwaite Crag from point 2331'

THE VIEW

The edges of the escarpments are better viewpoints than the cairn, the steep declivities giving remarkable depth to the scene. While the view from the western edge of the summit is the more extensive, that from the eastern reveals the most striking picture, that of Hayeswater below.

Principal Fells

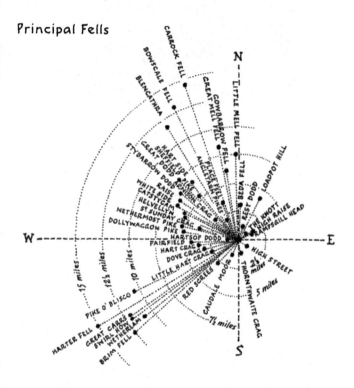

Lakes and Tarns

NNW: *Ullswater* (upper reach)

S: The small sheet of water seen above Threshthwaite Mouth is *Dubbs Reservoir*, Applethwaite Common. *Windermere* can be seen in the same direction by walking 300 yards along the ridge: it is especially well seen from point 2331'.

Hayeswater is brought into view by walking 50 yards in the direction of Rampsgill Head from the cairn, *Brothers Water* by walking 80 yards in the direction of Helvellyn.

Cascades above former filter house

Hayeswater Gill

Wath Bridge

Grey Crag

2093'

OS grid ref: NY497072

from Shipman Knotts

▲ HARTER FELL

▲ TARN CRAG

▲ KENTMERE PIKE　　▲ GREY CRAG

road summit

Longsleddale　　Huck's Bridge

Garnett Bridge　　• Selside

MILES

0　1　2　3　4　5

NATURAL FEATURES

Shap Fells are the high link between the Pennines and Lakeland. They form a broad upland area of smooth grassy slopes and plateaux, inexpressibly wild and desolate but riven by deep valleys having each its lonely sheepfarm ; gradually the ground rises in undulating ridges towards a focal point above the head of Longsleddale at the 2000 feet contour. The place of convergence of the ridges is Grey Crag, where is the first evidence, in rocky outcrops and low crags, of the characteristics so peculiar to Lakeland, although the influences of the Pennines persist in the form of peat hags and marshes. These ridges, on a map, rather resemble the spread fingers and thumb of a hand, with Grey Crag as the palm.

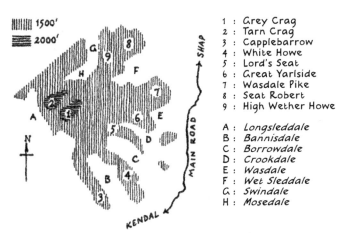

1 : Grey Crag
2 : Tarn Crag
3 : Capplebarrow
4 : White Howe
5 : Lord's Seat
6 : Great Yarlside
7 : Wasdale Pike
8 : Seat Robert
9 : High Wether Howe

A : *Longsleddale*
B : *Bannisdale*
C : *Borrowdale*
D : *Crookdale*
E : *Wasdale*
F : *Wet Sleddale*
G : *Swindale*
H : *Mosedale*

There is nothing remarkable about Grey Crag, but here Lakeland may be said to start and moorland country to end — and the transition is sudden : the quiet beauty gives place to romantic beauty, placid scenery to exciting. One looks east, and the heart is soothed ; west, and it is stirred. Longsleddale, at the western base of the fell, is a lovely valley and, at its head, typically Lakeland. Nearby, across a slight depression north-west, is a twin height, Tarn Crag ; between them is Greycrag Tarn, which more usually resembles a marsh than a stretch of water.

Grey Crag 3

MAP

For approaches from the east, readers are advised to use the Ordnance Survey 1:25,000 map OL7 (the English Lakes, south-eastern area), or, if they prefer Harvey maps, the 1:25,000 Lakeland East and Lakeland South-East maps.

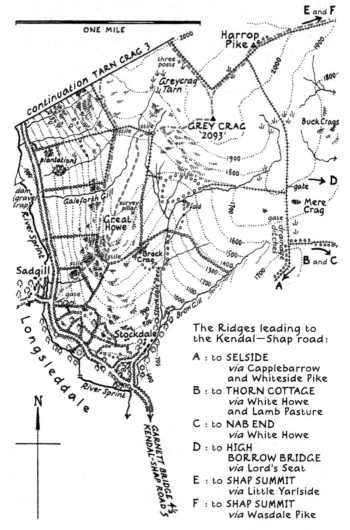

The Ridges leading to the Kendal—Shap road:

A : to SELSIDE
   via Capplebarrow
   and Whiteside Pike

B : to THORN COTTAGE
   via White Howe
   and Lamb Pasture

C : to NAB END
   via White Howe

D : to HIGH
   BORROW BRIDGE
   via Lord's Seat

E : to SHAP SUMMIT
   via Little Yarlside

F : to SHAP SUMMIT
   via Wasdale Pike

ASCENT FROM LONGSLEDDALE
1500 feet of ascent: 1½ miles from Sadgill

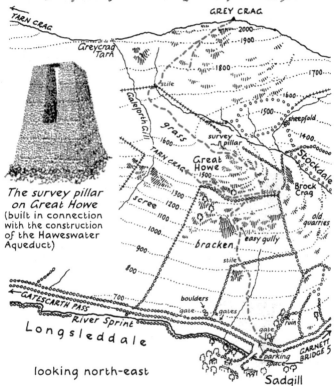

The survey pillar on Great Howe (built in connection with the construction of the Haweswater Aqueduct)

looking north-east

The hurdle across the gap in the wall at the top of the first enclosure was once awkward to negotiate, being too frail to climb. Ladies, and gentlemen with short legs, mindful of their dignity, will be glad to note that a stile has now been provided. It is dog-friendly, too, with access for four-legged fellwalkers.

Great Howe is an excellent viewpoint for Longsleddale, looking down on Sadgill and up the valley towards Buckbarrow Crag and the rocky gorge of the River Sprint. See illustration on page 9.

The ascent should be commenced from Sadgill Bridge, the more direct Stockdale route being much less attractive than the climb over Great Howe. The first thousand feet is steep but the views are beautiful. In mist, the ascent has nothing to commend it.

ASCENTS FROM THE KENDAL~SHAP ROAD

Grey Crag may be approached from the eastern fringe of the district along any of four clearly defined ridges, each of which has independent and distinct summits — and all of which descend to the main Kendal—Shap road, as well as two subsidiary ridges that also descend to the A6. These approaches are described on this and the next three pages.

A	B	C
from **SELSIDE**	*from* **THORN COTTAGE**	*from* **NAB END**
1700 feet of ascent	*1700 feet of ascent*	*1650 feet of ascent*
7 miles	*7 miles*	*6 miles*

Refer to the notes on the facing page

These are the ridges featured on *pages 7 and 8*

This Borrowdale is not to be confused with its famous Cumberland namesake.

looking north-north-west

The circuit of Bannisdale by the ridges is itself an excellent walk. The better way round is clockwise, ascending *via* Capplebarrow and descending *via* White Howe. Details of this walk can be found in *The Outlying Fells of Lakeland*.

ASCENTS FROM THE KENDAL - SHAP ROAD

It should be noted particularly that these routes lie across very lonely territory; there are thin or no paths along the ridges, and visitors are infrequent. The desolation is profound. Solitary walkers who want a decent burial should bear in mind that if an accident befalls them in this wilderness their bones are likely to adorn the scene until they rot and disintegrate.

These walks are more Pennine than Lakeland in character: there is very little rock but much tough grass and heather, and peat hags and marshes are unwelcome features. Because of the nature of the ground, the traverse of the ridges should be undertaken only after a period of dry weather; they are best left alone on a wet day or during a rainy season or if under snow. Subject to the disabilities mentioned, it may be stated at once that the ridges offer easy and exhilarating walking in impressive surroundings, while the wide horizons and the vast skyscapes deserve the brush of a Turner.

This is fine open country, but it is not Lakeland.

FROM SELSIDE

This approach, along a ridge that splits Longsleddale and the shy Bannisdale, which is concealed from the main road by a screen of trees and low hills, is long, and an early start is necessary. Clear weather is advisable, too, because the way, although largely following a wall and/or fence from just before Todd Fell onwards, is not clear at the finish.

The first section is the best, the rising path to Whiteside Pike looking more like a climb out of Newlands or Buttermere than this far eastern outpost, with the rocky little summit of the Pike, clad in heather and grass, being a delectable place. A pretty descent follows to a wall stile, which is when the nature of the walk changes to that of a moorland tramp. Visit Todd Fell and Capplebarrow for views.

Starting point (foot of lane leading to Mosergh Farm) : SD530998.

FROM THORN COTTAGE

Finding the starting point is the first step: Bannisdale High Bridge and nearby Thorn Cottage lie on a narrow loop road off a winding section of the A6. There is some verge parking north of the cottage.

As in the route from Selside, the early section holds much promise, but once past the height of Lamb Pasture the approach slips from pastoral beauty into grassy mediocrity, only relieved by the summit of White How and, higher up, the rocky Mere Crag.

Starting point (gate beside Thorn Cottage) : NY542013.

FROM NAB END

The impressive Nab End holds the promise of much to come, and there is some other early interest with a series of shooting butts and a sketchy path through some heathery ups and downs, but then the drudgery begins as the route merges with that above.

Starting point (gate below Nab End) : NY548030.

Mere Crag

All three routes shown on the facing page visit this remarkably 'clean' face of rock, which shows no sign of decay; lush grass grows up to its base. Climbers will enjoy its slabs.

ASCENTS FROM THE KENDAL-SHAP ROAD

D	E	F
from HIGH BORROW BRIDGE	from THE A6 ROAD SUMMIT via Little Yarlside	from THE A6 ROAD SUMMIT via Wasdale Pike
1700 feet of ascent	1000 feet of ascent	1200 feet of ascent
5 miles	5 miles	6 miles

looking west-north-west

Refer to the notes on the facing page

Shap Fell and the road summit

Before the Lancaster to Penrith section of the M6 motorway was completed in 1970, the way between north-west England and Scotland meant a crossing of Shap Fell via the A6, a route that, in winter months, was bedevilled with ice and snow; in such conditions truck drivers at the foot of the pass had to fix chains on their wheels to make any upward progress. In particularly harsh conditions, lorries became marooned in snow drifts and local folk had to come to the aid of stranded drivers. A memorial stone at the southern end of the layby at the summit states:

This memorial pays tribute to the drivers and crews of vehicles that made possible the social and commercial links between north and south on this old and difficult route over Shap Fell before the opening of the M6 motorway. Remembered too are those who built and maintained the road and the generations of local people who gave freely of food and shelter to stranded travellers in bad weather.

ASCENTS FROM THE KENDAL – SHAP ROAD

FROM HIGH BORROW BRIDGE

If approaching on the A6 from Kendal, bear left on an unsignposted road shortly after Kendal Caravans as the A6 bends right and climbs. If coming from Shap, turn sharp right as soon as the caravans come into view. There is room to park on the verge after crossing Borrow Beck. Continue along the road (which was the original road to Shap) to the last broken wall on the left 250 yards before an old barn on the right, and start the climb from here. There is a very thin path initially on the steep climb to High House Bank, beyond which a good path leads to the beacon on Robin Hood (1613') and Lord's Seat (1719'). The rest of the climb is a dull trudge.
Starting point (road below High House Gate) : NY552051.

FROM THE ROAD SUMMIT (*via* Little Yarlside)

From the gate opposite the summit layby a fence and wall leads unerringly to the summit of Little Yarlside (1691') and on to Great Yarlside (1986'). From here it is an easy walk to the prominent cairn on Harrop Pike with a further half-mile stroll on grass to Grey Crag's top.
Starting point (summit gate) : NY554063.

The cairn on Harrop Pike

FROM THE ROAD SUMMIT (*via* Wasdale Pike)

One hundred yards north of the summit's only structure (a disused substation), cross a stile and keep right following the edge of a former plantation. The route descends to Wasdale on the way to the rather sad ruins of Wasdale Head, a long-derelict farm. Follow a fence, crossing it at a junction with another, then strike out across grass to Wasdale Pike where a path leads to Great Yarlside.   *Starting point* (stile) : NY553068

Details of routes D, E and F can be found in *The Outlying Fells of Lakeland* in the chapters on the Crookdale and Wasdale horseshoes.

Avoiding treading the same ground twice

It *is* possible, if you are a superman, to ascend *via* route A, descend *via* route F and walk back to your starting point, but for lesser mortals a trek of 20 miles is out of the question. However, walkers can combine each route with the nearest alternative, keeping road walking to a minimum, as well as other combinations:
A–B, B–C, C–D, C–E, C–F, D–E, D–F and E–F.

THE SUMMIT

The top of the fell is extensive, but the highest point, indicated by a cairn, is not in doubt although it stands but little above a wide expanse of small outcrops and peat hags.

DESCENTS : In clear weather, with ample time in hand, a way may be made to the Kendal—Shap road by any of the eastern ridges. If Longsleddale is the objective, the descent should be made by Great Howe in preference to a direct route *via* Stockdale.

The head of Longsleddale from Great Howe

In bad conditions, the descent to the Kendal-Shap road must not be undertaken lightly. Note that only the Yarlside ridge has a continuous fence or wall all the way to the road. For Longsleddale, *in mist*, pick a way straight down into Stockdale to avoid the scarps on Great Howe.

- - - - - - - - - - - - - - - - - - -

RIDGE ROUTE

To TARN CRAG, 2176'

¾ mile : N then NW and SSW
Depression at 1940'
250 feet of ascent

Straightforward walking.
A direct route runs foul of Greycrag Tarn, a boggy morass to be avoided. Instead, skirt the marshes by keeping along the side of the fence (which is still wet in places) and turn off towards the summit on a thin path.

HALF A MILE

THE VIEW

Grey Crag is the most easterly of the Lakeland fells, but is not of sufficient elevation to provide the panorama across the district that might be expected from its position. Higher neighbours around the head of Longsleddale conceal most of the better known mountains, but the Coniston group is quite prominent and there is a peep of the Scafells over the saddle between Yoke and Ill Bell.

Principal Fells

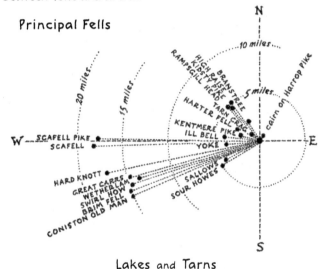

Lakes and Tarns

SSW: *Skeggles Water*
SW: *Windermere* (two sections)

Although the view towards Lakeland is disappointingly restricted, there can be no complaint of the quality of the prospects in other directions. On a clear day the panorama is remarkably extensive and very beautiful; there is a vastness, a spaciousness, about it that is usually lacking in the views from Lakeland summits. Just to the right of the cairn on Harrop Pike, Cross Fell and the twin Dun Fells start a glorious sweep of the Pennines extending south as far as Pendle Hill, with the principal heights of Mickle Fell, the Mallerstang fells, Whernside and Ingleborough all prominent. The nearer Howgill Fells, which always look attractive, are excellently grouped. Southwards is Kendal and the Kent Valley, and, beyond, Morecambe Bay silvers the horizon round to the isolated mass of Black Combe. There can be few better views in the country — but the days on which it is fully visible are also few, unfortunately.

Hallin Fell

1271'

OS grid ref: NY433198

from above Mellguards

Hallin Fell, beautifully situated overlooking a curve of Ullswater and commanding unrivalled views of the lovely secluded hinterland of Martindale, may be regarded as the motorists' fell, for the sandals and slippers and polished shoes of the numerous car owners who park their properties on the crest of the road above the Howtown zig-zags on Sunday afternoons have smoothed to its summit a wide track that is seldom violated by the rough boots of fellwalkers. In choosing Hallin Fell as their weekend picnic place and playground the Penrith and Carlisle motorists show commendable discrimination, for the rich rewards its summit offers are out of all proportion to the slight effort of ascent.

HALLIN FELL
Sandwick   ▲ Howtown
PLACE ▲   ▲ BEDA
FELL   FELL
● Patterdale
MILES
0   1   2   3

MAP

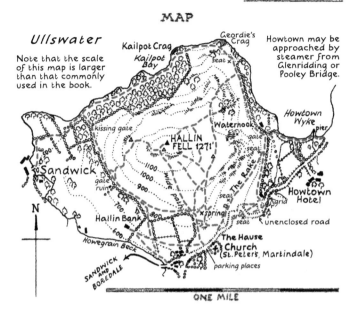

Ullswater

Note that the scale of this map is larger than that commonly used in the book.

Kailpot Crag

Kailpot Bay

Geordie's Crag

Howtown may be approached by steamer from Glenridding or Pooley Bridge.

seat

kissing gate

Waternook

Howtown Wyke

pier

gate

HALLIN FELL 1271'

1100

1000

900

wide path

The Rake

Sandwick

gate ruin

700

seat

800

spring

seat

Howtown Hotel

aerial

unenclosed road

N

Hallin Bank

600

Howegrain Beck

The Hause

Church (St. Peters, Martindale)

parking places

SANDWICK AND BOREDALE

ONE MILE

ASCENTS

FROM ST PETER'S CHURCH — *550 feet of ascent : ½ mile*

There is one royal road to the top : this is the wide grass path leaving the Hause opposite the church, and it can be ascended comfortably in bare feet ; in dry weather the short smooth turf is slippery. Another track from the Hause visits the large cairn overlooking Howtown, and offers an alternative route to the top. A third way up is to climb the grassy path on the western flank which starts above the intake wall beside a ruin.

FROM HOWTOWN — *800 feet of ascent : 1½ miles*

Go past Waternook on the lakeside path. About 300 yards before Geordie's Crag, at a point where a tree grows over the wall from the right, a grassy path heads steeply up the fellside and into a wide shallow gully, almost a valley. At a crossroads of paths, turn right. The gradients to the summit knoll are now very gentle.

FROM SANDWICK — *850 feet of ascent : 1 mile*

Follow the popular lakeside path for 600 yards then turn right and through the kissing gate above the intake wall. A grassy path heads up the fell's western flank above a small ruin.

Incidentally (although this has nothing to do with fellwalking!) the lakeside path *via* Kailpot Crag is entirely delightful. A circuit of the fell starting from The Hause, anti-clockwise *via* The Rake and returning *via* the kissing gate, is a splendid walk.

THE SUMMIT

In 2014 the top of the cairn was expertly rebuilt and it is now about six inches higher than shown here, with a much flatter top.

The man who built the summit cairn of Hallin Fell did more than indicate the highest point: he erected for himself a permanent memorial. This 12' obelisk, a landmark for miles around, is a massive structure of squared and prepared stone. Built into the cairn is a plaque bearing various initials and the date 1864. A small cairn, with a good view of the twin valleys of Boredale and Martindale, lies 70 yards south-south-west.

The Martindale skyline, from the top of Hallin Fell

DESCENTS : The temptation to descend east directly to Howtown should be resisted for the slope above The Rake is rough and unpleasant.

The easiest way off, and the quickest, is by the path going down to the church on the Hause. *In mist*, no other route can safely be attempted.

The lower reach of Ullswater from north of the summit

THE VIEW

The bird's eye view of Ullswater is dramatic, but the classic scene unfolded is an intimate one of green fields and steep fells, the Martindale district, for which this is the best viewpoint.

The panorama is good considering the modest elevation.

Principal Fells

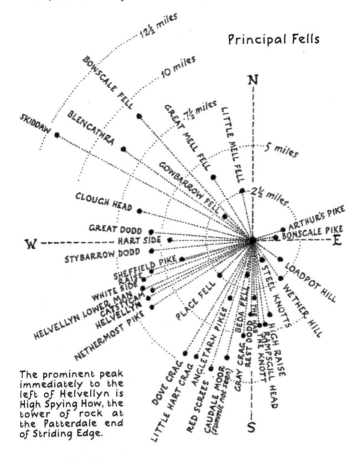

The prominent peak immediately to the left of Helvellyn is High Spying How, the tower of rock at the Patterdale end of Striding Edge.

Lakes and Tarns

WSW to NE: *Ullswater* (upper reach)
(all of the middle and lower reaches)

Harter Fell

2552'

OS grid ref: NY460093

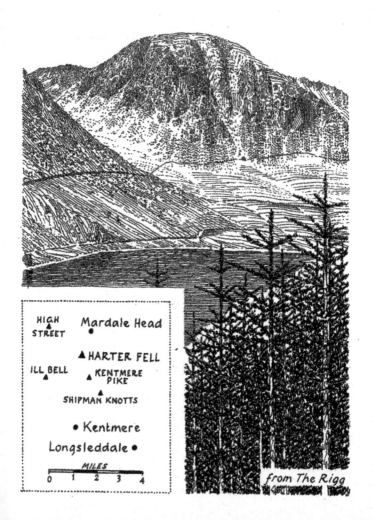

HIGH STREET ▲   Mardale Head ●

▲ HARTER FELL

ILL BELL ▲   ▲ KENTMERE PIKE

▲ SHIPMAN KNOTTS

● Kentmere

Longsleddale ●

MILES
0 1 2 3 4

from The Rigg

NATURAL FEATURES

A broad wedge of lonely upland country rises from the valley of the Kent at Burneside and continues north, narrowing, between the valleys of Kentmere and Longsleddale for nine miles; until, having very gradually attained its maximum height on Harter Fell, the ground suddenly collapses in a tremendous wall of crags, falling swiftly to the head of Mardale amongst wild and romantic surroundings — one of the noblest mountain scenes in the district. This northern face is Harter Fell's chief glory, for here, too, a shelf cradles Small Water, which is the finest of Lakeland's tarns in the opinion of many qualified to judge: seen in storm, the picture is most impressive and awe-inspiring. The other slopes have less of note although Drygrove Gill is an interesting example of landslip and Wren Gill has extensive (and dangerous) quarries. Harter Fell is one of the few fells that can claim a well known pass on either side of its summit: Nan Bield Pass on the west and Gatescarth Pass on the east link Kentmere and Longsleddale respectively with Mardale, but since the hamlet of Mardale Head was 'drowned' by Haweswater (shame!) these passes have largely fallen from favour.

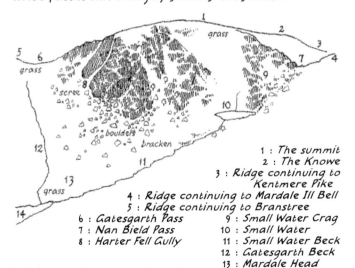

1 : The summit
2 : The Knowe
3 : Ridge continuing to Kentmere Pike
4 : Ridge continuing to Mardale Ill Bell
5 : Ridge continuing to Branstree
6 : Gatesgarth Pass
7 : Nan Bield Pass
8 : Harter Fell Gully
9 : Small Water Crag
10 : Small Water
11 : Small Water Beck
12 : Gatesgarth Beck
13 : Mardale Head
14 : Haweswater

looking south-east

MAP

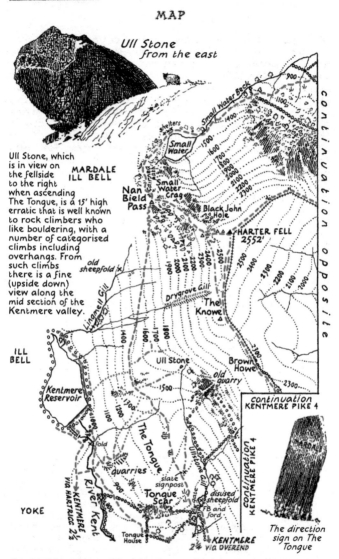

Ull Stone
from the east

Ull Stone, which
is in view on
the fellside
to the right
when ascending
The Tongue, is a 15' high
erratic that is well known
to rock climbers who
like bouldering, with a
number of categorised
climbs including
overhangs. From
such climbs
there is a fine
(upside down)
view along the
mid section of the
Kentmere valley.

MARDALE
ILL BELL

Nan
Bield
Pass

shelters

Small
Water

Small
Water
Crag

Black John
Hole

HARTER FELL
2552'

continuation opposite

old
sheepfold

Lingmell Gill

Drygrove Gill

The
Knowe

Brown
Howe

ILL
BELL

Kentmere
Reservoir

Ull Stone

old
quarry

continuation
KENTMERE PIKE 4

fold

The Tongue

quarries

Ullstone Gill

slate
signpost

Tongue
Scar

disused
sheepfold

FB and
ford

Tongue
House

YOKE

River Kent

KENTMERE
VIA HARTRIGG 2½

KENTMERE
2¼ VIA OVEREND

continuation KENTMERE PIKE 4

The direction
sign on The
Tongue

An old slate signpost giving directions to Mardale may be found near the
junction of the track across The Tongue and a thin branch to the right that
used to be the main route to Nan Bield Pass. It is 40 yards from the junction.

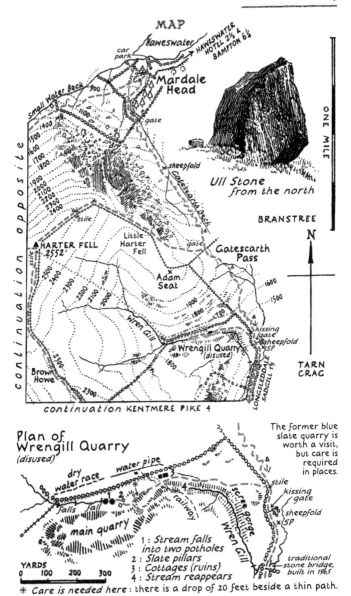

MAP

Haweswater

car park

HAWESWATER
HOTEL 2¾ 4
BAMPTON 6¼

Mardale
Head

Small Water Beck

900

1000

1100

gate

sheepfold

Gatescarth Beck

ONE MILE

Ull Stone
from the north

BRANSTREE

N

1400
1500
1600
1700
1800
1900
2000
2100
2200
2300
2400

stile

HARTER FELL
2552'

stile

Little
Harter
Fell

gate

Gatescarth Pass

1600

1500

Adam
Seat

2500
2400
2300
2200
2100
2000

Wren Gill

1900

1800

1700

kissing
gate
sheepfold
SP

Wrengill Quarry
(disused)

1800

continuation opposite

2300

Brown
Howe

2300

LONGSLEDDALE
SADGILL 1¾

TARN
CRAG

continuation KENTMERE PIKE 4

Plan of
Wrengill Quarry
(disused)

The former blue
slate quarry is
worth a visit,
but care is
required
in places.

dry
water race

water pipe

falls

fall

1 2

main quarry

railway

scree gorge

Wren Gill

stile

kissing
gate

sheepfold
SP

1 : Stream falls
into two potholes
2 : Slate pillars
3 : Cottages (ruins)
4 : Stream reappears

traditional
stone bridge,
built in 1965

YARDS
0   100   200   300

* Care is needed here: there is a drop of 20 feet beside a thin path.

The west face of Harter Fell
from the north-east ridge of Ill Bell

ASCENT FROM KENTMERE
2200 feet of ascent
5¼ miles via Nan Bield Pass : 4¼ miles via Kentmere Pike

looking north

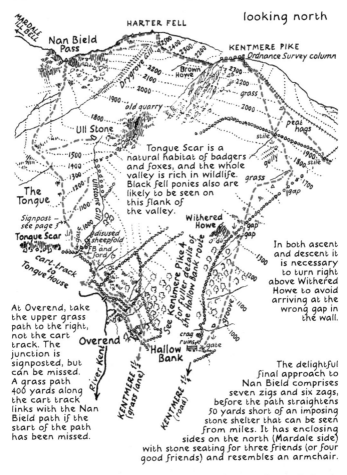

MARDALE ILL BELL

HARTER FELL

Nan Bield Pass

KENTMERE PIKE
Ordnance Survey column

2500
2400
2300
2200

Drygrove Gill

Brown Howe

2300
2200

grass

2100
2000

1900

old quarry

2000

peat hags

1800

Ull Stone

stile

1500
1400
1300

gully

1900 stile
1800

1200

grass

1700

The Tongue

Ullstone Gill

1100

gap

Signpost – see page 5

Tongue Scar is a natural habitat of badgers and foxes, and the whole valley is rich in wildlife. Black fell ponies also are likely to be seen on this flank of the valley.

Withered Howe

gap
gap

Tongue Scar

gate 1000

disused sheepfold
FB and ford

In both ascent and descent it is necessary to turn right above Withered Howe to avoid arriving at the wrong gap in the wall.

cart-track to Tongue House

1300

1200

See Kentmere Pike 4 for fuller details of the hollow bank route

groove

1100

At Overend, take the upper grass path to the right, not the cart track. The junction is signposted, but can be missed. A grass path 400 yards along the cart track links with the Nan Bield path if the start of the path has been missed.

Overend

crag ruins

gate

1000

Hallow Bank

River Kent

KENTMERE 1¼ (grass lane)

KENTMERE 1¼ (road)

The delightful final approach to Nan Bield comprises seven zigs and six zags, before the path straightens 50 yards short of an imposing stone shelter that can be seen from miles. It has enclosing sides on the north (Mardale side) with stone seating for three friends (or four good friends) and resembles an armchair.

Two routes are shown. That from Hallow Bank is both easier and shorter, that from Overend much the more beautiful and interesting. The round journey serves as an excellent introduction to upper Kentmere. The sharp-crested Nan Bield is the finest of Lakeland passes.

ASCENT FROM LONGSLEDDALE
1950 feet of ascent : 4¼ miles from Sadgill

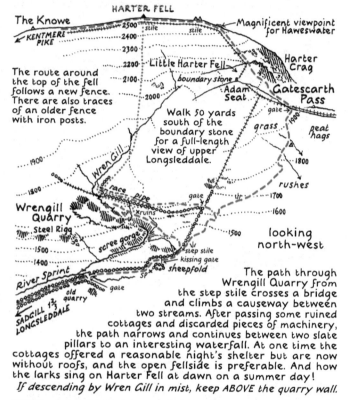

HARTER FELL

The Knowe
KENTMERE PIKE

2500   stile   stile

2400

Magnificent viewpoint
for Haweswater

2300

2200   Little Harter Fell

The route around
the top of the fell
follows a new fence.
There are also traces
of an older fence
with iron posts.

2100   boundary stone

2000

Harter
Crag

Adam
Seat

Gatescarth
Pass

Walk 50 yards
south of the
boundary stone
for a full-length
view of upper
Longsleddale.

gate

1900

grass

peat
hags

1900   Wren Gill

1800   race pipe

Wrengill
Quarry
Steel Rigg

1800

rushes

gate

1700

1600

1500

looking
north-west

ruins

scree gorge

1500

1400

step stile
kissing gate
sheepfold

River Sprint

gate

SADGILL 1¾   old quarry
LONGSLEDDALE

The path through
Wrengill Quarry from
the step stile crosses a bridge
and climbs a causeway between
two streams. After passing some ruined
cottages and discarded pieces of machinery, the
path narrows and continues between two slate
pillars to an interesting waterfall. At one time the
cottages offered a reasonable night's shelter but are now
without roofs, and the open fellside is preferable. And how
the larks sing on Harter Fell at dawn on a summer day!
If descending by Wren Gill in mist, keep ABOVE the quarry wall.

The disappearance of Wren Gill

The Gatescarth route
is particularly easy : a
hands-in-pockets stroll
with no steep climbing,
the top being reached
with surprising lack of
effort. Nonagenarians
will find it eminently
suitable. An alternative
visiting Wren Gill is
interesting, *but should
be avoided in mist.*

ASCENT FROM MARDALE
1750 feet of ascent : 2 miles from the road end

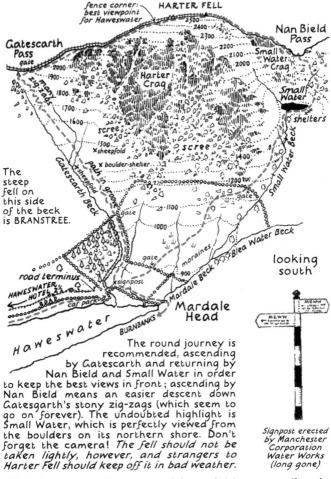

looking
south

Signpost erected
by Manchester
Corporation
Water Works
(long gone)

The round journey is
recommended, ascending
by Gatescarth and returning by
Nan Bield and Small Water in order
to keep the best views in front; ascending by
Nan Bield means an easier descent down
Gatescarth's stony zig-zags (which seem to
go on forever). The undoubted highlight is
Small Water, which is perfectly viewed from
the boulders on its northern shore. Don't
forget the camera! *The fell should not be
taken lightly, however, and strangers to
Harter Fell should keep off it in bad weather.*

This is an excellent expedition, richly rewarding in
intimate scenes of Harter Fell's grand northern cliffs
and in the views of Haweswater from its summit, yet
short in distance and needing much less effort in
execution than its formidable appearance suggests.

THE SUMMIT

A mild shock awaits anyone reaching the top of the fell on a first visit, especially in mist, for there is a spectral weirdness about the two highest cairns (one of which is a double cairn). The stones support an elaborate superstructure of iron fence posts and railings, which, having served their original mission, now act as an adornment that has a nightmarish quality. The summit cairn, illustrated above, now has a higher proportion of stones to metal.

The highest part of the fell, a graceful curve, is a long grassy sheep-walk. The pedestrian route across the top follows a wire fence. The paths are clear on hard ground, in places ten yards wide or more. Only at the peat bed is there any significant moisture to be found.

The fence corner is the setting for the illustration opposite, which was used to introduce the author's television programmes in the 1980s.

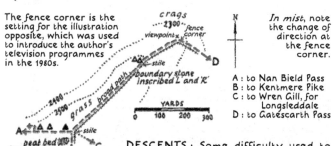

In mist, note the change of direction at the fence corner.

A : to Nan Bield Pass
B : to Kentmere Pike
C : to Wren Gill, for Longsleddale
D : to Gatescarth Pass

DESCENTS : Some difficulty used to arise in locating the ridge west going down to Nan Bield Pass, which cannot be seen from the summit, but the path from the summit cairn, arrow-straight in the direction of Red Screes, is now much clearer and is cairned, so there should be no problems. Other routes follow the fence, although a quick way down to Wren Gill may also be noted. In mist, head directly west for the ridge to Nan Bield Pass. Keep to the line of the fence on other routes.

*Haweswater
from the fence corner*

THE VIEW
(with distances in miles)

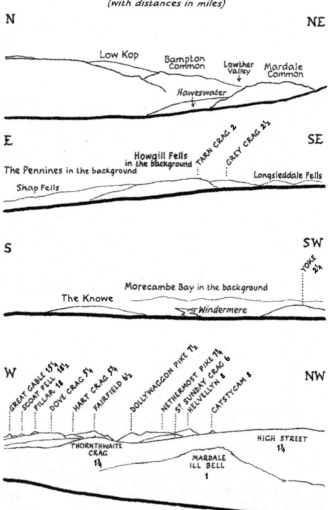

Three of Lakeland's 3000-footers are in view: Scafell Pike, Scafell and Helvellyn. Skiddaw can be seen from the double cairn to the north-east.

THE VIEW

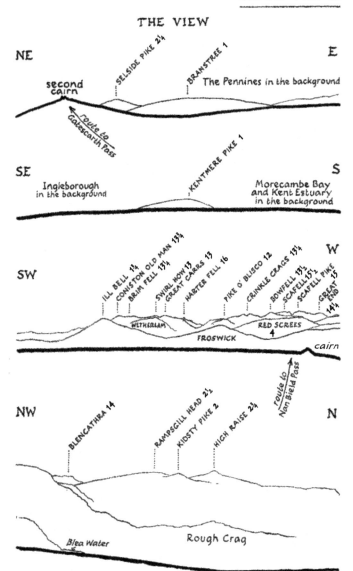

NE / **E**

SELSIDE PIKE 2¼ · BRANSTREE 1

second cairn

The Pennines in the background

route to Gatescarth Pass

SE / **S**

Ingleborough in the background

KENTMERE PIKE 1

Morecambe Bay and Kent Estuary in the background

SW / **W**

ILL BELL 1¾ · CONISTON OLD MAN 13¾ · BRIM FELL 13½ · SWIRL HOW 13 · GREAT CARRS 13 · HARTER FELL 16 · PIKE O' BLISCO 12 · CRINKLE CRAGS 13¼ · BOWFELL 13½ · SCAFELL 15½ · SCAFELL PIKE 15 · GREAT END 14¼

WETHERLAM

RED SCREES 4

FROSWICK

cairn

route to Nan Bield Pass

NW / **N**

BLENCATHRA 14 · RAMPSGILL HEAD 2½ · KIDSTY PIKE 2 · HIGH RAISE 2¾

Blea Water

Rough Crag

Blea Water cannot be seen from the cairn, but is brought into view by walking a few yards north-west.

RIDGE ROUTES

TO KENTMERE PIKE, 2397': 1¼ miles
S then SSE
Depression at 2275': 150 feet of ascent

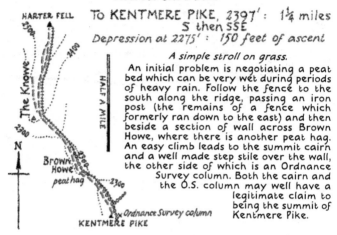

A simple stroll on grass.

An initial problem is negotiating a peat bed which can be very wet during periods of heavy rain. Follow the fence to the south along the ridge, passing an iron post (the remains of a fence which formerly ran down to the east) and then beside a section of wall across Brown Howe, where there is another peat hag. An easy climb leads to the summit cairn and a well made step stile over the wall, the other side of which is an Ordnance Survey column. Both the cairn and the O.S. column may well have a legitimate claim to being the summit of Kentmere Pike.

TO BRANSTREE, 2339': 2 miles : NE then SE and NE
Depression at 1875' (Gatescarth Pass) : 465 feet of ascent

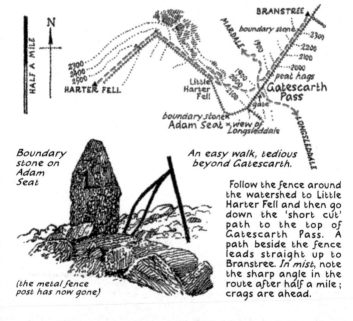

Boundary stone on Adam Seat

An easy walk, tedious beyond Gatescarth.

Follow the fence around the watershed to Little Harter Fell and then go down the 'short cut' path to the top of Gatescarth Pass. A path beside the fence leads straight up to Branstree. *In mist*, note the sharp angle in the route after half a mile; crags are ahead.

(the metal fence post has now gone)

RIDGE ROUTE

To MARDALE ILL BELL, 2496′: W, then WNW and NW
1 mile
Depression at 2100′ (Nan Bield Pass):   450 feet of ascent

An excellent crossing of a fine pass, with beautiful and impressive views.
  Aim west (in the direction of Red Screes) along a cairned path until the ridge going down to Nan Bield is seen below: this is a delectable descent, Small Water being a striking feature. Nan Bield is marked by a big cairn shelter; round the outcrop beyond on the left side. When the gradient starts to ease, take the path slanting up to the right and watch for the white boulders that indicate the final rise to the summit. *In mist,* in the days when there were no paths across the top Mardale Ill Bell was confusing and dangerous; nowadays it is a safe place to venture, *but care is still needed.*

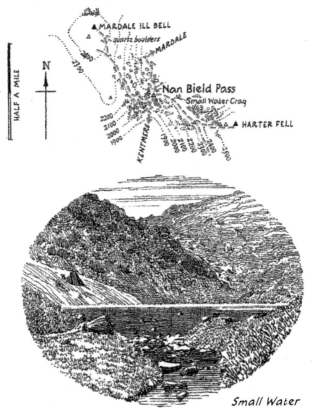

Small Water

Hartsop Dodd

2028'

OS grid ref: NY411119

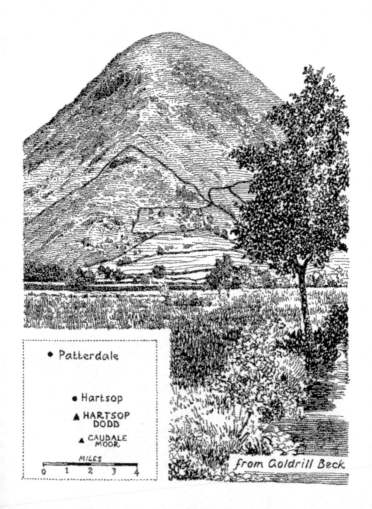

- Patterdale
- Hartsop
- ▲ HARTSOP DODD
- ▲ CAUDALE MOOR

MILES
0 1 2 3 4

from Goldrill Beck

NATURAL FEATURES

For a few miles along the road from Patterdale to Kirkstone, Hartsop Dodd has the form of a steep sided conical hill, rising like a giant tumulus from the flat floor of the valley; a high ridge connecting with the loftier Caudale Moor behind is unseen and unsuspected. After the fashion of many subsidiary fells in this area, the imposing front is a sham, for the Dodd is no more than the knuckled fist at the end of one of the several arms of Caudale Moor. It rises from pleasant places, pastures and woods and water, and quite rightly has been named from the delightful hamlet nestling unspoilt among trees at its foot.

It is interesting to note that Hartsop Dodd (*Low* Hartsop Dodd), at 2028' has a greater elevation than its counterpart *High* Hartsop Dodd (1702') on the far side of the valley beyond Caudale Bridge (see *Book One: The Eastern Fells*). The prefixes relate to their geographical positions in the valley, not to their altitudes.

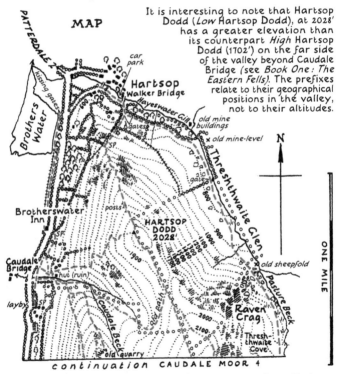

MAP

A new path from the layby to the Brotherswater Inn alleviates the need for road walking between the two. It also connects the start of three paths: the zig-zag shepherd's track direct to Hartsop Dodd; the more roundabout Caudale Beck path; and the path ascending Caudale Moor's north-west ridge.

ASCENT FROM HARTSOP

A feature of the paths leading up Hartsop Dodd is that, for much of their length, they run in well-engineered grooves that help considerably in defining the routes. The best way up is by the steep north ridge, a beautiful climb. Cross Walker Bridge and then go right when the Threshthwaite path swings left.

ASCENT FROM CAUDALE BRIDGE

The former shepherds' path zig-zagging steeply up the west flank is seldom used but is distinct, although obstructed by bracken in the summer. The only easy route follows Caudale Beck at first and gains the ridge between the Dodd and Caudale Moor; this way is dull.

THE SUMMIT

The fence post in the illustration is still there but getting more weather beaten with every passing year. The wall has crumbled behind it; this is actually the highest point of Hartsop Dodd. The summit cairn is on a gentle mound about ten yards away in the direction of Dollywaggon Pike.

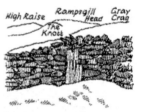

RIDGE ROUTE

HARTSOP DODD

Raven Crag

Threshthwaite Cove

ONE MILE

N

CAUDALE MOOR

DESCENTS: The grooves do not continue onto the summit. To find the path going down to the west, walk in the direction of Dove Crag — the top of the groove lies straight ahead. The path along the north ridge now leads to the car park at Walker Bridge. The old path from the ridge between Hartsop Dodd and Caudale Moor to Caudale Bridge (marked on the map on *Hartsop Dodd 2*) is to be preferred to the more direct route when the bracken is high.

In mist, the path on the west is very difficult to find, and the start of the old path beside Caudale Beck is also vague. The safest way down is to follow the path north down the ridge to Hartsop.

To CAUDALE MOOR, 2502'
1½ miles : SSE, then S
Depression at 1900' : 620 feet of ascent

An easy climb on grass, safe in mist. The wall drearily links the two summits. In fine weather, interest may be introduced into the walk by following the edge of the escarpment on the left, the views from there down into Threshthwaite being very striking.

Patterdale

THE VIEW

The view of Dove Crag and Dovedale across the gulf of the Patterdale valley is exceedingly impressive, a classic amongst views. Red Screes, too, rises majestically and steeply from the depths of Kirkstone. The edges of the summit, rather than the top, give the best views.

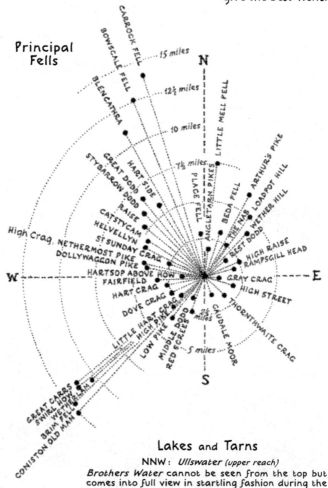

Principal Fells

Lakes and Tarns

NNW: *Ullswater (upper reach)*

Brothers Water cannot be seen from the top but comes into full view in startling fashion during the descent by the north ridge.

Dovedale

High Raise

OS grid ref: NY448135

Howtown
Martindale
Bampton
▲ WETHER HILL
Measand
▲ HIGH RAISE
▲ Riggindale
HIGH STREET

MILES

0   1   2   3   4

from the col
below The Knott

NATURAL FEATURES

Second in altitude among the fells east of Kirkstone and Ullswater, High Raise is overtopped only by High Street itself. Topographically, it cannot be said to occupy an important position, for it commands no valleys and it is not a meeting place of ridges; yet, nevertheless, its summit cone rises distinctively from the lofty watershed of the main range, and it is the last fell, going north, with the characteristics of a mountain — beyond are rolling foothills. Flanking it on the west is the valley of Ramps Gill, to which falls abruptly a featureless wall of grass and scree. Much more extensive, and much more interesting, are the eastern declivities, going down to Haweswater: here natural forces have scooped out a great hollow just below the subsidiary summit of Low Raise, leaving a mile-long fringe of crags between two airy ridges.

There are considerable streams on this flank, and all flow into Haweswater. Formerly these waters helped to irrigate the fertile Lowther and Eden valleys, but nowadays only the most favoured do so: the fate of the majority is captive travel along less pleasurable routes to the taps of Manchester, there to serve the needs of man in other ways.

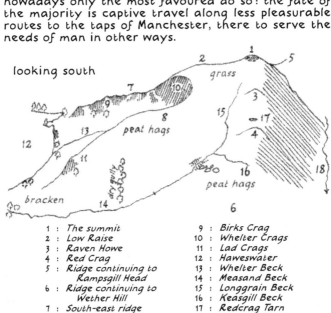

looking south

1 : The summit
2 : Low Raise
3 : Raven Howe
4 : Red Crag
5 : Ridge continuing to Rampsgill Head
6 : Ridge continuing to Wether Hill
7 : South-east ridge
8 : North-west ridge
9 : Birks Crag
10 : Whelter Crags
11 : Lad Crags
12 : Haweswater
13 : Whelter Beck
14 : Measand Beck
15 : Longgrain Beck
16 : Keasgill Beck
17 : Redcrag Tarn
18 : Rampsgill Beck

MAP

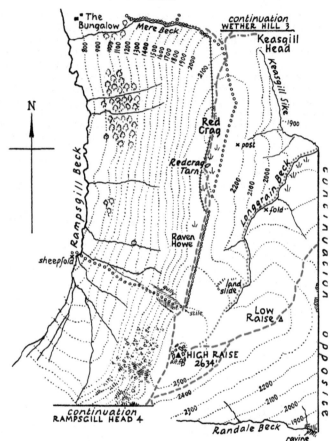

The lonely valley of Ramps Gill is entirely within the Martindale Deer Forest. Walkers are requested not to enter this area to avoid disturbing the deer. See *The Nab 2 and 3*.

Subsidiary summits

High Raise has three subsidiary summits. The most obvious is Low Raise (2473'), just over half a mile away to the east with a prominent cairn — see summit details on *page 9*. The ridge north of High Raise, the course of the High Street Roman road, swells first to Raven Howe (2345') and then Red Crag (2333').

MAP

ONE MILE

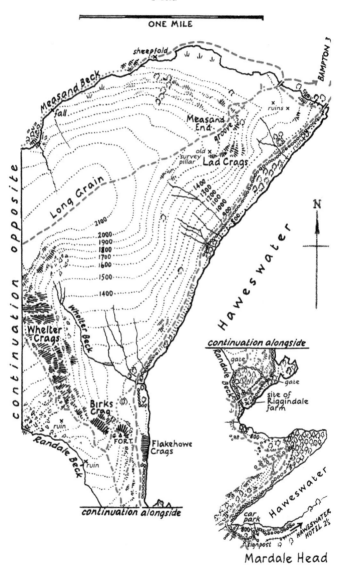

Mardale Head

ASCENTS FROM PATTERDALE AND HARTSOP
2400 feet of ascent : 5¼ miles from Patterdale
2250 feet of ascent : 3½ miles from Hartsop

There are a number of paths across the top of Rampsgill Head and *in mist* there could be confusion. Consult the summit diagram on *Rampsgill Head 7* if in any doubt.

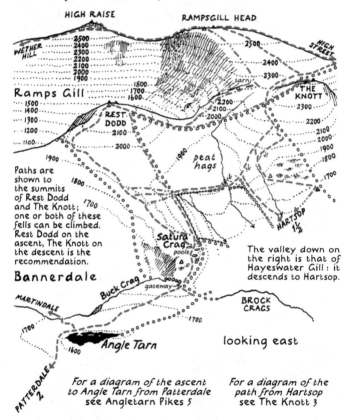

HIGH RAISE   RAMPSGILL HEAD

WETHER HILL

HIGH STREET

Ramps Gill

tarn

THE KNOTT

REST DODD

peat hags

Paths are shown to the summits of Rest Dodd and The Knott; one or both of these fells can be climbed. Rest Dodd on the ascent, The Knott on the descent is the recommendation.

HARTSOP 1½

Bannerdale

Satura Crag

pools

The valley down on the right is that of Hayeswater Gill: it descends to Hartsop.

MARTINDALE

Buck Crag

gateway

BROCK CRAGS

Angle Tarn

looking east

PATTERDALE 2

For a diagram of the ascent to Angle Tarn from Patterdale see Angletarn Pikes 5

For a diagram of the path from Hartsop see The Knott 3

This is a most enjoyable excursion with a succession of widely differing views, all excellent; and the route itself, being rather 'cross country', is an interesting puzzle to unravel. In bad weather, however, there will be some difficulty, and a stranger may run into trouble on top of Rampsgill Head, where there are crags.

ASCENT FROM MARTINDALE
2100 feet of ascent : 5 miles from Martindale (Old Church)

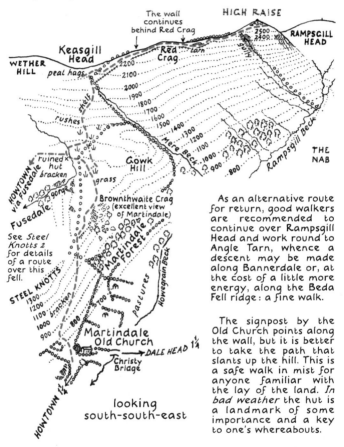

As an alternative route for return, good walkers are recommended to continue over Rampsgill Head and work round to Angle Tarn, whence a descent may be made along Bannerdale or, at the cost of a little more energy, along the Beda Fell ridge : a fine walk.

The signpost by the Old Church points along the wall, but it is better to take the path that slants up the hill. This is a safe walk in mist for anyone familiar with the lay of the land. *In bad weather* the hut is a landmark of some importance and a key to one's whereabouts.

From Howtown, the ruined hut may be reached more quickly by a direct route along Fusedale. For details of this attractive alternative approach, see *Wether Hill 7.*

This is the only full-size mountain expedition conveniently available from the neighbourhood of Martindale and Howtown. It hardly lives up to its early promise, the middle section being dull, but the views are excellent throughout.

ASCENTS FROM MARDALE
1900 feet of ascent
3½ miles from Mardale Head ; 3½ miles from Measand

NOTE : To the ascent from Measand must be added a mile and a half of road walking from the nearest settlement (Burnbanks).

Kidsty Howes:
See Kidsty Pike 3 and 4.

South-east ridge:
The zig-zag path opposite Speaking Crag at the foot of the ridge is difficult to find and follow ; the path from Flakehowe Crags crosses a tricky scree slope. Probably best is to walk through the plantation and find a gate at the foot of the ridge. All who ascend by this route are recommended to make a detour to visit the remains of the ancient fort, which occupied a striking position, and even today its ruins are a stimulus to the imagination. A steep, direct route to the fort is possible, starting from near Whelter Beck bridge.

North-east ridge:
Very easy gradient once the peat hags are reached. A fast way down.

Measand Beck:
The best part of any of the routes is the path alongside the Forces, which is a continuous succession of delights. Cross the beck at a bridge and take the good path to the sheepfold. The rest of the way is pathless.

Three ridges and a shy valley offer a good variety of ascents from the Haweswater shoreline path. All the routes are interesting, and the ascent *via* the south-east ridge especially is an attractive climb.

Haweswater, from Measand
at the foot of the north-east ridge

The British Fort
on the south-east ridge
with Haweswater beyond

THE SUMMIT

BRANSTREE TARN CRAG Gatescarth Pass HARTER FELL Nan Bield Pass MARDALE ILL BELL

The true fellwalker appreciates best a summit with rocks; failing that, a summit with stones. He will, therefore, have an affectionate regard for High Raise, especially if his visit follows a tour of the neighbouring fells, for its top is crowned with stones in a quantity uncommon amongst the heights of the High Street range, which are usually grassy — they are rough weathered and colourful stones, a pleasure to behold. Some have been used in the erection of a large cairn; others form an effective wind shelter alongside. The old High Street, here merely a narrow track, crosses the top below the cap of stones, 100 yards west of the cairn.

A long half-mile away, reached by a decent path slightly north of east, is the rounded hump of Low Raise. Here all is grass except for a remarkable oasis of bleached stones, obviously transported — a tumulus. These stones were a convenient quarry for later generations whose preference it was to build cairns rather than tumuli, and a really handsome edifice has been constructed which also includes a substantial shelter with several flat stones that have been well placed to provide seating.

The tumulus and cairn on Low Raise

DESCENTS

Since the friendly inn and farmsteads of Mardale were so cruelly sacrificed for the common good (*sic*), the summit of High Raise has been remote from tourist accommodation. The only beds in Mardale are in the Haweswater Hotel, which is on the wrong side of the lake for walkers, and which, unlike the old Dun Bull, is much more a motorists' resort than a refuge for foot travellers and shepherds.

Ample time should be allowed for descents, which are lengthy in all directions, and confusing in all directions except to the east, especially so in bad weather.

The natural inclination to scramble down into Ramps Gill must be resisted: this valley offers sanctuary for deer, and there is neither welcome nor lodging for two-legged animals.

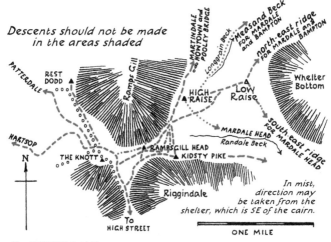

Descents should not be made in the areas shaded

In mist, direction may be taken from the shelter, which is SE of the cairn.

ONE MILE

To PATTERDALE: An interesting and beautiful walk in good weather, but an anxious and complicated journey in bad. Note that Rampsgill Head must first be climbed before the descent properly commences (note, too, the number of paths radiating from the depression between High Raise and Rampsgill Head), and that The Knott is rounded on its north side. *In bad weather, after crossing the wall between The Knott and Rest Dodd, descend directly to Hayeswater and Hartsop.*

To MARDALE: The north-east ridge particularly is a good way down, and the best if Burnbanks or Bampton is the objective. The south-east ridge is rougher, with excellent views, but leads only to the uninhabited head of the valley: for the Haweswater Hotel, however, it is a useful route. *In mist, the streams are safe guides to the lakeside, but care is needed along Measand Beck.*

To MARTINDALE, HOWTOWN and POOLEY BRIDGE: Follow the ridge north, turning down left at Keasgill Head for Martindale and Howtown — *and, in bad weather, for Pooley Bridge also.* Consult the map on *Wether Hill 3.*

THE VIEW

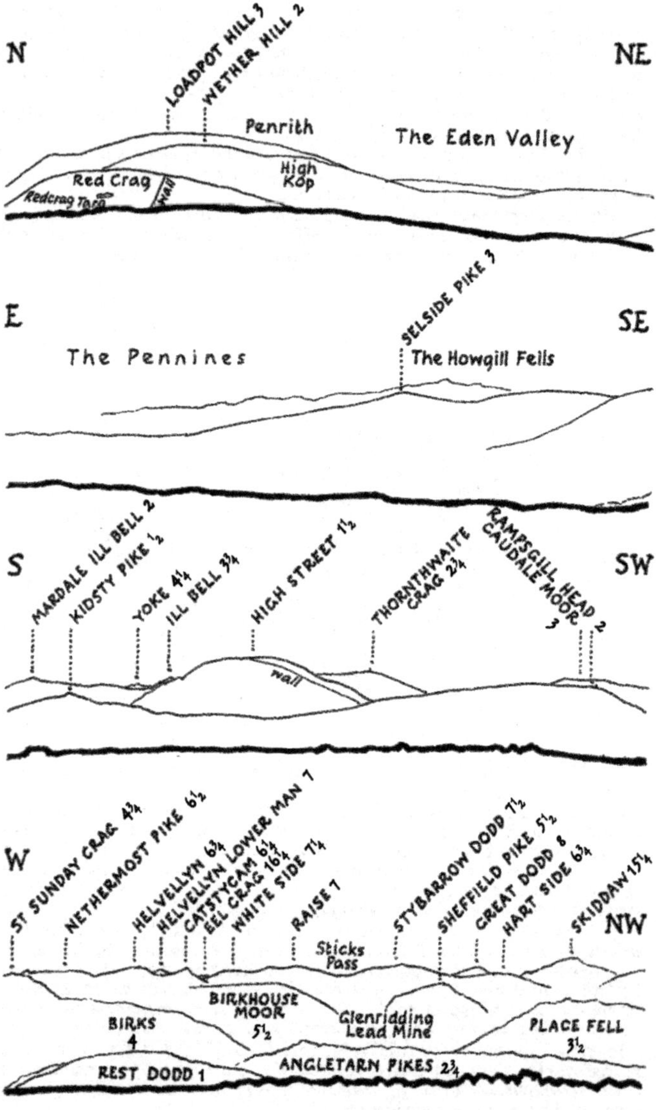

N

NE

LOADPOT HILL 3
WETHER HILL 2

Penrith

The Eden Valley

Red Crag

High Kop

Redcrag Tarn

Wall

E

SE

The Pennines

SELSIDE PIKE 3

The Howgill Fells

S

SW

MARDALE ILL BELL 2
KIDSTY PIKE 1½
YOKE 4¼
ILL BELL 3¾
HIGH STREET 1½
THORNTHWAITE CRAG 2¼
RAMPSGILL HEAD 2
CAUDALE MOOR 3

Wall

W

NW

ST SUNDAY CRAG 4¼
NETHERMOST PIKE 6½
HELVELLYN 6¾
HELVELLYN LOWER MAN 1
CATSTYCAM 6¼
EEL CRAG 16¼
WHITE SIDE 7¼
RAISE 7
STYBARROW DODD 7½
SHEFFIELD PIKE 5½
GREAT DODD 8
HART SIDE 6¾
SKIDDAW 15¼

Sticks Pass

BIRKS 4

BIRKHOUSE MOOR 5½

Glenridding Lead Mine

PLACE FELL 3½

REST DODD 1

ANGLETARN PIKES 2¾

THE VIEW
(with distances in miles)

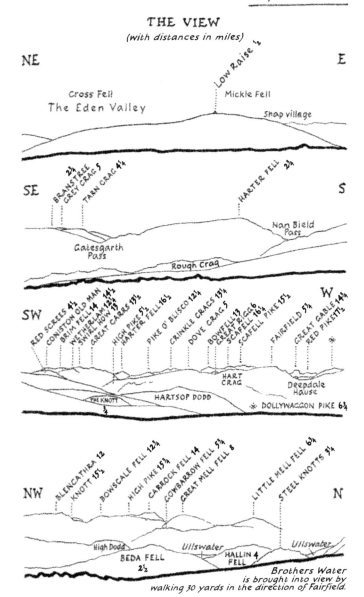

NE   E

Cross Fell
The Eden Valley

Low Raise ½

Mickle Fell

Shap village

SE   S

Branstree 2¾
Grey Crag 5
Tarn Crag 4¼

Harter Fell 2¾

Nan Bield Pass

Gatesgarth Pass

Rough Crag

SW   W

Red Screes 4½
Coniston Old Man 14½
Brim Fell 14 14½
Wetherlam 12½
Swirl How 13
Great Carrs 13½
High Pike 5½
Harter Fell 16½
Pike o' Blisco 12¼
Crinkle Crags 13¾
Dove Crag 3¼
Bowfell 13
Great Rigg 6
Scafell Pike 16¼
Scafell Pike 15½
Fairfield 5½
Great Gable 14½
Red Pike 17½

HART CRAG

THE KNOTT ¾

HARTSOP DODD

Deepdale Hause

☀ DOLLYWAGGON PIKE 6¾

NW   N

Blencathra 12
Knott 15½
Bowscale Fell 12¾
High Pike 15¾
Carrock Fell 14
Cowbarrow Fell 5¾
Great Mell Fell 8
Little Mell Fell 6¾
Steel Knotts 5¾

High Dodd
Beda Fell 2½
Ullswater
Hallin Fell 4
Ullswater

Brothers Water
is brought into view by
walking 30 yards in the direction of Fairfield.

RIDGE ROUTES

To WETHER HILL, 2210': 2¼ miles: NNE
Depression at 2150': 100 feet of ascent

A long easy walk, safe in mist.

Facing north, incline left to join the path (the old High Street), which continues to Wether Hill and beyond. The course of the path has changed considerably in recent times and it is reasonable to assume that it has changed even more over the course of many centuries. It is known that the Roman High Street ran along the ridge, but it is unlikely that any of the paths currently in use follows it exactly.

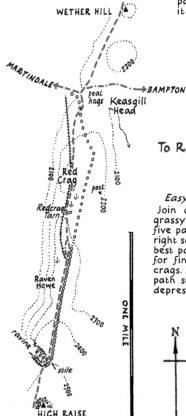

Redcrag Tarn

To RAMPSGILL HEAD, 2598'
¾ mile: SW
Depression at 2450': 140 feet of ascent

Easy, but needing care in mist.

Join and follow the path to the grassy depression south-west. Here five paths meet, the one on the far right somewhat indistinct; this is the best path to follow in good weather for fine views of Rampsgill Head's crags. *In mist,* take the more distinct path second on the right from the depression.

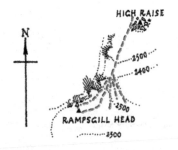

Whelter Beck and Whelter Crags

High Street

2718'

OS grid ref: NY441110

from the north ridge of Branstree

NATURAL FEATURES

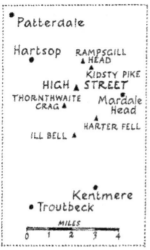

Most of the high places in Lakeland have no mention in history books, and, until comparatively recent times, when enlightened men were inspired to climb upon them for pleasure and exercise, it was fashionable to regard them as objects of awe and terror, and their summits were rarely visited. Not so High Street, which has been known and trodden, down through the ages, by a miscellany of travellers on an odd variety of missions : by marching soldiers, marauding brigands, carousing shepherds, officials of the Governments, and now by modern hikers. Its summit has been in turn a highway and a sports arena and a racecourse, as well as, as it is today, a grazing ground for sheep.

The long whale-backed crest of High Street attains a greater altitude than any other fell east of Kirkstone. Walking is easy on the grassy top: a factor that must have influenced the Roman surveyors to throw their road along it. But High Street is much more than an elevated and featureless field, for its eastern flank, which falls precipitously from the flat top to enclose the splendid tarn of Blea Water in craggy arms, is a striking study in grandeur and wildness ; on this side a straight narrow ridge running down to Mardale is particularly fine. The western face drops roughly to Hayeswater. To north and south, high ground continues to subsidiary fells along the main ridge.

The River Kent has its birth in marshes on the south slope but most of the water draining from the fell flows northwards to Haweswater and Hayeswater. The water for the former is forever destined for the taps of Greater Manchester, but Hayeswater is no longer a reservoir serving Penrith.

Rough Crag
from
Long Stile

NATURAL FEATURES
The main High Street range
illustrating the complexity of the valley systems

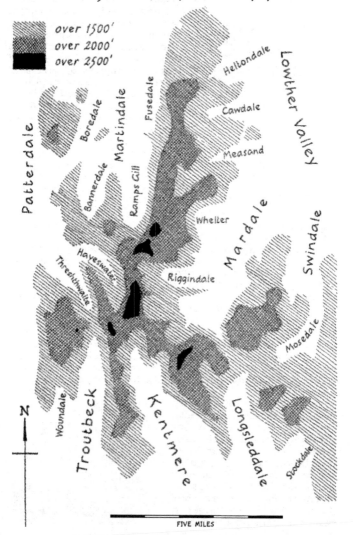

over 1500'
over 2000'
over 2500'

Patterdale

Boredale

Martindale

Fusedale

Hellondale

Lowther Valley

Cawdale

Measand

Bannerdale

Ramps Gill

Wheter

Mardale

Swindale

Haweswater

Threshthwaite

Riggindale

Mosedale

Woundale

Troutbeck

Kentmere

Longsleddale

Stockdale

N

FIVE MILES

MAP

Walkers with an eye for these things might consider Short Stile, beside the Straits of Riggindale, as a potential ascent route. When seen from Kidsty Pike, however, it is clear that the start of the ridge is defended by a fearsome band of crags and that considerable outflanking would be needed to bypass these rocks.

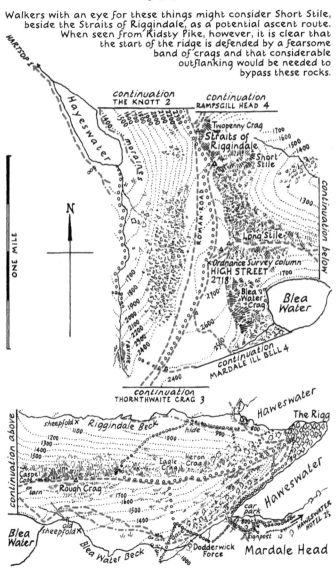

ASCENTS FROM PATTERDALE AND HARTSOP
2450 feet of ascent : 5½ miles from Patterdale
2300 feet of ascent : 3¾ miles from Hartsop

Proceed from the Straits of Rigindale to the summit
not by the wall nor by the Roman Road (which are
dull trudges) but by following the thin path on the edge
of the eastern face (which has excellent views) until the
Ordnance Survey column comes into sight.

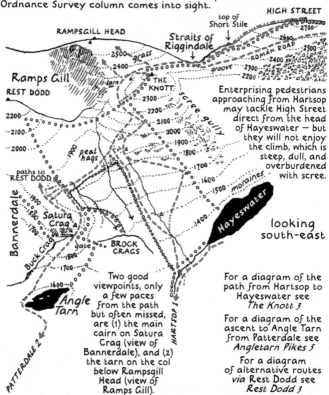

RAMPSGILL HEAD

top of
Short Stile

HIGH STREET

Straits of
Rigindale

ROMAN ROAD

Ramps Gill

REST DODD

THE KNOTT

Enterprising pedestrians
approaching from Hartsop
may tackle High Street
direct from the head
of Hayeswater — but
they will not enjoy
the climb, which is
steep, dull, and
overburdened
with scree.

peat hags

paths to
REST DODD

Bannerdale

Satura Crag

Buck Crag

Hayeswater

moraines

looking
south-east

gate

BROCK CRAGS

Angle Tarn

Two good
viewpoints, only
a few paces
from the path
but often missed,
are (1) the main
cairn on Satura
Crag (view of
Bannerdale), and (2)
the tarn on the col
below Rampsgill
Head (view of
Ramps Gill).

For a diagram of the
path from Hartsop to
Hayeswater see
The Knott 3

For a diagram of the
ascent to Angle Tarn
from Patterdale see
Angletarn Pikes 5

For a diagram
of alternative routes
via Rest Dodd see
Rest Dodd 3

PATTERDALE 2

The route *via* Hayeswater Gill has changed now that the dam on
the former reservoir has been dismantled, with a new footbridge
crossing Hayeswater Gill downstream. See *The Knott 2* for details.

This is the least exciting approach to High Street; it
is, nevertheless, a very enjoyable walk, with a series
of varied and beautiful views; and the tracking of
the path, which has many unexpected turns and
twists, is interesting throughout.

ASCENT FROM MARDALE

2050 feet of ascent   3 miles from the road end

HIGH STREET

2700
2600
2500   Blea Water Crag
2400

steep
scree slopes

Long Stile

Caspel
Gate
tarn

Riggindale

Blea Water

grass slope

Rough Crag

The ridge route may safely be attempted in mist, being so well defined that it is impossible to go astray — but it should be kept in mind that there are crags close by on both sides for most of the route, the Riggindale flank (north) in particular being precipitous.

Caspel Gate is the name of a grassy depression on the ridge: there is no gate. The tarn there dries up in times of drought.

dam
old sheepfold
1500
grass
1400
Blea Water Beck
boulders
gate

1800
1700
1600

Eagle Crag

Heron Crag

Dodderwick Force

NAN BIELD PASS
gate
gate

Swine Crag

Mardale Head

signpost
car park

bracken
1000

BURNBANKS

Haweswater

The Rigg

Haweswater

Although a rather easier alternative via Blea Water is illustrated, it is a poor substitute for the ridge. It does, however, give an intimate introduction to one of Lakeland's finest mountain tarns; from the small concrete dam the wall of crags stretching from Mardale Ill Bell to High Street is very impressive. Use this route when descending from the summit in bad weather.

looking west

The ridge of Rough Crag and the rocky stairway of Long Stile together form the connoisseur's route up High Street, the only route that discloses the finer characteristics of the fell. The ascent is a classic, leading directly along the crest of a long, straight ridge that permits of no variation from the valley to the summit. The views are excellent throughout.

ASCENT FROM TROUTBECK
2350 feet of ascent : 6 miles

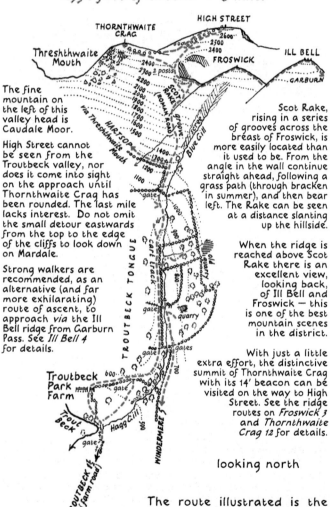

The fine mountain on the left of this valley head is Caudale Moor.

High Street cannot be seen from the Troutbeck valley, nor does it come into sight on the approach until Thornthwaite Crag has been rounded. The last mile lacks interest. Do not omit the small detour eastwards from the top to the edge of the cliffs to look down on Mardale.

Strong walkers are recommended, as an alternative (and far more exhilarating) route of ascent, to approach *via* the Ill Bell ridge from Garburn Pass. See *Ill Bell 4* for details.

Scot Rake, rising in a series of grooves across the breast of Froswick, is more easily located than it used to be. From the angle in the wall continue straight ahead, following a grass path (through bracken in summer), and then bear left. The Rake can be seen at a distance slanting up the hillside.

When the ridge is reached above Scot Rake there is an excellent view, looking back, of Ill Bell and Froswick — this is one of the best mountain scenes in the district.

With just a little extra effort, the distinctive summit of Thornthwaite Crag with its 14' beacon can be visited on the way to High Street. See the ridge routes on *Froswick 3* and *Thornthwaite Crag 12* for details.

looking north

The route illustrated is the direct way and is easy and pleasant throughout, steep only on the initial part of the climb to the ridge. It is safe in mist, and a very quick route when used for descent.

ASCENT FROM KENTMERE
2300 feet of ascent
5½ miles via Hall Cove: 6 miles via Nan Bield Pass

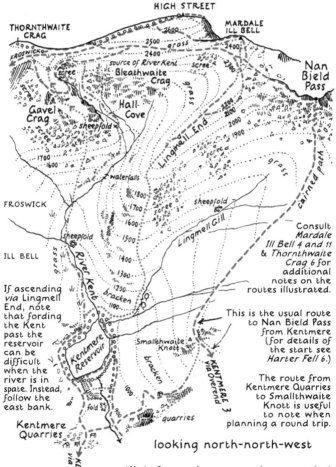

HIGH STREET

THORNTHWAITE CRAG

MARDALE ILL BELL

Nan Bield Pass

FROSWICK

source of River Kent

Bleathwaite Crag

Hall Cove

scree

scree

grass

2600
2500 grass
2400
2300
2200
2100
2000
1900

Gavel Crag

sheepfold

Lingmell End

1700
1600

waterfalls

1800
1700
scree
1600
1500

sheepfold

FROSWICK

sheepfold

Lingmell Gill

grass

cairned path

ILL BELL

grass

River Kent

1400
1300
1200
1100

bracken

If ascending *via Lingmell End*, note that fording the Kent past the reservoir can be difficult when the river is in spate. Instead, follow the east bank.

Consult *Mardale Ill Bell 4 and 11 & Thornthwaite Crag 6* for additional notes on the routes illustrated.

Smallthwaite Knott

KENTMERE via Overend

This is the usual route to Nan Bield Pass from Kentmere (for details of the start see *Harter Fell 6*.)

Kentmere Reservoir

fold

1000

bracken

quarries

The route from Kentmere Quarries to Smallthwaite Knott is useful to note when planning a round trip.

Kentmere Quarries

KENTMERE via Hartrigg 2½

looking north-north-west

High Street is commonly ascended from Kentmere by way of the Ill Bell ridge (the best route) or *via Mardale Ill Bell*, but it may be climbed direct by following the River Kent to its source in Hall Cove (or by a variation over Gavel Crag): an interesting expedition.

Haweswater, from above Long Stile

Hayeswater, from the Roman Road
(the tarn is now slightly smaller in area following the dismantling of the reservoir dam)

THE SUMMIT

The summit is barren of scenic interest, and only visitors of lively imagination will fully appreciate their surroundings. Any person so favoured may recline on the turf and witness, in his mind's eye, a varied pageant of history, for he has been preceded here, down the ages, by the ancient Britons who built their villages and forts in the valleys around; by the Roman cohorts marching between their garrisons at Ambleside and Brougham; by the Scots invaders who were repulsed on the Troutbeck slopes; by the shepherds, dalesmen and farmers who, centuries ago, made the summit their playground and feasting place on the occasion of their annual meets; by racing horses (the summit is still named Racecourse Hill on the large-scale Ordnance Survey maps).....and let us not forget Dixon of immortal legend, whose great fall over the cliff while fox hunting is an epic in enthusiasm.

Nowadays all is quiet here and only the rising larks disturb the stillness. A pleasant place, but — to those unfortunate folk with no imagination — so dull!

There is no summit cairn, just a space south-east of the O.S. column where one used to be. The column is the accepted top.

DESCENTS should be made only by the regular routes. It must be emphasised that there is only one direct way to Mardale — by Long Stile, the top of which is indicated by a cairn. Direct descents into Kentmere may lead to trouble, the best plan being to aim for Nan Bield Pass, in clear weather.

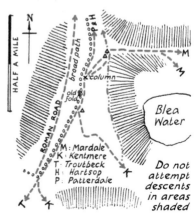

M: Mardale
K: Kentmere
T: Troutbeck
H: Hartsop
P: Patterdale

Blea Water

Do not attempt descents in areas shaded

In mist, consult the maps. For Mardale, stick to the crest of Long Stile, but at Caspel Gate turn right to Blea Water. Kentmere can be reached by descending into Hall Cove at a point 100 yards south-east of the end of the High Street wall, or, better still, *via* Mardale Ill Bell and Nan Bield Pass. Avoid the Hayeswater face.

THE VIEW

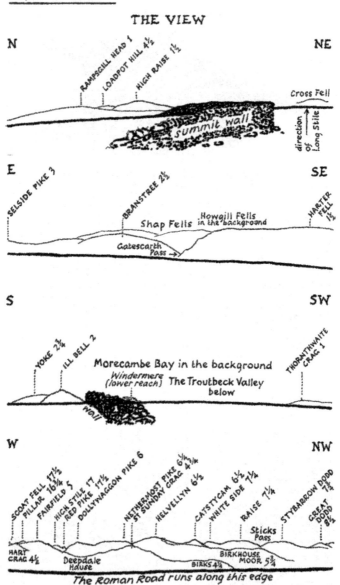

N — RAMPSGILL HEAD 1, LOADPOT HILL 4½, HIGH RAISE 1½, Cross Fell, summit wall, direction of Long Stile — **NE**

E — SELSIDE PIKE 3, BRANSTREE 2½, Shap Fells, Howgill Fells in the background, Gatescarth Pass →, HARTER FELL 1½ — **SE**

S — YOKE 2¾, ILL BELL 2, Morecambe Bay in the background, Windermere (lower reach), The Troutbeck Valley below, Wall, THORNTHWAITE CRAG 1 — **SW**

W — SCOAT FELL 17½, PILLAR 16¾, FAIRFIELD 5, HIGH STILE 17, RED PIKE 17½, DOLLYWAGGON PIKE 6, NETHERMOST PIKE 6½, ST SUNDAY CRAG 4½, HELVELLYN 6½, CATSTYCAM 6½, WHITE SIDE 7¼, RAISE 7¼, STYBARROW DODD 7¾, GREAT DODD 8¼, Sticks Pass, HART CRAG 4½, Deepdale Hause, BIRKS 4½, BIRKHOUSE MOOR 5¾, The Roman Road runs along this edge — **NW**

THE VIEW
(with distances in miles)

NE   E

The Pennines in the background

View of Haweswater and Blea Water from this edge

SE   S

KENTMERE PIKE 2½
MARDALE ILL BELL ¾

Ingleborough

Morecambe Bay
and the Kent Estuary

The Kentmere Valley
below

SW   W

CONISTON OLD MAN 13¼
BRIM FELL 13
SWIRL HOW 12½
GREAT CARRS 12¼
RED SCREES 3
HARTER FELL 1½
PIKE O' BLISCO 11½
CRINKLE CRAGS 12½
BOWFELL 12½
SCAFELL 14¼
SCAFELL PIKE 14¼
GREAT END 13½
GREAT GABLE 14½

CAUDALE MOOR 1½

DOVE CRAG 4

The Roman Road runs along this edge

NW   N

SKIDDAW 15¾
HART SIDE 7¼
ANGLETARN PIKES 3
BLENCATHRA 12½
PLACE FELL 4¼
BOWSCALE FELL 13¾
HIGH PIKE 16½
CARROCK FELL 15¾
REST DODD 1¾
GREAT MELL FELL 9½
THE KNOTT 1
BEDA FELL 4
LITTLE MELL FELL 8

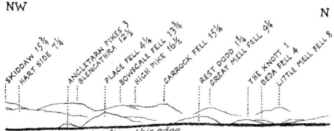

View of Hayeswater from this edge

RIDGE ROUTES

To RAMPSGILL HEAD, 2598' : 1¼ miles : N then NE
Depression at 2340' · 250 feet of ascent

An easy and interesting walk.

To enjoy the best views, from the cairn above Long Stile follow the sketchy path along the edge of the escarpment north to the cairn at the top of Short Stile and the narrow Straits of Riggindale, a dramatic spot. *In mist,* stick to the good path beside the wall all the way until the turn-off right opposite Twopenny Crag, which is a very clear path.

To MARDALE ILL BELL, 2496' : ⅘ mile : SE then ESE
Depression at 2350' · 150 feet of ascent

An easy walk with fine views.

Follow the edge of the escarpment south-east; there are various points close to the edge with fine views of Blea Water. *In mist,* it is better to use the path.

To THORNTHWAITE CRAG, 2569' 1¼ miles : SW then W and NW
Depression at 2475' 100 feet of ascent

A simple stroll, safe in mist.

The walk from the top of High Street to the wall corner is a very 'quick' one, the gentle gradient inducing speed — and there is little of interest to detain the walker.

High Street from Mardale Ill Bell

Blea Water Crag

Ill Bell

2484′

OS grid ref: NY437077

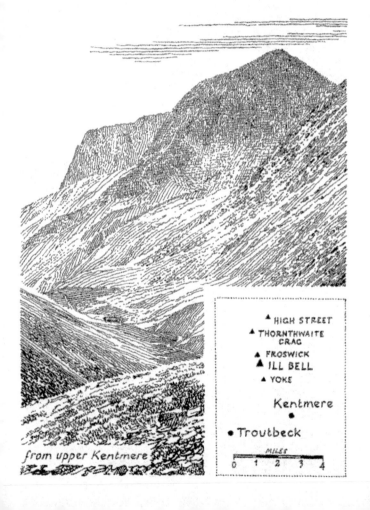

from upper Kentmere

▲ HIGH STREET
▲ THORNTHWAITE CRAG
▲ FROSWICK
▲ ILL BELL
▲ YOKE

Kentmere
●

● Troutbeck

MILES

0   1   2   3   4

NATURAL FEATURES

The graceful cone of Ill Bell is a familiar object to most residents of this part of Cumbria and those visitors who approach Lakeland by way of Kendal and Windermere, although few who know it by sight can give it a name and fewer still its correct name. It is the dominating height on a steep-sided ridge, running north to High Street from the foothills of Garburn, and forms a most effective and imposing barrier between the Troutbeck and upper Kentmere valleys. It is linked by easy slopes to its neighbours, Yoke and Froswick, but both flanks are excessively steep: the Kentmere side in particular is very rough and the aspect of the fell from the upper reaches of the valley is magnificent. Crags descend northwards from the small summit. Ill Bell is distinctive and of good appearance, its peaked shape making it easily identifiable. The ridge on which it stands is probably the most popular fell walk east of Kirkstone: the Kentmere Horseshoe.

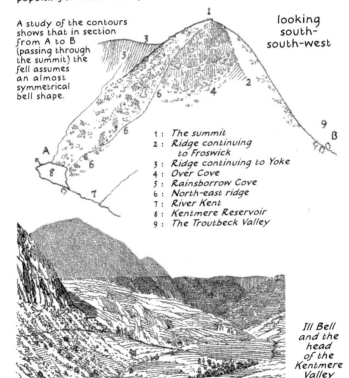

A study of the contours shows that in section from A to B (passing through the summit) the fell assumes an almost symmetrical bell shape.

looking south-south-west

1 : The summit
2 : Ridge continuing to Froswick
3 : Ridge continuing to Yoke
4 : Over Cove
5 : Rainsborrow Cove
6 : North-east ridge
7 : River Kent
8 : Kentmere Reservoir
9 : The Troutbeck Valley

Ill Bell and the head of the Kentmere Valley

Ill Bell 3

MAP

An alternative way to climb Ill Bell from Troutbeck is *via* Scot Rake and Froswick, the fell immediately to the north. For an ascent diagram, see *Thornthwaite Crag 5.*

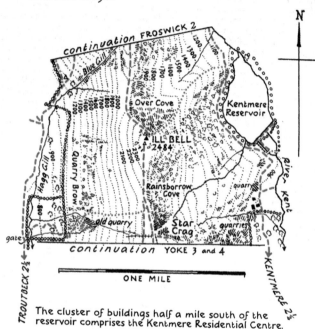

The cluster of buildings half a mile south of the reservoir comprises the Kentmere Residential Centre.

Parking in Troutbeck and Kentmere

Ill Bell is invariably climbed from the villages in the valleys on either side, but the map above does not show these approaches: see *Yoke 3* and *4* for a southern extension. The fell is deservedly popular, but that means parking spaces are at a premium in both valleys: at busy times, particularly weekends and holidays, it is advisable to get there early.

The usual way up from Troutbeck is *via* the Garburn Road, which leaves the A592 Kirkstone road about 250 yards south of Church Bridge. There is a small parking area a short way away from the bridge beside the road to Town End.

Parking is even more at a premium in Kentmere. The roads are narrow so please desist from leaving your vehicle in a passing place. Most drivers will leave their cars in the spaces just past the church, on the side of the road where the village telephone box is situated. In this area there is room for about a dozen cars in total.

O.S. grid references:
Church Bridge, Troutbeck : NY412027.
Village phone box, Kentmere : NY456041.

ASCENT FROM GARBURN PASS
1050 feet of ascent : 2½ miles

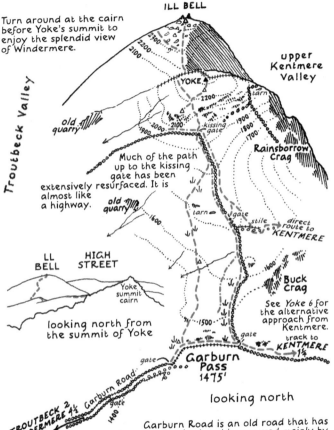

ILL BELL

Turn around at the cairn before Yoke's summit to enjoy the splendid view of Windermere.

upper Kentmere Valley

YOKE

Troutbeck Valley

old quarry

tarn

Rainsborrow Crag

kissing gate

Much of the path up to the kissing gate has been extensively resurfaced. It is almost like a highway.

old quarry

tarn

gate

stile

direct route to KENTMERE

LL BELL   HIGH STREET

Yoke summit cairn

Buck Crag

See *Yoke 6* for the alternative approach from Kentmere.

looking north from the summit of Yoke

gate

track to KENTMERE 1¾

Garburn Pass 1475'

gate

looking north

Garburn Road

TROUTBECK 2
WINDERMERE 4½

gate

Garburn Road is an old road that has never been modernised and is now used mainly by walkers and mountain bikers. From whichever direction the pass is approached it is preferable to use the left (western) path in this diagram; the old path beside the wall is abominably marshy and progress can be painfully slow weaving in and out of peat bogs.

This is the obvious route to Ill Bell, and the only easy one. As far as Yoke it is a dull walk although the dreary foreground in this section is relieved by the splendid views to the west. From the summit of Yoke onwards the ridge is a joy.

ASCENT FROM KENTMERE RESERVOIR

1500 feet of ascent : ⅔ mile
From Kentmere village : 2200 feet of ascent : 4 miles

The ascent of the north-east ridge falls neatly into four sections:

A to B: Pathless on a broad, grassy shoulder. Aim for the rocks half right;

B to C: On the ridge proper, still grassy with the faintest of paths in places (there will be relief that some walkers have been this way before!) From an easy gradient the steepest section ahead looks rocky and difficult;

C to D: It *is* rocky in places, and it most certainly is steep, but it is not difficult to pick through the rock outcrops and boulders; only occasionally will hands be needed. From the top of this section the views into the coves either side of the ridge and down to the reservoir are superb;

D to summit: The slope eases at a photogenic rocky outcrop which is a splendid spot. It is just a short walk to the summit cairn.

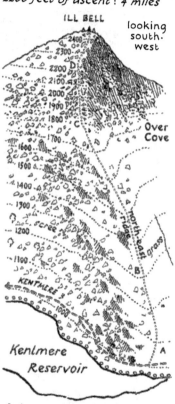

ILL BELL · looking south-west.

2400
2300
2200
2100
2000
1900
1800
1700
C
1600
1500
1400
1300
scree
1200
1100
north-east ridge
KENTMERE
1000
Over Cove
B
A
Kentmere Reservoir

summit cairn

It is more than three miles from Kentmere village to the foot of the ridge *via* Hartrigg (see map on *Yoke 4*). A variation can be made in return, crossing the River Kent at the quarry and following the track to Hallow Bank; this adds another mile to the journey. See maps on *Harter Fell 3* and *Kentmere Pike 4.*

For walkers with a touch of mountaineering blood in their veins, this ascent will set their pulses racing; the rough upper slopes appear intimidating but steepness is the only difficulty. *Avoid in wintry conditions unless an expert.*

ASCENT FROM HAGG GILL, TROUTBECK

1700 feet of ascent : 1¼ miles
From Troutbeck village :
2000 feet of ascent : 4 miles

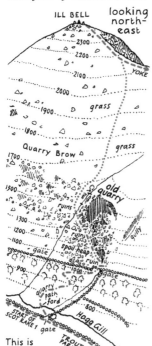

This is the second quarry in Hagg Gill (not the first). Turn right after the gate below the quarry, and then left, and left again (past a ruin). Carry on up the fellside on a straight ramp and continue the climb beyond the stream : a long featureless slope follows. *In mist*, the quarry is dangerous when descending.

Ill Bell's steep western flank is a challenge to those who prefer a direct route to a summit.

THE SUMMIT

Only the three cairns on the right remain. The summit is far right.

The walker who toils up to the top of Ill Bell may be pardoned for feeling that he has achieved a major climb that has played a part of some consequence in mountaineering history, for he finds himself confronted by an imposing array of fine cairns that would do credit to a Matterhorn. And in fact this is a real mountain top, small in extent and very rough ; it is one of the most distinctive summits in Lakeland. Only one post remains of the wire fence that used to follow the ridge.

DESCENTS : The Troutbeck flank is steep, the Kentmere side is very steep and rough. Neither is suitable for descent, nor is there need to attempt them, for all destinations south are much more easily reached by way of the ridge to Garburn Pass.

In mist, Garburn Pass must be the objective. Take the path to the depression south of the summit, ascend Yoke and continue on a good path to the pass.

THE VIEW

Although higher fells northwards restrict the distant view in that direction, elsewhere it is good, the Scafells being prominent on the western skyline. Ill Bell is one of the classic 'stations' for viewing Windermere.

Principal Fells

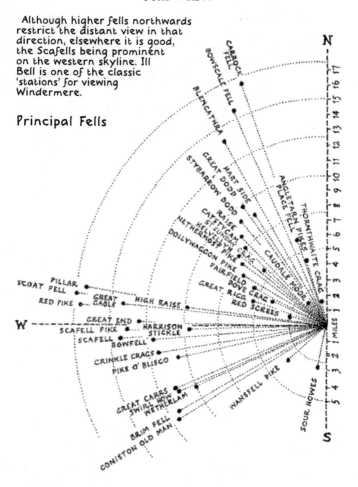

Lakes and Tarns

SSW: *Windermere*
SW: *Blelham Tarn*
NNW: A tiny strip of *Ullswater* is visible from the northern edge of the summit, 35 yards from main cairn.
E: *Kentmere Reservoir* is brought suddenly into view by walking 40 yards towards Harter Fell.

THE VIEW

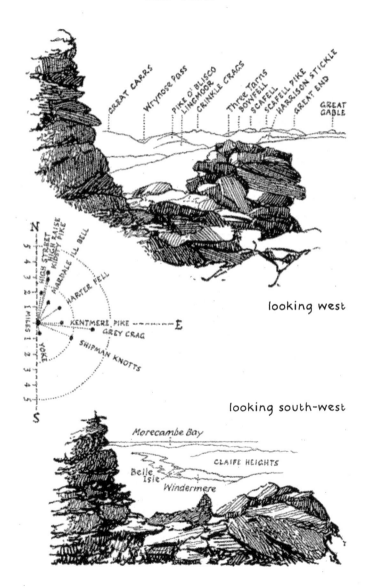

GREAT CARRS
Wrynose Pass
PIKE O' BLISCO
LINGMOOR
CRINKLE CRAGS
Three Tarns
BOWFELL
SCAFELL
SCAFELL PIKE
HARRISON STICKLE
GREAT END
GREAT GABLE

looking west

N
5
4
3
2
1
MILES
1
2
3
4
5
S
E

HIGH STREET
MARDALE ILL BELL
RAMPSGILL RAISE
KIDSTY PIKE
HARTER FELL
KENTMERE PIKE
GREY CRAG
SHIPMAN KNOTTS
YOKE

looking south-west

Morecambe Bay
CLAIFE HEIGHTS
Belle Isle
Windermere

Thornthwaite Crag
and Froswick

Two views
from the
summit

Rainsborrow Cove
and Yoke

RIDGE ROUTES

To FROSWICK, 2359' : ⅔ mile : NW then N
Depression at 2075' : 285 feet of ascent

Rough at first, then easy walking.

Turn west by the most northerly cairn, over stones (*care needed in mist*), and follow the path which goes down north-west to the depression, beyond which is an easy climb on grass to the neat summit cone that is like a miniature Ill Bell. There is just a solitary cairn, however, and any resemblance to its bigger neighbour is illusory.

ONE MILE

To YOKE, 2316' : ⅔ mile : S
Depression at 2180' : 130 feet of ascent

An easy walk, safe in mist.

Descend by the southerly cairn, following a clear path. Cross the depression: at the far end, where the path bifurcates, take the left branch along the edge of the escarpment. A wire leads to the cairn and the path is good all the way. For an excellent view of Kentmere Reservoir, turn off left near the fence corner and follow a thin path to above Star Crag, *but not in mist.*

The Ill Bell Ridge from Stile End

Kentmere Pike

2397'

OS grid ref: NY466078

HIGH STREET ▲
● Mardale Head
HARTER FELL ▲
ILL BELL ▲
KENTMERE PIKE ▲ ▲ TARN CRAG
SHIPMAN KNOTTS ▲
● Kentmere
Longsleddale ●

MILES
0 1 2 3 4

from Ill Bell
(north-east ridge)

NATURAL FEATURES

A high ridge, a counterpart to the Ill Bell range across Kentmere, rises steeply to enclose the upper part of that valley on the east. This is the south ridge of Harter Fell, which, soon after leaving the parent summit, swells into the bare, rounded top of Kentmere Pike, a fell of some importance and of more significance to the inhabitants of the valley, as its name suggests, than Harter Fell itself. The Kentmere slope, wooded at its foot and craggy above, is of little interest, but the eastern flank is altogether of sterner stuff, falling precipitously into the narrow jaws of Longsleddale: a most impressive scene. Here, abrupt cliffs riven by deep gullies tower high above the crystal waters of the winding Sprint and give to the dalehead a savageness that contrasts strikingly with the placid sweetness of the Sadgill pastures just out of their shadow. Of these crags, Goat Scar is the most spectacular.

looking north-west

1 : The summit	8 : Settle Earth
2 : Shipman Knotts	9 : Ullstone Gill
3 : Ridge continuing	10 : River Kent
to Harter Fell	11 : Wren Gill
4 : Goat Scar	12 : River Sprint
5 : Steel Pike	13 : Sadgill Woods
6 : Steel Rigg	14 : Kentmere
7 : Raven Crag	15 : Longsleddale

The River Sprint is said to be one of England's fastest-rising rivers, and downstream of Kentmere Pike it is popular with canoeists. It is a tributary of the River Kent, joining its near neighbour just south of Burneside.

Steel Pike, from the quarry road

looking down a scree gully, eastern flank

MAP

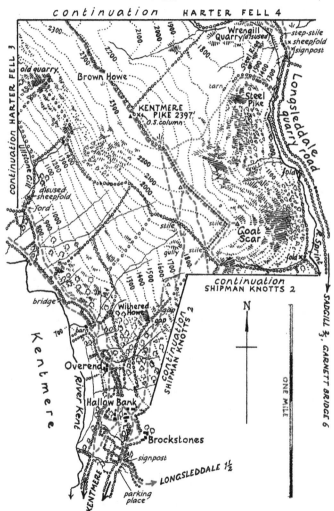

The farm at Hallow Bank is at the junction of two routes: to the right there is an old grooved path that crosses the flank of Kentmere Pike above Withered Howe; to the left there is a path that leads to Overend, the final settlement on the eastern side of the valley. Here there is a further split: left, to Kentmere Reservoir; right to Nan Bield Pass.

ASCENT FROM KENTMERE
1900 feet of ascent : 3 miles

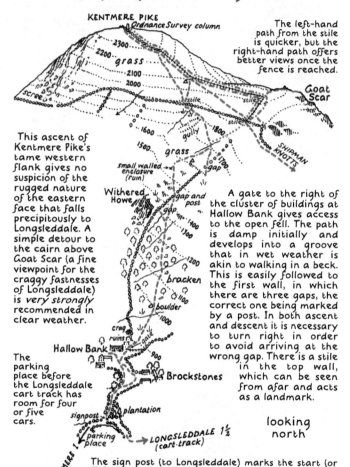

The left-hand path from the stile is quicker, but the right-hand path offers better views once the fence is reached.

KENTMERE PIKE
Ordnance Survey column
2300
2200
grass
2100
2000
scree
1600
gully
1500
grass
stile
stile
stile
Goat Scar
SHIPMAN KNOTTS
1800
1700
gap
small walled enclosure (ruin)
Withered Howe
gap and post
gap
1400
1300
1200
bracken
1100
boulder
1000
crag ruins
gate
900
Hallow Bank
Brockstones
plantation
signpost
parking place
LONGSLEDDALE 1½ (cart-track)
KENTMERE 1

This ascent of Kentmere Pike's tame western flank gives no suspicion of the rugged nature of the eastern face that falls precipitously to Longsleddale. A simple detour to the cairn above Goat Scar (a fine viewpoint for the craggy fastnesses of Longsleddale) is *very strongly* recommended in clear weather.

The parking place before the Longsleddale cart track has room for four or five cars.

A gate to the right of the cluster of buildings at Hallow Bank gives access to the open fell. The path is damp initially and develops into a groove that in wet weather is akin to walking in a beck. This is easily followed to the first wall, in which there are three gaps, the correct one being marked by a post. In both ascent and descent it is necessary to turn right in order to avoid arriving at the wrong gap. There is a stile in the top wall, which can be seen from afar and acts as a landmark.

looking north

The sign post (to Longsleddale) marks the start (or finish) of the Kentmere Horseshoe ridge walk: Shipman Knotts, Kentmere Pike, Harter Fell, Mardale Ill Bell, Thornthwaite Crag, Froswick, Ill Bell and Yoke.

A pleasant, well graded climb along an old grooved path, with excellent views of Kentmere, although the last mile is dull. This is the easiest way onto the Harter Fell ridge. The route shown is safe *in mist*.

ASCENT FROM LONGSLEDDALE
1850 feet of ascent : 3 miles from Sadgill

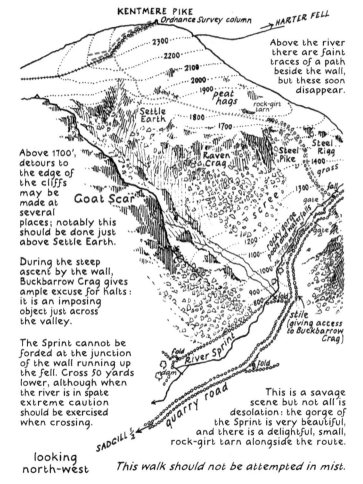

KENTMERE PIKE
Ordnance Survey column → HARTER FELL

Above the river there are faint traces of a path beside the wall, but these soon disappear.

2300
2200
2100
2000
1900
peat hags
rock-girt tarn
Settle Earth
1800
1700
Steel Rigg
Raven Crag
Steel Pike
1400 grass
Goat Scar
scree
1300 fall
gate
1200
rocky gorge pools and waterfalls
gate
1100
1000
900
fold
800
stile (giving access to Buckbarrow Crag)
fold
River Sprint
fold
dam
quarry road
SADGILL ½

Above 1700', detours to the edge of the cliffs may be made at several places; notably this should be done just above Settle Earth.

During the steep ascent by the wall, Buckbarrow Crag gives ample excuse for halts : it is an imposing object just across the valley.

The Sprint cannot be forded at the junction of the wall running up the fell. Cross 50 yards lower, although when the river is in spate extreme caution should be exercised when crossing.

This is a savage scene but not all is desolation: the gorge of the Sprint is very beautiful, and there is a delightful, small, rock-girt tarn alongside the route.

looking north-west

This walk should not be attempted in mist.

This route has been devised for walkers who have a liking for impressive rock scenery — it is the only practicable way up the rough eastern face, and it affords striking views of the crags, first from below then in profile and lastly from above.

THE SUMMIT

The top of the fell, an unattractive and uninteresting place, is robbed of any appeal it might otherwise have had by a high wall that bisects it from end to end. A triangulation station of the Ordnance Survey in the form of a short column stands in the shelter of the east side of the wall, on a small rise, but its claim to occupy the highest point is disputed by a cairn on the other side of the wall. The two are linked by a well made stone stile, the type of structure so needed at neighbouring Shipman Knotts (*see Shipman Knotts 3*).

DESCENTS: To Kentmere: The middle section of the path down to Hallow Bank, between 1700' and 1300', is difficult to follow. Anyone unfamiliar with the route should continue by the ridge over Shipman Knotts to the Sadgill—Kentmere cart track: *in mist, this route is safest.* For Longsleddale, too, it is best to make this cart track the objective. *Much of the Longsleddale flank is craggy and dangerous,* although the route described as an ascent on page 6 is a safe way off in clear weather.

The eastern face, with Harter Fell beyond, from Goat Scar

THE VIEW

The distant view of Lakeland is interrupted by the nearer heights across Kentmere; it is interesting to note that the summit cone of Ill Bell exactly conceals Scafell Pike. More satisfactory prospects are south-east, towards the Pennines, and south-west, over Windermere to Morecambe Bay.

Principal Fells

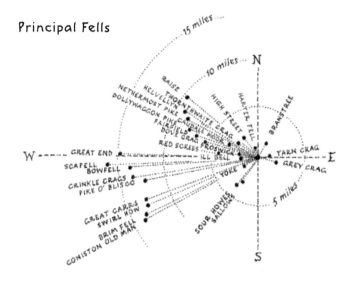

Lakes and Tarns

SSW: *Windermere*
Kentmere Reservoir is brought into view by walking
  50 yards in the direction of Ill Bell.

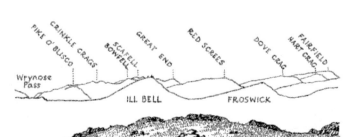

RIDGE ROUTES

HARTER FELL

The Knowe

2500
2400
2300
2300
2300

Brown Howe
peat hags — 2300

▲× Ordnance Survey column
KENTMERE PIKE

HALF A MILE

To HARTER FELL, 2552': 1¼ miles
NNW then N

Depression at 2275': 290 feet of ascent
Easy walking on grass; safe in mist.

Walls at first and then fences link the two summits (with traces of an earlier fence on the broad top of Harter Fell) and indicate the route; the path is distinct.

N

KENTMERE PIKE
▲ Ordnance Survey column

2300
2200
2100

peat hags
2000 --- stile
1900

stile

1900

SHIPMAN KNOTTS
×

Goat
▲ Scar

HALF A MILE

N

To SHIPMAN KNOTTS, 1926'
1¼ miles : SE then S
Depression at 1875': 80 feet of ascent

Easy walking; safe in mist, but
care is needed on the eastern route.

Continuous walls and fences link the summits but, in clear weather, a short detour (100 yards) should be made to the cairn on Goat Scar — an excellent viewpoint for Longsleddale. A scree gully and a steep crag distinguish the depression. There is no stile or gate at the summit of Shipman Knotts, so reaching the highest point (to the east of the wall) is not easy. *See Shipman Knotts 3 for the alternatives.*

Branstree and the head of Longsleddale, from Goat Scar

Goat Scar
from
Longsleddale

Kidsty Pike

2560′

OS grid ref: NY447126

• Patterdale

Hartsop
•

▲ HIGH RAISE
RAMPSGILL HEAD
▲ ▲ KIDSTY PIKE

Riggindale
•
▲ HIGH STREET

MILES

0 1 2 3 4

from Twopenny Crag

NATURAL FEATURES

Travellers on the road and railway at Shap, looking west to the long undulating skyline of the High Street range, will find their attention focussing on the most prominent feature there, the sharp peak of Kidsty Pike. This distinctive summit, which unmistakably identifies the fell whenever it is seen in profile, is formed by the sudden breaking of the gently rising eastern slope in a precipice of crags and scree that falls very abruptly into the depths of Riggindale. The summit is the best feature of the fell. The Riggindale face is everywhere steep, but other slopes are easy except for Kidsty Howes, an extensive area of rock halfway down the long eastern shoulder.

It is interesting to note that the raising of the level of Haweswater gave Kidsty Pike a 'footing' on the shore of the lake, for the first time — previously the confining becks of Randale and Riggindale united before reaching the lake, but now each enters as a separate feeder and the small strip of shore between — barely 200 yards — is the new terminus of the fell.

The summit crags

MAP

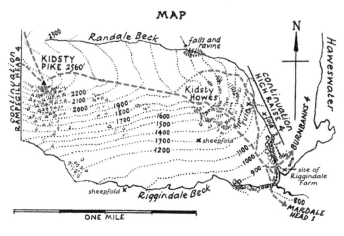

ASCENT FROM MARDALE
1900 feet of ascent : 3 miles from the road end

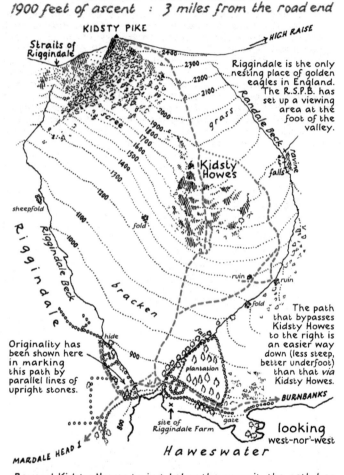

KIDSTY PIKE

→ HIGH RAISE

Straits of Rigindale

2400
2300
2200
2100

Rigindale is the only nesting place of golden eagles in England. The R.S.P.B. has set up a viewing area at the foot of the valley.

scree

Randale Beck

2000
1900
1800
1700
1600
1500
1400
1300
1200
1100
1000

grass

Kidsty Howes

ravine
falls

sheepfold

Rigindale

Rigindale Beck

fold

ruin
ruin
fold

bracken

The path that bypasses Kidsty Howes to the right is an easier way down (less steep, better underfoot) than that via Kidsty Howes.

hide

900

falls
plantation

Originality has been shown here in marking this path by parallel lines of upright stones.

800

→ BURNBANKS

MARDALE HEAD ↓

× site of Rigindale Farm

gate

looking west-nor'-west

Haweswater

Beyond Kidsty Howes to just below the summit, the path has been extensively repaired. It is part of the Coast to Coast route and takes much foot traffic, particularly in summer.

The path over Kidsty Howes replaces an old route which made use of neglected and fading paths ascending to the right of the plantation, crossing Randale Beck at the ruin. It is a much better approach. At the top of the steep ascent the path enters an interesting world of little rocky hills.

THE SUMMIT

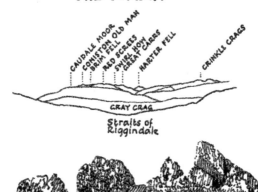

The summit is an eyrie perched high above Riggindale. The cairn, which is quite a bit larger than in the illustration above, sprawls untidily on grass amongst the boulders of the top pedestal, and crags are immediately below. The situation is dramatic.

DESCENTS : For Patterdale or Hartsop, make a beeline over Rampsgill Head and join the path below The Knott. For Mardale use the path over Kidsty Howes. Further down, the alternative route to the left of Kidsty Howes is pathless initially but is the easier descent. Obviously there is no direct way into Riggindale.

In mist, keep to the Straits of Riggindale track if bound for Patterdale or Hartsop. For Mardale, follow the ridge to the east (at first east-north-east) ; there is a clear path all the way to Haweswater. Avoid the route to the left of Kidsty Howes, the start of which is not easy to find in poor visibility.

RIDGE ROUTE

HALF A MILE

To RAMPSGILL HEAD, 2598'
⅓ mile : WNW
Depression at 2525'
60 feet of ascent

This is merely a five-minute stroll, but *in mist* it is well to remember that Rampsgill Head has crags.

THE VIEW

The bulky masses of High Street, Rampsgill Head and High Raise, all in close proximity, cut out big slices of the distant panorama ; but in those directions where the view is unrestricted, it is good.

Principal Fells

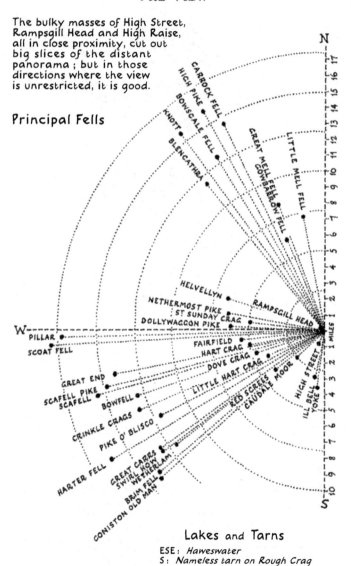

Lakes and Tarns

ESE: *Haweswater*
S: *Nameless tarn on Rough Crag*

THE VIEW

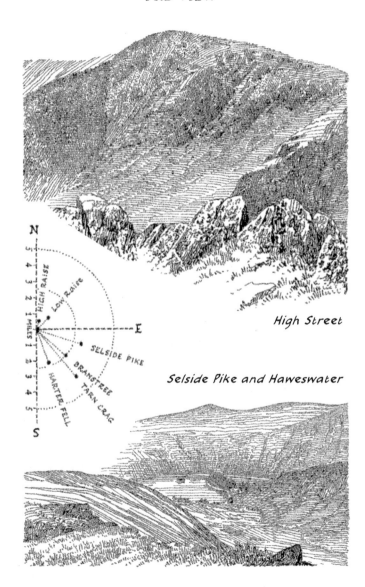

High Street

Selside Pike and Haweswater

The Knott

2423'

OS grid ref: NY437127

Patterdale

Hartsop
▲ HIGH RAISE
▲ ▲ RAMPSGILL HEAD
THE KNOTT
▲ HIGH STREET

MILES
0 1 2 3 4

from Hayeswater Gill

NATURAL FEATURES

The steep western slope descending from Rampsgill Head is arrested below the summit, just as the fall is gathering impetus, by a protuberance that takes the shape of a small conical hill. This is The Knott, a key point for walkers in this area, and although its short side rises barely a hundred feet from the main fell, its appearance is imposing when seen from other directions and especially when approached from the Hartsop valley. Fans of scree litter its western flank, which goes down steeply to Hayeswater; a tremendous scree gully here is The Knott's one interesting feature (seen in the illustration opposite).

MAP

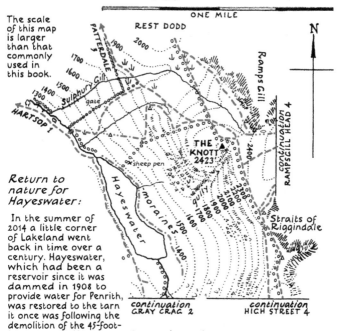

The scale of this map is larger than that commonly used in this book.

Return to nature for Hayeswater:

In the summer of 2014 a little corner of Lakeland went back in time over a century. Hayeswater, which had been a reservoir since it was dammed in 1908 to provide water for Penrith, was restored to the tarn it once was following the demolition of the 45-foot-long stone and concrete dam at its outlet.

There is now no crossing of the gill at the tarn outlet. For walkers heading for The Knott and the High Street range this presents no problem, but those using the zig-zag path from The Knott *in descent* will find that the path ends 200' above the outlet; because of this it is likely that a continuation of this path will spring up, bridging the gap to the main path from the new footbridge, which is 250 yards downstream of the old one.

The Knott 3

ASCENT FROM HARTSOP
1850 feet of ascent : 2 miles

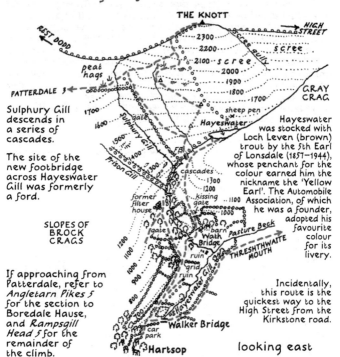

THE KNOTT

HIGH STREET

REST DODD

scree gully

2300
2200
2100 scree
2000
1900
1800
1700 scree

PATTERDALE 3

peat hags

GRAY CRAG

1700

sheep pen

Hayeswater

1600

Sulphury Gill

1500

FB

Prison Gill

1400

1300

cascades

1300

1200

former filter house

kissing gate

1100

1000

1000

gate

barn

Pasture Beck

Wath Bridge

THRESHTHWAITE MOUTH

ruin

1200

1100

ruin

1000

900

Hayeswater Gill

800

car park

Walker Bridge

Hartsop

looking east

Sulphury Gill descends in a series of cascades.

The site of the new footbridge across Hayeswater Gill was formerly a ford.

SLOPES OF BROCK CRAGS

If approaching from Patterdale, refer to *Angletarn Pikes 5* for the section to Boredale Hause, and *Rampsgill Head 5* for the remainder of the climb.

Hayeswater was stocked with Loch Leven (brown) trout by the 5th Earl of Lonsdale (1857–1944), whose penchant for the colour earned him the nickname the 'Yellow Earl'. The Automobile Association, of which he was a founder, adopted his favourite colour for its livery.

Incidentally, this route is the quickest way to the High Street from the Kirkstone road.

As far as the footbridge 250 yards before Hayeswater, this is a fine approach, with a number of attractive cascades in Hayeswater Gill; beyond, it deteriorates into a dull trudge.

THE SUMMIT

The small top of the fell is without interest. A broken wall crosses the summit, forming an angle; a few paces away is the summit cairn, which is much larger than illustrated, right.

DESCENTS: Follow the wall either way to join the path.

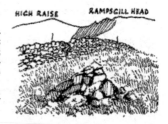

HIGH RAISE   RAMPSGILL HEAD

THE VIEW

Principal Fells

Eastwards the view is severely confined to the High Street range, but in other directions it is excellent.

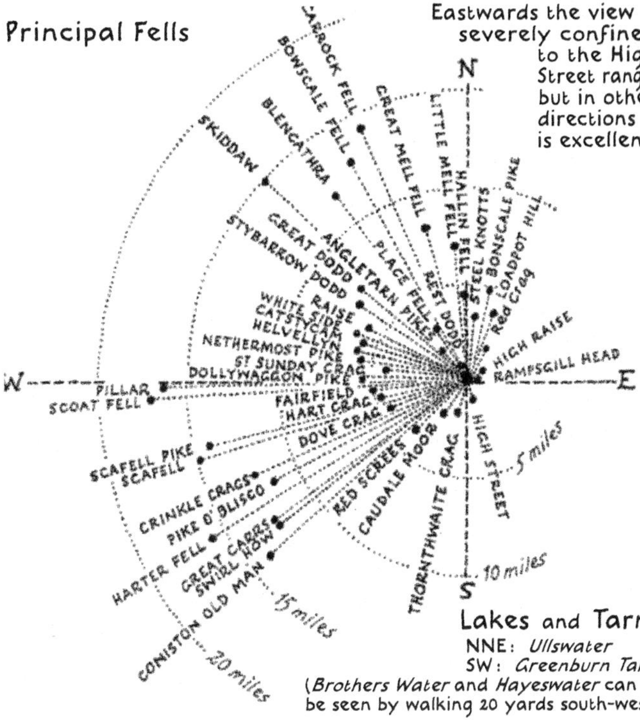

Fells shown on the diagram (clockwise): CARROCK FELL · BOWSCALE FELL · BLENCATHRA · SKIDDAW · GREAT MELL FELL · LITTLE MELL FELL · HALLIN FELL · STEEL KNOTTS · BONSCALE PIKE · LOADPOT HILL · GREAT DODD · ANGLETARN PIKES · PLACE FELL · REST DODD · STYBARROW DODD · Red Crag · WHITE SIDE · RAISE · CATSTYCAM · HELVELLYN · NETHERMOST PIKE · ST SUNDAY CRAG · DOLLYWAGGON PIKE · HIGH RAISE · RAMPSGILL HEAD · PILLAR · SCOAT FELL · FAIRFIELD · HART CRAG · DOVE CRAG · SCAFELL PIKE · SCAFELL · RED SCREES · CAUDALE MOOR · HIGH STREET · CRINKLE CRAGS · PIKE O'BLISCO · GREAT CARRS · SWIRL HOW · HARTER FELL · THORNTHWAITE CRAG · CONISTON OLD MAN

N · W · E · S

5 miles · 10 miles · 15 miles · 20 miles

Lakes and Tarns
NNE: *Ullswater*
SW: *Greenburn Tarn*
(*Brothers Water* and *Hayeswater* can be seen by walking 20 yards south-west)

RIDGE ROUTES

To RAMPSGILL HEAD, 2598′ : ½ mile : E
Depression at 2360′ : 225 feet of ascent
An easy walk, care needed in mist.
The better way is the *via* the tarn (which sometimes dries up) and the sketchy path direct to Rampsgill Head.
In mist, the safest route is by the much clearer path 250 yards to the east.

(map labels: RAMPSGILL HEAD · 2500 · tarn · 2400 · viewpoint · THE KNOTT 2300 · REST DODD · 2100-2000 · N · QUARTER MILE)

To REST DODD, 2283′ : ¾ mile : NNW
Depression at 1925′ · 360 feet of ascent
A straightforward walk, safe in mist.
Follow the wall until it turns left, then directly ahead to the top on a clear path. The summit is the second cairn.

Loadpot Hill

2201'

OS grid ref: NY457181

from Sandwick

• Pooley Bridge
Askham

Helton •

▲ ARTHUR'S PIKE

• Howtown

LOADPOT
▲ HILL
Bampton •

▲ WETHER HILL

MILES
0   1   2   3   4

The beacon on The Pen

NATURAL FEATURES

The High Street range, narrow-waisted at the impressive Straits of Riggindale, thereafter develops buxom girth as it proceeds north. Although the western flank continues steep to its extremity on Arthur's Pike, the eastern slopes descend gradually and irresolutely, halting often in wide plateaux and covering a considerable tract of moorland that is intersected by a succession of deep-cut gills, all of which join the main lateral valley of Mardale and the River Lowther. Nowhere is this characteristic manifest more than in Loadpot Hill, and because Loadpot Hill is the last of the principal eminences of the range it also has northern slopes, no less extensive, which exhibit the same reluctance to depart from the high places: hence the gradients are easy, with subsidiary hillocks arresting the decline. By Lakeland standards (which demand at least a glimpse of *rock* in every scene) territory of this type is uninteresting, for all hereabouts is tough grass and heather except for the single shattered scree-rash of Brock Crag, above Fusedale; yet there is a haunting attractiveness about these far-flung rolling expanses. There is the appearance of desolation, but no place is desolate that harbours so much life: in addition to the inevitable sheep, hardy fell ponies roam and graze at will, summer and winter alike, and the Martindale deer often cross the watershed; in springtime especially, the number and variety of birds is quite unusual for the fells. There is little to disturb these creatures. Man is not the enemy, only the fox and the buzzard. Loadpot Hill is a natural sanctuary for all wildlife.

1 : *The summit*
2 : *Arthur's Pike*
3 : *Bonscale Pike*
4 : *Brock Crag*
5 : *The Pen*
6 : *Brown Rigg*
7 : *Moor Divock*
8 : *River Lowther*
9 : *Cawdale Beck*
10 : *Heltondale Beck*
11 : *Aik Beck*
12 : *Swarthbeck Gill*
13 : *Fusedale Beck*
14 : *Ullswater*

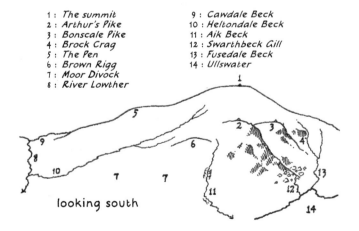

looking south

Cop Stone
and an oddly sited
signpost

The antiquities and oddities of Moor Divock

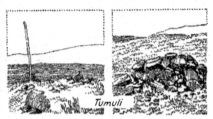

Tumuli

Man may (and does) neglect Loadpot Hill nowadays, but it was not always so. There is plenty of evidence of the esteem with which it was regarded in the past. Even before the Romans traversed it with their High Street, its slopes were the home and meeting place of man. Until recently there was a stone circle created by human agency near the headwaters of Swarthbeck Gill. There are Bronze Age remains and other curiosities in surprising profusion on Moor Divock on the 1050'

A boundary stone

contour, while, nearer our own time, men have laboured to erect an elaborate system of parochial boundary stones and posts along Loadpot's top and down its flanks. One of these, known as 'Lambert Lad', is unsquared and appears to be much older than the rest. And no other Lakeland fell has a concrete living-room

A boundary post

floor and the remains of a domestic chimney stack almost on its summit!

Moor Divock is of very special interest to the antiquarian and archaeologist, and has long been a happy hunting ground for them. The geologist will be concerned with investigating the crater-like hollows or sinkholes (locally known as swallows), which incidentally have been found to contain carcasses and skeletons. The humbler pedestrian, not versed in the sciences, will be impressed by the spaciousness and loneliness of the scene and the excellence of its principal path.

Stone Circles

MAP

Loadpot Hill is the principal eminence of the High Street range at the northern extremity, and is extensive in area. Five pages of maps are necessary in order to show fully the main approaches to the fell from the villages at its base.

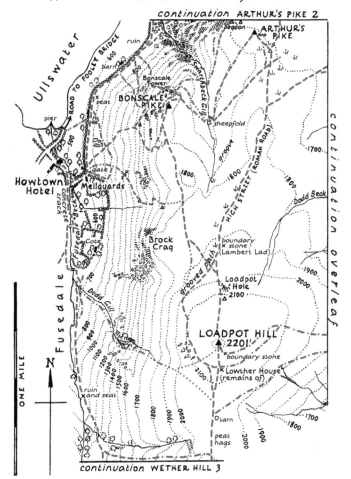

The thin path that follows the southern bank of Dodd Gill before petering out higher up the fell is particularly clogged with bracken during the late summer.

MAP

Reference should be made to the note at the top of page 8 before this map is consulted.

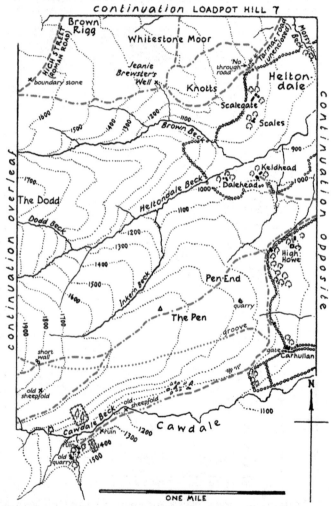

There are numerous quad-bike tracks made by farmers across Loadpot Hill's vast eastern slopes.

MAP

Reference should be made to the note at the top of page 8 before this map is consulted.

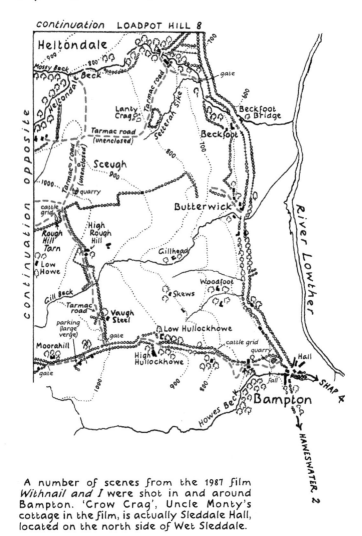

A number of scenes from the 1987 film *Withnail and I* were shot in and around Bampton. 'Crow Crag', Uncle Monty's cottage in the film, is actually Sleddale Hall, located on the north side of Wet Sleddale.

MAP

Reference should be made to the note at the top of the facing page before this map is consulted.

If the ascent is commenced from Pooley Bridge, a visit to Arthur's Pike should be considered: such a detour en route entails little extra time, is a pleasanter way to the tops, and offers rewarding views of Ullswater. For details, see *Arthur's Pike 3.*

Ullswater Steamers ferries operate from Pooley Bridge, with connections to Howtown and Glenridding.

Heughscar Hill is featured in *The Outlying Fells of Lakeland.*

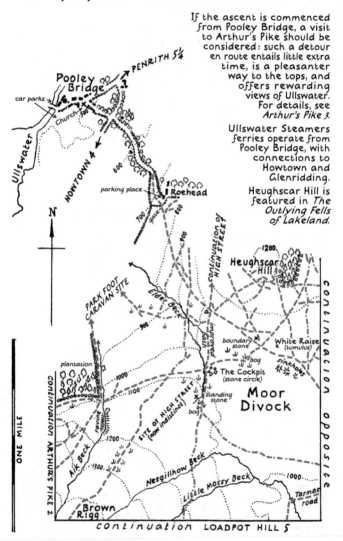

MAP

NOTE on the Loadpot Hill maps:

Walkers bound for the summit, especially from the north and east, may have difficulty in finding access to the fell: routes cannot be determined by observation from valley level because of intervening tracts of cultivated farmland, which must be traversed before open ground is reached. A maze of byways and walled enclosures and farmsteads complicates the approaches. Many variations may be made, but the accompanying maps illustrate only the most direct routes, and, to depict them more clearly, *much unnecessary detail in the cultivated areas has been omitted.*

Those walkers who, like the author, do not enjoy encounters with cows and young bulls and the sundry other mammals that commonly frequent confined farmyards will be relieved to learn that the routes illustrated have been specially selected to reduce this possibility to a minimum, and nowhere is it necessary to pass through a farmyard.

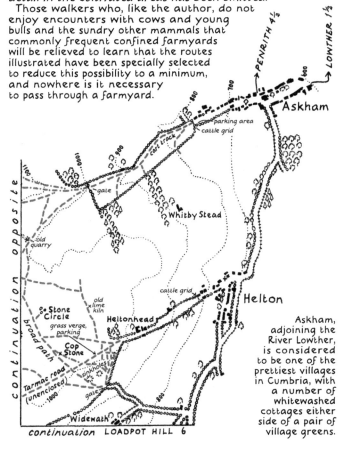

Askham, adjoining the River Lowther, is considered to be one of the prettiest villages in Cumbria, with a number of whitewashed cottages either side of a pair of village greens.

continuation LOADPOT HILL 6

ASCENTS FROM BAMPTON AND HELTON
1650 feet of ascent
4½ miles from Bampton ; 5½ miles from Helton

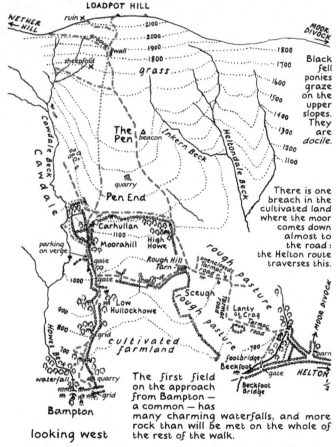

LOADPOT HILL

NETHER HILL

ruin ✕

2100
2000
1900
1800

wall

sheepfold ✕

grass

The Pen △ beacon

Inkern Beck

Heltondale Beck

quarry

Pen End

Cawdale Beck

Cawdale

parking on verge

gate

Carhullan

1100

Moorahill

High Howe

Rough Hill Tarn

gate

1000

900

800

Low Hullockhowe

grid

Hones Beck

waterfall

quarry

grid

rough pasture

unenclosed Tarmac road

Sceugh

rough pasture

Tarmac road

Lanty Crag

Tarmac road

footbridge

Beckfoot

gate

Beckfoot Bridge

MOOR DIVOCK

700

barn

HELTON

½

MOOR DIVOCK

1800
1700
1600
1500
1400
1300
1200
1100

Black fell ponies graze on the upper slopes. They are docile.

There is one breach in the cultivated land where the moor comes down almost to the road : the Helton route traverses this.

cultivated farmland

Bampton

looking west

The first field on the approach from Bampton — a common — has many charming waterfalls, and more rock than will be met on the whole of the rest of the walk.

Two routes are shown, both of which take advantage of The Pen, Loadpot Hill's broad eastern ridge. If starting from Bampton, note that it is now possible to get from Moorahill to Carhullan along the lane; an alternative route following the wall beside Cawdale Beck is marshy. A drier (but longer) variation visits Rough Hill Tarn, joining the route from Helton.

ASCENT FROM MOOR DIVOCK
1300 feet of ascent : 4½ miles

Full route from POOLEY BRIDGE
1800 feet of ascent : 6 miles

Full route from ASKHAM
1600 feet of ascent : 6½ miles

Fell ponies are likely to be seen on these slopes where they live all the year. When the fell is under deep snow they are fed from the farms. In former times such ponies worked in coal pits.

Jeanie Brewster's Well is not easily found.

Bridge in Heltondale

looking south-south-west

This is not a walk for a wet or misty day, and ample time should be allowed. The gradients are everywhere simple; even the most decrepit hiker will surmount them with ease. The High Street of the Romans is now, at best, only a line of ruts in the grass. The ascent *via* Arthur's Pike is recommended for its superior views.

ASCENT FROM HOWTOWN
1750 feet of ascent : 2¼ miles

LOADPOT HILL

× ruin

HIGH RAISE

←BAMPTON

Loadpot
Hole

2100

WETHER HILL

2000

HIGH STREET
(ROMAN ROAD)

1900

←MOOR DIVOCK

1800

1700

1800

1600

1500

Brock
Crag

1400

1300

1200

1100

1000

BONSCALE
PIKE

1800

In late summer
tall bracken
impedes
progress
here

WETHER HILL

1600

scree

1300

dry scree gully

good path

groove

Dodd Gill

Fusedale Beck

FUSEDALE

1200

900

800

700

Cote

bracken

1000

concrete
track

MOOR DIVOCK←

Mellguards

gate

grid

500

looking
south-east

Howtown Hotel

There are two
approaches: the
route *via Mellguards*
has a clearer path,
whereas that *via
Dodd Gill* has the
better scenery.

The approach to Loadpot Hill from Howtown is the
shortest and far the best, the dullness of the climb being
relieved by the beautiful retrospect over Martindale.

Fusedale and
Ullswater
from Dodd Gill

Brock Crag
and Ullswater

THE SUMMIT

Reference has already been made to the attention paid to Loadpot Hill since ancient times, and this is also manifest in the cairn on the summit — somebody, at some time, has gone to the trouble to collect, somewhere, a number of handsome stones foreign to the immediate neighbourhood, all prominently displaying a glittering quartz content, and transport them, somehow, to the highest point; at one time these formed a cairn around the base of a boundary stone, as in the illustration above, but now this stone lies on top of the cairn and some of the quartz stones have been dispersed.

Apart from this cairn, and a triangulation column (no. 10789), the summit is unremarkable. All is grass and all is flat, and more like a 30-acre field than a mountain top.

DESCENTS : Descents may be made easily and safely in any direction. (Loadpot *Hole* is not a hazard to avoid — it is not a hole one can fall into but a shallow landslip, which, because it faces north, holds the last snow on the fell every spring.)

In mist, the walker should not be here at all, but if he is his best plan is probably to descend northwards to the High Street (a rut in the grass) and follow it to Moor Divock. *If conditions are bad,* go west, crossing the High Street, down the steepening bracken slopes into Fusedale (for Howtown).

Chimney of Lowther House (now fallen)

Just below and south of the summit are the remains of Lowther House, formerly a shooting lodge. In the 1950s its stone chimney stack was still to be seen pointing forlornly at the sky — a landmark that distinguished this fell from all others. Today, all that is left is part of the concrete floor and a pile of stones.

THE VIEW

Principal Fells

One half of the panorama is Lakeland, dominated by the high, imposing range of Helvellyn; the other half is Pennine, with Cross Fell and its satellites prominent.

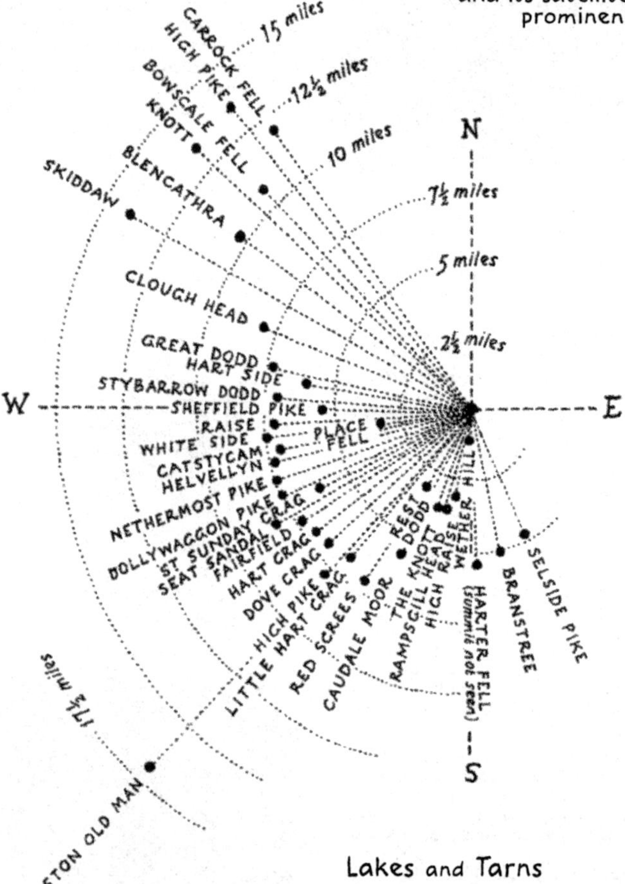

CARROCK FELL
HIGH PIKE
BOWSCALE FELL
KNOTT
BLENCATHRA
SKIDDAW
CLOUGH HEAD
GREAT DODD
HART SIDE
STYBARROW DODD
SHEFFIELD PIKE
RAISE
WHITE SIDE
CATSTYCAM
HELVELLYN
PLACE FELL
NETHERMOST PIKE
DOLLYWAGGON PIKE
ST SUNDAY CRAG
SEAT SANDAL CRAG
FAIRFIELD
HART CRAG
DOVE CRAG
HIGH PIKE
LITTLE HART CRAG
RED SCREES
CAUDALE MOOR
RAMPSGILL HEAD
THE KNOTT
HIGH RAISE
REST DODD
WETHER HILL
HARTER FELL (summit not seen)
BRANSTREE
SELSIDE PIKE
CONISTON OLD MAN

15 miles
12½ miles
10 miles
7½ miles
5 miles
2½ miles
17½ miles

N
W — E
S

Lakes and Tarns

Because of the extent and flatness of the top, the view from the cairn is of heights, not of valleys, and no lakes are visible. *Ullswater*, however, can be seen by walking 150 yards towards the west.

RIDGE ROUTES

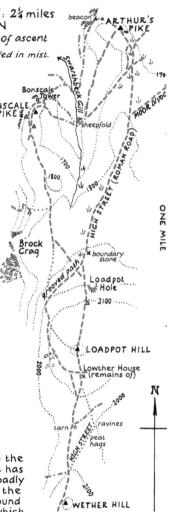

To ARTHUR'S PIKE, 1747': 2¼ miles
NW, then NNE and N
Minor depressions: 50 feet of ascent

An easy walk, not recommended in mist.

Follow the path north until
it joins the High Street,
and keep straight on for
about a mile. Then bear
left for the summit.
Visit the beacon for the
best view of Ullswater.

To BONSCALE PIKE, 1718'
1½ miles: NW, then N
*Minor depressions:
50 feet of ascent*

An easy walk, not safe in mist.

Descend the easy western
slope to the High Street,
and near the start of the
grooved section leave it
and continue north over
sundry grassy mounds
(good path) to the summit
cairn. Two prominent pillars
should be visited,
the *lower* of the two being
Bonscale Tower. The views
of Ullswater are striking.

To WETHER HILL, 2210'
1 mile: S
*Depression at 2025'
200 feet of ascent*

An easy walk, safe in mist

The High Street inclined to the
left below Lowther House, but has
become indistinct and is now badly
cut about by peat hags in the
depression. Easier walking is found
on the path, easy to follow, which
crosses the depression on its right
(*i.e.* west) side, away from the hags. There should be no
difficulty in mist: all gradients are easy — if steep ground is
encountered the route is lost.

Mardale Ill Bell 2496'

OS grid ref: NY448101

from the north ridge of
Branstree

HIGH STREET
▲
Mardale
● Head
MARDALE ▲
ILL BELL ▲ HARTER FELL

▲ ILL BELL

● Kentmere

MILES
0 1 2 3 4

NATURAL FEATURES

Mardale Ill Bell has received scant mention in Lakeland literature, and admittedly is mainly of nondescript appearance, yet one aspect of the fell is particularly good and appeals on sight to all who aspire to a little mild mountaineering. This is to the north-east, where a boulder-strewn shoulder leaves the summit and soon divides into two craggy ridges, enclosing a rocky corrie;

the rugged surroundings on this side are greatly enhanced in impressiveness by the two splendid tarns of Blea Water (below High Street) and Small Water (below Harter Fell), each of them occupying a volcanic crater and deeply inurned amongst crags. These tarns, with their streams, are collectively known as Mardale Waters, and greatly contribute to the fine scenic quality of this typical Lakeland landscape.

To the west the fell merges gently and dully into High Street, with a fringe of crag throughout on the north; and south of the linking high ground is a wall of steep rock,

Waterfalls
River Kent
below Hall Cove

Bleathwaite Crag, bounding the silent hollow of Hall Cove, the birthplace of the River Kent. On the south also is the most pronounced shoulder of the fell, Lingmell End, thrusting far into the valley of Kentmere, and from it descends a short spur to the top of Nan Bield Pass.

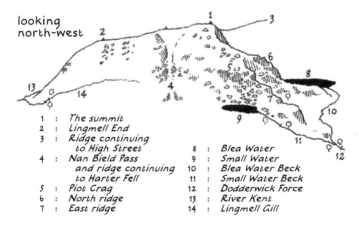

looking north-west

1 :	The summit
2 :	Lingmell End
3 :	Ridge continuing to High Street
4 :	Nan Bield Pass and ridge continuing to Harter Fell
5 :	Piot Crag
6 :	North ridge
7 :	East ridge
8 :	Blea Water
9 :	Small Water
10 :	Blea Water Beck
11 :	Small Water Beck
12 :	Dodderwick Force
13 :	River Kent
14 :	Lingmell Gill

MAP

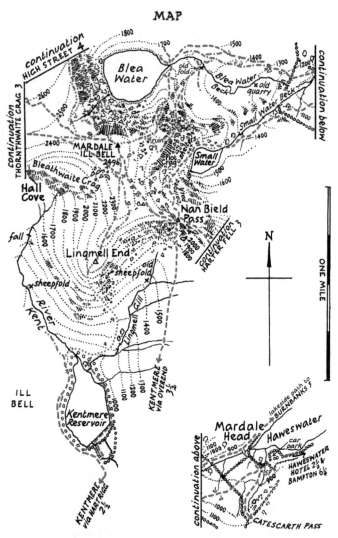

The signpost at the junction of the paths from the road-end car park indicates three routes : *Public Byway—Gatesgarth Pass* ; *Public Bridleway—Nan Bield Pass Kentmere*; and *Public Footpath—fellside path to Bampton*. This latter sign really should read *lakeside path to Burnbanks* (from Burnbanks to Bampton involves road walking).

ASCENT FROM KENTMERE
2100 feet of ascent : 4¾ miles

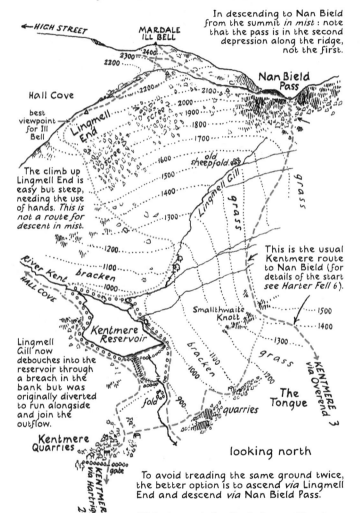

In descending to Nan Bield from the summit *in mist* : note that the pass is in the second depression along the ridge, not the first.

←—HIGH STREET

MARDALE ILL BELL

Nan Bield Pass

Hall Cove

best viewpoint for Ill Bell

Lingmell End

scree

old sheepfold

The climb up Lingmell End is easy but steep, needing the use of hands. *This is not a route for descent in mist.*

Lingmell Gill

grass

bracken

River Kent

HALL COVE

This is the usual Kentmere route to Nan Bield (for details of the start see Harter Fell 6).

Kentmere Reservoir

grass

Smallthwaite Knott

grass

1500
1400
1300

Lingmell Gill now debouches into the reservoir through a breach in the bank but was originally diverted to run alongside and join the outflow.

bracken

The Tongue

KENTMERE via Overend 3

fold

quarries

Kentmere Quarries

KENTMERE via Hartrigg 2½

gate

looking north

To avoid treading the same ground twice, the better option is to ascend *via* Lingmell End and descend *via* Nan Bield Pass.

This is a dull climb but affords a good introduction to the fine Kentmere valley head. Nan Bield, the perfect Lakeland pass, is the best feature.

ASCENT FROM MARDALE
1700 feet of ascent : 2 miles from the road end

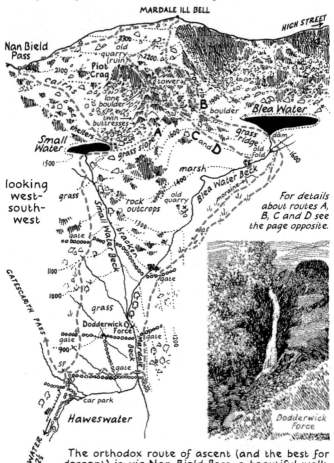

MARDALE ILL BELL

HIGH STREET

Nan Bield Pass

2300
old quarry (ruin)
2200.
2100
Piot Crag
cairns
tower
lone boulder
twin buttresses
shelters
B
boulder
Blea Water
A
grass slope
C and D
grass ridge
dam
old fold
1600

Small Water
1500

looking west-south-west

grass
marsh
1400
Blea Water Beck
moraine
old quarry
rock outcrops
Small Water Beck
bracken
1300

For details about routes A, B, C and D see the page opposite.

GATESCARTH PASS

gate
1100
1000
grass
Dodderwick Force
gate
900
SP
gate
Mardale Beck
gate
1200

car park

Haweswater

HAWESWATER HOTEL 2¾

Dodderwick Force

The orthodox route of ascent (and the best for descent) is *via* Nan Bield Pass, a beautiful walk. *In mist this is the only safe route, up or down.*

Of the many excellent climbs available from Mardale Head the direct ascent of Mardale Ill Bell ranks high, the walk being favoured by striking views of two of the finest tarns in Lakeland, each set amongst crags in wild and romantic surroundings.

ASCENT FROM MARDALE

route A, via Small Water and the east ridge

Access to the ridge is gained *via* a grassy slope from Small Water where a thin path makes a gradual appearance. The path stays below the ridge line as it passes above two prominent rock buttresses, then swings round a rocky part of the ridge (*route C joins here*) and on to a wide grassy col dominated by solitary boulder (*route D joins here*). A wide bouldery gully behind the buttress of Piot Crag leads to a flat grassy ridge and the ruin at the foot of a tiny quarry. A thin path continues; bear right up a wide grassy slope when it peters out.

route B, via Blea Water and the north ridge

From the dam at Blea Water, follow a path that climbs gently on a grassy ridge towards a prominent boulder at the foot of a steep, rocky section. This looks daunting, but a thin path, sometimes barely footprints, utilises short grassy ramps to avoid most of the bouldery outcrops. A rocky tower can be passed on either side, that on the right being the more obvious route.

routes C and D, via the north-east corrie

From the old sheepfold on the bank of Blea Water Beck a good path heads into the north-east corrie. Where it splits, *route C* goes left, hugs rocks on the right and continues on grass and finally up a boulder-strewn slope to a prominent col on the east ridge where it joins *route A*.

More straightforward is *route D*, with a thin path heading right from the bifurcation and following the line of a grassy gully which curves gently towards the lone boulder on the skyline; here it joins *routes A and C*.

The north face from Blea Water

THE SUMMIT

A large cairn, which sprawls much more than shown in the illustration, crowns the undulating top on a small rocky knoll. The area around is characterised by soft turf, patches of brown stones and occasional outcrops. There is nothing here to suggest the presence of fine crags close by, and a visit to them (north) adds interest to the summit, *but not in mist.*

DESCENTS : The usual way off is *via* Nan Bield Pass (the wall shelter on the top of the pass is plainly visible from the summit cairn) ; to reach it, follow the path south-east from the summit which joins the more substantial track from Thornthwaite Crag. Both the north and east ridges are rough and the Lingmell End route is steep.

▌ *In mist,* aim for Nan Bield Pass, noting that it crosses the *second* depression reached, *not the first.*

The stone shelters at Small Water

Testimony to the former importance of Nan Bield Pass as a route for travellers and trade are the three shelters alongside the track where it crosses the bouldery shore of Small Water — erected for wayfarers overtaken by bad weather or darkness. These shelters are roughly but soundly built and roofed, but they are low and can be entered only by crawling. Once the body is insinuated snugly in their spider-infested recesses, however, the weather may be defied.

THE VIEW

Outstanding in the moderate view is the neighbouring ridge of Ill Bell, which, displaying its steep and rugged eastern face, looks magnificent from this angle. The long curve of High Street hides most of the western fells, and only the tips of the Bowfell group are visible above the rising skyline of Thornthwaite Crag.

Principal Fells

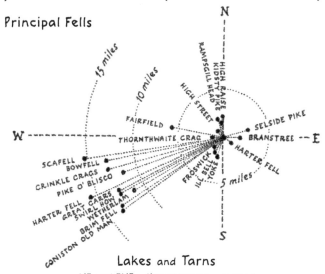

N

15 miles
10 miles

HIGH RAISE
KIDSTY PIKE
RAMPSGILL HEAD
HIGH STREET

FAIRFIELD

THORNTHWAITE CRAG

SELSIDE PIKE

W — — — — — — — — — — — — — — — — — — — BRANSTREE – – E

HARTER FELL

SCAFELL
BOWFELL
CRINKLE CRAGS
PIKE O' BLISCO

FROSWICK
ILL BELL
YOKE

5 miles

HARTER FELL
GREAT CARRS
SWIRL HOW
WETHERLAM
BRIM FELL
CONISTON OLD MAN

S

Lakes and Tarns

NE and ENE : *Haweswater (two sections)*

Neither *Blea Water* nor *Small Water* can be seen from the cairn but both are worth the detour necessary to obtain bird's eye views of them, the former from a break in the crags 100 yards north, the latter from above Piot Crag a quarter of a mile due east.

*The summit crags
from the north ridge*

RIDGE ROUTES

To HIGH STREET, 2718': ⅔ mile : WNW then NW
Depression at 2350': 400 feet of ascent

An easy walk with excellent views via the escarpment.

There is a very clear path from the summit to the broken wall along the spine of High Street, but it is preferable to follow the edge of the escarpment above Blea Water. Turn off the cairned path to High Street at the point where a repaired gravel surface commences and cross a grassy depression to the edge of the cliffs. A sketchy path follows the escarpment and at three places, marked A, B and C on the map, there are sensational downward views of Blea Water. Midway between B and C it is possible to take a direct line to the Ordnance Survey column which marks the summit of High Street, but a better alternative is to continue to the top of Long Stile where there are two parallel paths (the furthest one very wide) which lead to the summit. *In mist, this route is dangerous; keep to the path instead.*

The view east from the edge of the escarpment at point B

To THORNTHWAITE CRAG, 2569'
1½ miles : WNW, then WSW, W & NW
Depressions at 2350' and 2475'
250 feet of ascent

Easy walking, confusing in mist.

Walk west until a thin path appears which joins the track coming up from Nan Bield Pass. When this bends left keep straight on along a fainter path to the wall corner. From there a path cuts across to the distinctive summit of Thornthwaite Crag with its 14' beacon unmissable. This ridge walk, and that to High Street at the top of the page, can be combined; if that is the chosen option, the better way round is anti-clockwise, ascending High Street first.

RIDGE ROUTES

To HARTER FELL, 2552': 1 mile : SE, then ESE and E
Depression at 2100' (Nan Bield Pass) : 500 feet of ascent

A rough but interesting walk, with beautiful and impressive views.

Aim first for the top of Nan Bield Pass (the wall shelter there is in view from the summit), following the path south-east until the cairned track from Thornthwaite Crag is reached. Beyond the pass, an interesting ridge rises in rocky steps to the flat top of Harter Fell. *In mist, this is safe : the broad path across the summit plateau is well cairned.*

*Haweswater and Small Water
from the Nan Bield ridge*

The Nab

OS grid ref: NY434152

from Rampsgill Beck

Howtown •
• Martindale
BEDA FELL ▲
WETHER
▲ HILL
• Patterdale
▲ THE NAB
REST DODD ▲
HIGH
▲ RAISE

MILES
0   1   2   3   4

The Nab is situated wholly within the Martindale Deer Forest, home to the oldest herd of native red deer in England. The boundaries of the Forest are principally defined by the 'Forest Wall', which encloses much of the Ramps Gill and Bannerdale valleys and crosses the high ground between. This wall does not confine the deer — they roam freely beyond the boundaries — but it marks their home, their only safe refuge, their one sanctuary.

Walkers are asked to keep to the preferred routes described on *page 3*, and to avoid disturbing the deer.

Red Deer Stag

NATURAL FEATURES

The Nab is, in character, akin to the three Dodds around Kirkstonefoot. Very steep-sided, soaring in symmetrical lines to a slender cone, it appears from the pastures of Martindale as a lofty wedge splitting the valley into two branches, Ramps Gill and Bannerdale: from this viewpoint it may well be thought to be a separate and solitary fell. But in fact, as is seen from neighbouring heights, it is merely the butt of the northern shoulder of Rest Dodd. Its lower slopes are of bracken, its higher reaches of grass, with occasional scree on both flanks and a few rocks on Nab End. In addition to its other distinctions it has, on the wide ridge behind the summit, a most unpleasant morass of peat hags, one of the worst in the district.

MAP

Martindale Deer Forest may be closed at times between September and February, and walkers are asked to keep away from the deer at calving time in June and July. It is advisable to check that access is available before you visit. The numbers to call are 017684 86450 or 86120.

to MARTINDALE CHURCH 1¼

Dale Head

The Bungalow

gate

Bannerdale Beck

Bannerdale

hurdle

Nab End

THE NAB 1887

N

Yewgrove Gill

Ramps Gill Beck

Ramps Gill

ONE MILE

Falls

flat boulder

continuation REST DODD 2

The Bungalow is a holiday cottage, green-coloured with a distinctive red roof, that sleeps up to twelve. It was built in 1910 as a shooting lodge by the Earl of Lonsdale for a visit of Kaiser Wilhelm II to the Martindale deer shoot.

ASCENTS

The 'Keep Out' notices, barricaded gates and miles of barbed wire have gone from The Nab and most of the fell is now public access land. However, it is a red deer conservation area and wandering within the boundaries of the Deer Forest is not encouraged. In the 1950s, the author carried out his explorations surreptitiously, and without permission (not caring to risk a refusal): he was not detected, but this may possibly have been due to his marked resemblance to an old stag, and others should not expect the same good fortune.

In general, walkers are requested to follow the informal agreement to approach the summit only by way of the ridge from Rest Dodd (*see page 2*) and to return the same way.

FROM MARTINDALE *via* Angle Tarn and Rest Dodd

The preferred route of ascent from Martindale is from Dale Head Farm, where walkers should follow the Patterdale path which goes through the wicket gate below the farmhouse onto the fell. The path climbs towards Angle Tarn (*see Angletarn Pikes 6*). On coming within sight of the tarn, swing east behind Buck Crag to the gate at Satura Crag and then onto Rest Dodd and The Nab (*see Rest Dodd 6, top and bottom*).

FROM MARTINDALE *via* High Raise and Rest Dodd

The longer ascent is from Martindale Old Church, on the east side of the valley above Gowk Hill onto High Raise (*see High Raise 6*) and then crossing the summit of Rampsgill Head to The Knott and on to Rest Dodd as before (*see High Raise 13, Rampsgill Head 8, The Knott 6 and Rest Dodd 6 for details*).

FROM PATTERDALE *via* Angle Tarn and Rest Dodd

This cross-country route takes in Angle Tarn, Satura Crag and Rest Dodd (*see Rampsgill Head 5 and Rest Dodd 6*).

FROM HARTSOP *via* Satura Crag and Rest Dodd

There are two ways possible : *via* Hayeswater Gill or the zig-zag path to Brock Crags. From Satura Crag onwards the routes coincide (*see Rest Dodd 3 and Brock Crags 2*).

THE SUMMIT

The summit, a shapely dome, is competely grassy. A few stones have been carried up and make an untidy cairn.

THE VIEW

Principal Fells

The view is 'open' only to the north. The most interesting feature, however, is the snug fit of Scafell Pike in the frame of Deepdale Hause.

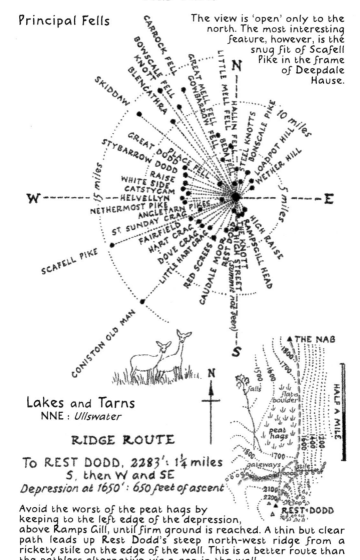

Lakes and Tarns

NNE : *Ullswater*

RIDGE ROUTE

To REST DODD, 2283': 1¼ miles
S, then W and SE
Depression at 1650': 650 feet of ascent

Avoid the worst of the peat hags by keeping to the left edge of the depression, above Ramps Gill, until firm ground is reached. A thin but clear path leads up Rest Dodd's steep north-west ridge from a rickety stile on the edge of the wall. This is a better route than the pathless alternative *via* a gap in the wall.

Place Fell

2154'

OS grid ref: NY406170

from Birks

Howtown •

▲ PLACE FELL
• Patterdale

MILES
0   1   2   3

Few fells are so well favoured as Place Fell for appraising neighbouring heights. It occupies an exceptionally good position in the curve of Ullswater, in the centre of a great bowl of hills; its summit commands a very beautiful and impressive panorama. On a first visit to Patterdale, Place Fell should be an early objective, for no other viewpoint gives such an appreciation of the design of this lovely corner of Lakeland.

NATURAL FEATURES

Place Fell rises steeply from the curve formed by the upper and middle reaches of Ullswater and its bulky mass dominates the head of the lake. Of only moderate elevation, and considerably overtopped by surrounding heights, nevertheless the fell more than holds its own even in such a goodly company: it has that distinctive blend of outline and rugged solidity characteristic of the true mountain. Many discoveries await those who explore: in particular the abrupt western flank, richly clothed with juniper and bracken and heather, and plunging down to the lake in a rough tumble of crag and scree, boulders and birches, is a paradise for the scrambler, while a more adventurous walker will find a keen enjoyment in tracing the many forgotten and overgrown paths across the fellside and in following the exciting and airy sheep tracks that so skilfully contour the steep upper slopes below the hoary crest.

The eastern face, overlooking Boredale, is riven by deepcut gullies and is everywhere steep. Northward two ridges descend more gradually to the shores of Ullswater after passing over minor summits; from a lonely hollow between them issues the main stream on the fell, Scalehow Beck, which has good waterfalls. To the south, Boredale Hause is a well known walkers' crossroads, and beyond this depression high ground continues to climb towards the principal watershed.

looking south

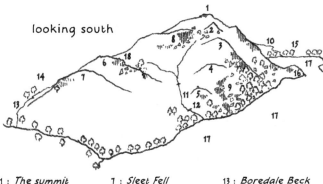

1 : The summit	7 : Sleet Fell	13 : Boredale Beck
2 : The Knight	8 : Mortar Crag	14 : Boredale
3 : Birk Fell	9 : Long Crag	15 : Patterdale
4 : Kilbert How	10 : Goldrill Beck	16 : Silver Point
5 : Low Birk Fell	11 : Scalehow Beck	17 : Ullswater
6 : High Dodd	12 : Scalehow Force	18 : Low Moss

MAP

It is the author's opinion that the lakeside path from Scalehow Beck, near Sandwick, to Patterdale (in that direction) is the most beautiful and rewarding walk in Lakeland.

The junction of paths at Silver Bay is marked by a large cairn.

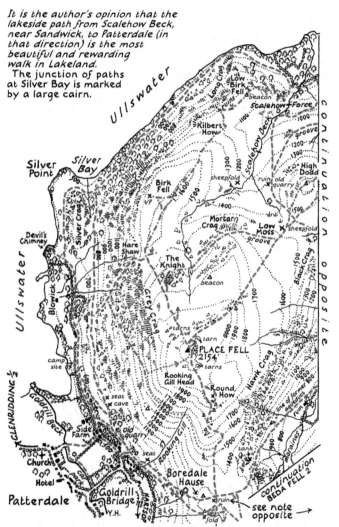

The heights of Place Fell's main subsidiary summits (in descending order) are: The Knight, 1778'; Birk Fell, 1680'; High Dodd, 1644'; Sleet Fell, 1240'; Low Birk Fell, 1225'. Silver Crag is 890' high.

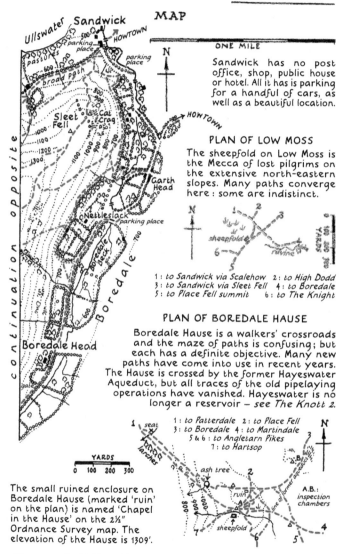

Sandwick MAP

ONE MILE

Sandwick has no post office, shop, public house or hotel. All it has is parking for a handful of cars, as well as a beautiful location.

PLAN OF LOW MOSS

The sheepfold on Low Moss is the Mecca of lost pilgrims on the extensive north-eastern slopes. Many paths converge here: some are indistinct.

1: to Sandwick via Scalehow 2: to High Dodd
3: to Sandwick via Sleet Fell 4: to Boredale
5: to Place Fell summit 6: to The Knight

PLAN OF BOREDALE HAUSE

Boredale Hause is a walkers' crossroads and the maze of paths is confusing; but each has a definite objective. Many new paths have come into use in recent years. The Hause is crossed by the former Hayeswater Aqueduct, but all traces of the old pipelaying operations have vanished. Hayeswater is no longer a reservoir – see The Knott 2.

1: to Patterdale 2: to Place Fell
3: to Boredale 4: to Martindale
5 & 6: to Angletarn Pikes
7: to Hartsop

A.B.: inspection chambers

YARDS
0 100 200 300

The small ruined enclosure on Boredale Hause (marked 'ruin' on the plan) is named 'Chapel in the Hause' on the 2½" Ordnance Survey map. The elevation of the Hause is 1309'.

The summit of Birk Fell is sometimes referred to as Bleaberry Knott. A path leads westwards 250 yards to a renowned Ullswater viewing platform, marked 'VP' on the map opposite.

ASCENT FROM PATTERDALE
1700 feet of ascent : 1¾ miles

The face of Place Fell overlooking Patterdale is unremittingly and uncompromisingly steep, and the ascent is invariably made by way of the easier gradients of Boredale Hause, there being a continuous path on this route. (From the valley there appear to be paths going straight up the fell, but these are not paths at all: they are incipient streams and runnels.)

Take the upper path at the fork near the seat. Watch for the zig-zag: if this is missed the walker naturally gravitates to the lower path. The prominent ash tree is on the upper path.

The path from Boredale Hause to Round How has been extensively repaired and for much of the way is smooth; there is a short rocky gully immediately below Round How.

Birk Fell   The Knight   PLACE FELL   Round How

Grey Crag

Silver Crag

juniper   bracken   SILVER BAY   low crags and scree

SILVER BAY

larches

Boredale Hause   ruin   ash tree   zig-zag

looking north-north-east   Side Farm   gate   bracken

Patterdale   →CROOKABECK

car park   White Lion Hotel   Goldrill Bridge   Goldrill Beck

GLENRIDDING 1   Y.H. HARTSOP 2 and KIRKSTONE PASS

As an alternative, an old track that branches from the higher path to Silver Bay is recommended: this slants leftwards to the skyline depression between Birk Fell and Grey Crag. It is difficult to locate from above and is better not used for descent as there is rough ground in the vicinity. The diversion of the old track from the higher path to Silver Bay occurs a full half-mile beyond the quarry at a point where there is a bluff of grey rock on the left above some larches. A flat boulder marks the junction, and a few ancient cairns along the route are also a help. Botanists will find much of interest here.

Note also, 200 yards up the old track, a faint path on the right: this climbs high across the face below Grey Crag, is lost on scree, but can be traced beyond, on the 1500' contour, all the way to the usual route via Boredale Hause — an exhilarating high-level walk. From this path the summit may be gained without difficulty after leaving Grey Crag behind and crossing a small ravine.

One cannot sojourn at Patterdale without looking at Place Fell and one cannot look long at Place Fell without duly setting forth to climb it. The time is very well spent.

ASCENT FROM SANDWICK
1700 feet of ascent : 2½ miles

Of the two routes shown from Low Moss to the summit, the one on the left is very much the better. An easy but longer alternative is *via* Boredale Hause. *See the map on page 4.*

looking south-west

Five alternatives are shown converging near the sheepfold on Low Moss, beyond which is a further choice. The best way of these is over Sleet Fell, although this is initially steep.
 A very different route is that *via* Low Birk Fell, Kilbert How, Birk Fell and The Knight, visiting subsidiary summits on Place Fell's western flank overlooking Ullswater (there are excellent viewpoints at the ruins just after Kilbert How and 250 yards west of Birk Fell). The route starts at a corner of the wall accompanying the lakeside track to Patterdale; a sketchy path picks its way through rock outcrops ahead of a wider, grassy ridge where it becomes more distinct up to the beacon on Low Birk Fell, which is a fine viewpoint. This little-used way up is a delight.

 Place Fell's extensive northern slopes offer a wide variety of ascents; starting from this side of the fell means different options are available for the return.

THE VIEW
(with distances in miles)

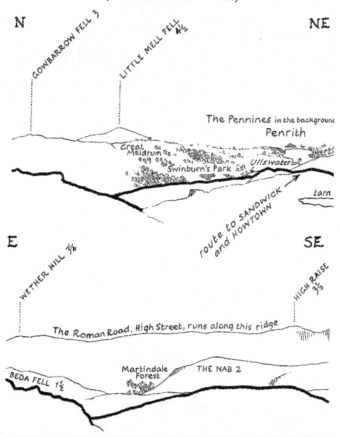

N

GOWBARROW FELL 3

LITTLE MELL FELL 4½

NE

The Pennines *in the background*
Penrith

Great
Meldrum
Swinburn's Park
Ullswater

route to SANDWICK and HOWTOWN

tarn

E

WETHER HILL ¾

SE

HIGH RAISE 2½

The Roman Road, High Street, runs along this ridge

BEDA FELL 1½

Martindale
Forest

THE NAB 2

THE SUMMIT

A rocky ridge overtops gently rising slopes
and has a cairn at one end and a
triangulation column at the other; the cairn
illustrated right is no longer as prominent.

DESCENTS: Routes of descent are
indicated in the illustration of the
view; that to Boredale Hause is
safest in bad weather.

THE VIEW

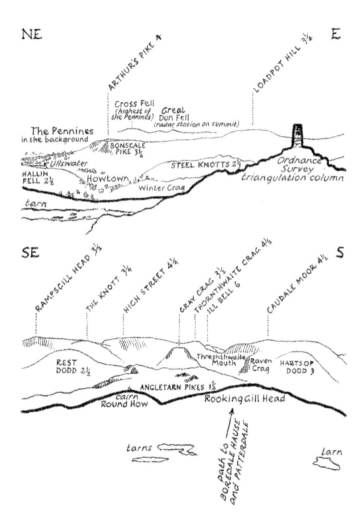

The thick black line marks the visible
boundaries of Place Fell from
the summit cairn.

continued

THE VIEW

continued

S   SW

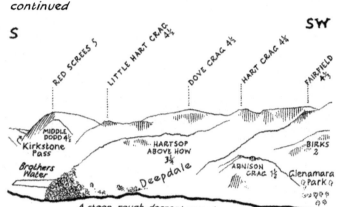

A steep, rough descent may be made to Patterdale
over this edge, but there is no path. The Boredale
Hause route is to be preferred, and takes no longer.

W   NW

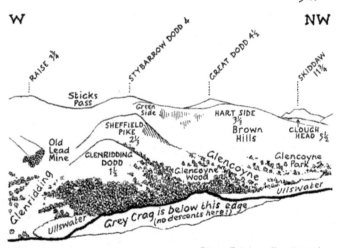

Place Fell is a fine location
to appreciate the number of side valleys
that lead westwards from Patterdale; from the summit can
be seen (from the left): Deepdale, Grisedale, the valley of Glenridding
Beck and Glencoyne. Only Dovedale, beyond the ridge of Hartsop
above How, is out of sight. No other Lakeland valley has so many
significant side branches.

THE VIEW

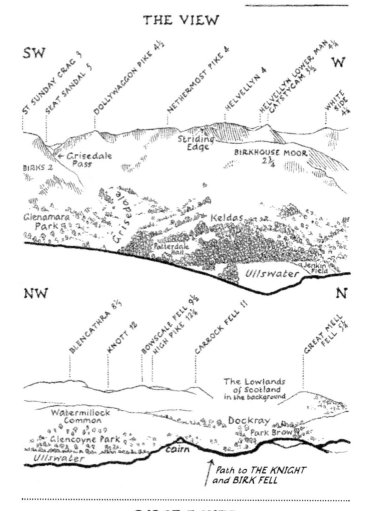

SW

ST SUNDAY CRAG 3
SEAT SANDAL 5
DOLLYWAGGON PIKE 4½
NETHERMOST PIKE 4
HELVELLYN 4
HELVELLYN LOWER MAN 4½
CATSTYCAM 3½
WHITE SIDE 4½

W

← Grisedale Pass
Striding Edge
BIRKHOUSE MOOR 2¾

BIRKS 2

Glenamara Park
Grisedale
Keldas
Patterdale Hall
Ullswater
Jenkin Field

NW

BLENCATHRA 8½
KNOTT 12
BOWSCALE FELL 9½
HIGH PIKE 12½
CARROCK FELL 11
GREAT MELL FELL 5¼

N

The Lowlands of Scotland in the background

Watermillock Common
Glencoyne Park
Ullswater
Cairn
Dockray
Park Brow

↑ Path to THE KNIGHT and BIRK FELL

....

RIDGE ROUTE

To ANGLETARN PIKES, 1851′

1¾ miles : S then SSE : *Depression at 1309′* : *600 feet of ascent*

Place Fell, strictly speaking, has no connecting ridges. However, near-neighbour Angletarn Pikes is commonly climbed as part of its ascent and the route *via* Boredale Hause is clear all the way. See maps on *Place Fell 3* and *Angletarn Pikes 4* and ascent diagram on *Angletarn Pikes 5.*

Rampsgill Head

2598'

OS grid ref: NY443129

Patterdale

Hartsop

HIGH RAISE
▲
RAMPSGILL HEAD
▲ ▲ KIDSTY PIKE

Riggindale

▲ HIGH STREET

MILES

0   1   2   3   4

from Gray Crag

NATURAL FEATURES

There is usually little difficulty in defining the boundaries of a mountain. If it rises in isolation there is no difficulty, and even if it is merely a high point on a ridge invariably its main slopes go down to valley level, probably on both flanks, and the limit of its extent in other directions is, as a rule, marked by watercourses falling from the cols or depressions linking it with adjacent heights. Rampsgill Head is, geographically, a 'key' point in the High Street range, for two independent ridges of some importance leave its summit, and it is, therefore, all the more remarkable that a neat and precise definition of its natural boundaries cannot be given, largely because lower secondary summits on the side ridges are also regarded as separate fells and claim to themselves territory that would otherwise be attributed to the parent fell. It is also unusual for so prominent a height to be without an official name. Rampsgill Head is properly the name of the semicircle of high ground enclosing the rough upper reaches of the valley of Ramps Gill but is now generally attached to all the fell above and beyond, although occasionally some writers have remedied the lack of a common title by referring to the whole mass hereabouts, east of the watershed, as Kidsty Pike, but this is incorrect.

The most impressive natural feature is the fringe of crags breaking abruptly at the edge of the summit facing Ramps Gill and the long slopes of boulder debris and scree below are an indication that, before the age of decay, the rock scenery here must have been very striking. Grass predominates elsewhere but there is another steep face of rock, Twopenny Crag, falling into Riggindale. Hayeswater lies at the foot of the western slope, but the principal becks from the fell act as feeders of Ullswater and Haweswater.

Twopenny Crag

Rampsgill Head 3

This fine arête (here seen from the south) starts from a
leaning pinnacle on the west face and
leads directly to the top of the
fell. It is littered with loose rock
and is obviously in a state
of decay; otherwise it
would surely deserve
the attention of
rock climbers.

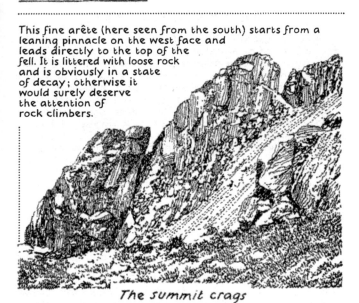

The summit crags

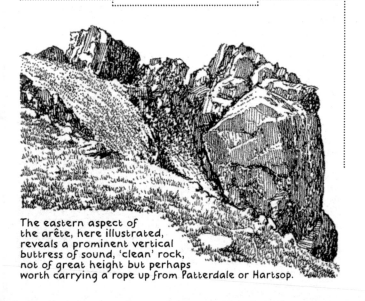

The eastern aspect of
the arête, here illustrated,
reveals a prominent vertical
buttress of sound, 'clean' rock,
not of great height but perhaps
worth carrying a rope up from Patterdale or Hartsop.

MAP

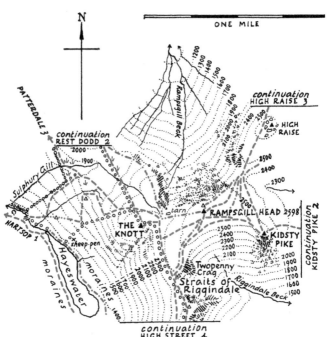

In the summer of 2014 the dam at Hayeswater was demolished, allowing the former reservoir to return to nature. This has affected a number of paths in the vicinity. For details about this major change to a corner of Lakeland, see *The Knott 2*.

The crags above the north-west face

ASCENTS FROM PATTERDALE AND HARTSOP
2200 feet of ascent : 4½ miles from Patterdale
2050 feet of ascent : 2¼ miles from Hartsop

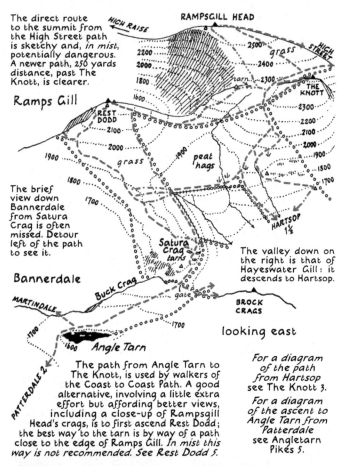

The direct route to the summit from the High Street path is sketchy and, *in mist*, potentially dangerous. A newer path, 250 yards distance, past The Knott, is clearer.

Ramps Gill

The brief view down Bannerdale from Satura Crag is often missed. Detour left of the path to see it.

Bannerdale

The valley down on the right is that of Hayeswater Gill: it descends to Hartsop.

looking east

The path from Angle Tarn to The Knott, is used by walkers of the Coast to Coast Path. A good alternative, involving a little extra effort but affording better views, including a close-up of Rampsgill Head's crags, is to first ascend Rest Dodd; the best way to the tarn is by way of a path close to the edge of Ramps Gill. *In mist this way is not recommended. See Rest Dodd 5.*

For a diagram of the path from Hartsop see The Knott 3.

For a diagram of the ascent to Angle Tarn from Patterdale see Angletarn Pikes 5.

This is a most enjoyable excursion with a succession of widely differing views, all excellent; and the route itself is an interesting puzzle to unravel. *In bad weather*, however, there will be some difficulty, and a stranger may run into trouble on top of Rampsgill Head, where there are crags.

ASCENT FROM MARDALE
1950 feet of ascent : 3½ miles from the road end

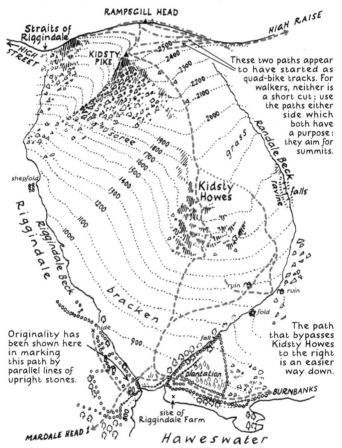

RAMPSGILL HEAD

HIGH RAISE

Straits of Riggindale

HIGH STREET

KIDSTY PIKE

2500
2400
2300
2200
2100
2000
1900
1800
1700
1600
1500
1400
1300
1200
1100
1000
900

scree

These two paths appear to have started as quad-bike tracks. For walkers, neither is a short cut; use the paths either side which both have a purpose: they aim for summits.

grass

Randale Beck ravine

Kidsty Howes

falls

shepfold

Riggindale

Riggindale Beck

bracken

ruin

ruin

fold

hide

Originality has been shown here in marking this path by parallel lines of upright stones.

fall

plantation

The path that bypasses Kidsty Howes to the right is an easier way down.

BURNBANKS

MARDALE HEAD 1

x site of Riggindale Farm

Haweswater

looking west-north-west

The ascent of Rampsgill Head from Mardale cannot really avoid the intervening summit of Kidsty Pike, nor should it: the climb, much of which follows the route of the Coast to Coast Path, is particularly good in the vicinity of Kidsty Hows (although rough in places) and the views are beautiful. The final section is a stroll.

THE SUMMIT

On the right sort of day, the top is a pleasant place to linger awhile. The turf is delightful, there is some outcropping rock to add interest, the rim of crags is worthy of a leisurely and detailed exploration, the views are good in all directions. A prominent, well built cairn stands on the edge of the abrupt north-west face; thirty yards away is the highest cairn — an untidy heap of stones.

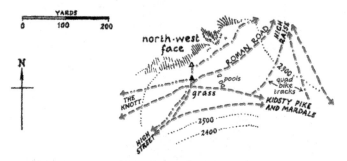

DESCENTS : For Patterdale and Hartsop, aim for The Knott to join the path there. For Mardale, use the ridge beyond Kidsty Pike, following the path over Kidsty Howes to Riggindale Beck, or take the alternative and easier route to the left that avoids Kidsty Howes, *but not in mist*. For more details see *Kidsty Pike 4*.

It should be noted that Mardale Head is uninhabited, and the only beds in the valley are at the Haweswater Hotel on the far side of the lake.

In mist, the edge of the escarpment is sufficiently defined to give direction, but care is needed following a sketchy path : keep the escarpment on the right hand if bound for either Patterdale or Hartsop and descend easy ground to the path. A clearer path, shown on the map above, meets the Patterdale—High Street path 300 yards further south. For Mardale, follow the path to Kidsty Pike and descend east-north-east then east from there on a good path.

RIDGE ROUTES

To HIGH RAISE, 2634' : ¾ mile : NE
Depression at 2450': 190 feet of ascent

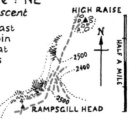

Follow the edge of the crags north-east (noting the arête on the way) and join a narrow path (the old High Street) that crosses the depression and continues up the easy grass slope of High Raise opposite. When the stony top is reached leave the path and pick a way among embedded boulders to the cairn.

To THE KNOTT, 2423': ⅓ mile : W
Depression at 2360' 65 feet of ascent

Descend the easy west slope to the wall corner in the depression (the good path crossed here is the Patterdale to High Street route), or take the clearer path to the south. He is tired indeed who cannot gain the summit of The Knott from the corner of the wall, and two minutes for the ascent is a generous time allowance.

To KIDSTY PIKE, 2560': ⅓ mile : ESE
Depression at 2525', 35 feet of ascent

Kidsty Pike is unmistakable. A thin path aims for it, which joins the main path from the Straits of Riggindale.

To HIGH STREET, 2718': 1¼ miles : SW then S
Depression at 2340': 400 feet of ascent

Go south and join the path from Kidsty Pike, which leads down to a narrow depression in impressive surroundings. This is (or these are) the Straits of Riggindale, and from here the top of High Street may be reached simply by following the broken wall, but it is better by far to arrive there by following the sketchy path which skirts the edge of the cliffs on the left, giving striking views. _Not in mist, however._

All these routes are easy, and, with care, safe in mist.

THE VIEW

Although the Helvellyn range conceals most of the western fells the view is very extensive and interesting. There is a commanding prospect of Ramps Gill from the larger cairn.

Principal Fells

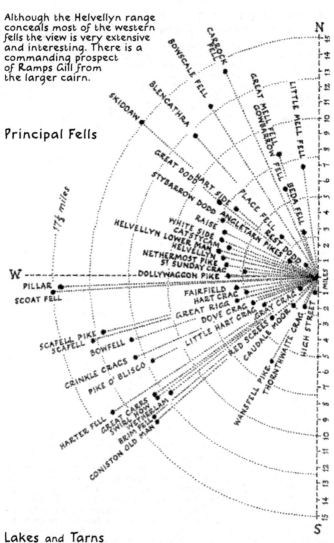

Lakes and Tarns

N: *Ullswater (two sections)*
W: *Brothers Water*

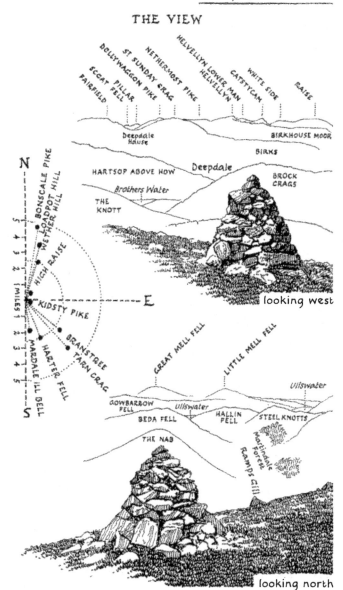

THE VIEW

FAIRFIELD
SCOAT FELL
PILLAR
DOLLYWAGGON PIKE
ST SUNDAY CRAG
NETHERMOST PIKE
HELVELLYN LOWER MAN
HELVELLYN
CATSTYCAM
WHITE SIDE
RAISE

Deepdale
Hause

BIRKHOUSE MOOR

BIRKS

HARTSOP ABOVE HOW   Deepdale

Brothers Water

BROCK
CRAGS

THE
KNOTT

looking west

N

BONSCALE PIKE
LOADPOT HILL
WETHER HILL

HIGH RAISE

5
4
3
2
1 (MILES 1)
2
3
4
5

KIDSTY PIKE

E

BRANSTREE
TARN CRAG
HARTER FELL
MARDALE ILL BELL

S

GREAT MELL FELL

LITTLE MELL FELL

Ullswater

GOWBARROW
FELL   Ullswater
BEDA FELL   HALLIN
FELL

STEEL KNOTTS

Martindale
Forest

THE NAB

Ramps Gill

looking north

Rest Dodd

2283'

OS grid ref: NY433137

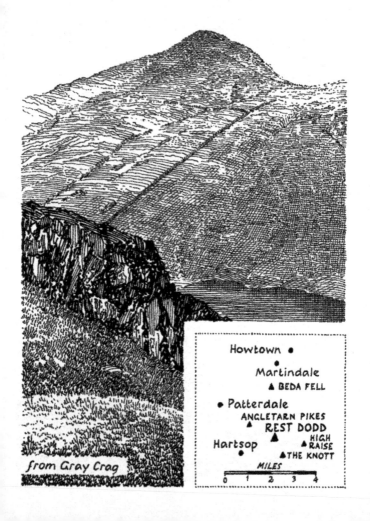

from Gray Crag

Howtown •

Martindale •

▲ BEDA FELL

• Patterdale

ANGLETARN PIKES
▲   **REST DODD**

Hartsop   ▲ HIGH
•   RAISE
▲ THE KNOTT

MILES

0   1   2   3   4

NATURAL FEATURES

The steep-sided ridge that divides Martindale into the secluded upper valleys of Bannerdale and Ramps Gill rises first to the shapely conical summit of The Nab and then more gradually to the rounded dome of Rest Dodd, which dominates both branches. It is a fell of little interest, although the east flank falls spectacularly in fans of colourful scree. Rest Dodd stands at an angle on the undulating grassy ridge coming down from the main watershed to the shores of Ullswater, and its south-west slope, which drains into Hayeswater Gill, is crossed by the track from Patterdale to High Street. Much of the fell is within the Martindale deer forest.

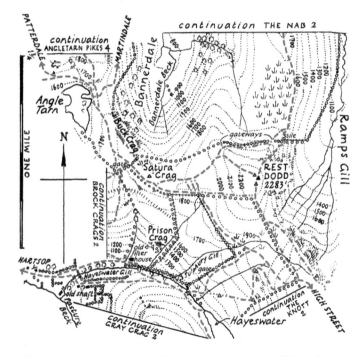

The dam at the outlet of Hayeswater was demolished in the summer of 2014 and the former reservoir has now reverted to its natural shape. For details about how this has affected paths in the immediate vicinity, see The Knott 2.

ASCENT FROM HARTSOP
1700 feet of ascent : 2 miles

REST DODD

looking east

The usual path up the valley (to Hayeswater) runs along the right (south) side of the gill above Wath Bridge, but it is possible to keep on the left side as far as the former filter house. Alternative routes are shown for the final climb up the fellside but no amount of inventiveness can make this dull trudge interesting or attractive.

Another approach is by way of Satura Crag, using the path that starts from the former filter house, traversing the flank of Brock Crags (*see Brock Crags 2*).

Initially the approach is good, for the valley of Hayeswater Gill is both beautiful and interesting, but beyond the quality of the scene deteriorates sadly.

ASCENT FROM PATTERDALE
1900 feet of ascent : 3½ miles

Take the usual route to High Street (*see Angletarn Pikes 5* and *High Street 5*), which traverses the slopes of Rest Dodd, but after crossing the top of Satura Crag continue up the ridge to the left, although the start of the path is a little indistinct. *In mist*, follow the fence and broken wall directly ahead, bearing left at the top.

(It is an interesting fact that the Patterdale—High Street route formerly followed this wall up to its top corner and down the south slope of Rest Dodd, an extra 300 feet of climbing which the present more direct path avoids.)

THE SUMMIT

A summit cairn with a flagpole! Such was once
Rest Dodd's distinction, but now the flagpole has
gone there is little to relieve the drabness of
the top of the fell. There are three cairns
and a natural obstacle in the shape of an
eroded peat hag on the grassy summit.

DESCENTS : Go down past the south cairn to the junction of two
broken walls. Follow the wall west to join the path from High
Street to Patterdale. Alternatively, use the path to the west.
 Do not attempt any descents to the east into Ramps Gill, which
is deer forest.

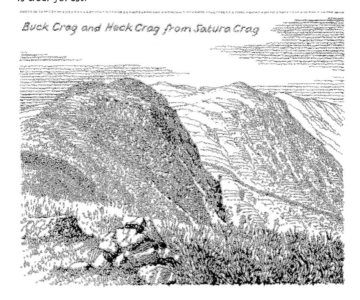

Buck Crag and Heck Crag from Satura Crag

THE VIEW

The view is neither so pleasing nor so extensive as that from The Knott nearby, although the full length of the Helvellyn range is well seen. The wild and lonely head of Ramps Gill is an impressive sight. In the west, Great Gable fits snugly into the deep depression of Deepdale Hause.

Principal Fells

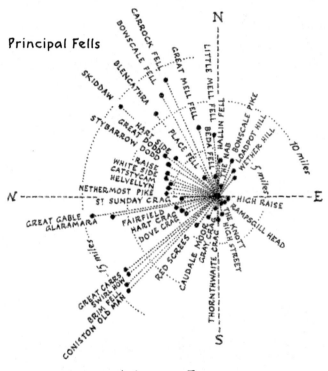

Lakes and Tarns

from the main cairn:
  NNE: *Ullswater*

from the south cairn:
  S: *Hayeswater*
  WSW: *Brothers Water*

from the west cairn:
  NNE: *Ullswater*
  WSW: *Brothers Water*
  WNW: *Angle Tarn*

RIDGE ROUTES

To ANGLETARN PIKES, 1857′: 1¾ miles: W, then NW

Depression at 1600′: 300 feet of ascent

An interesting walk, full of variety.

From the west cairn go down the shoulder to Satura Crag, where the path to Patterdale is joined. *(In mist, descend by the wall.)* At Angle Tarn there is a choice: bear right onto the path to Beda Fell and left at the top of the hill; or continue on the Patterdale path and climb directly to the summit.

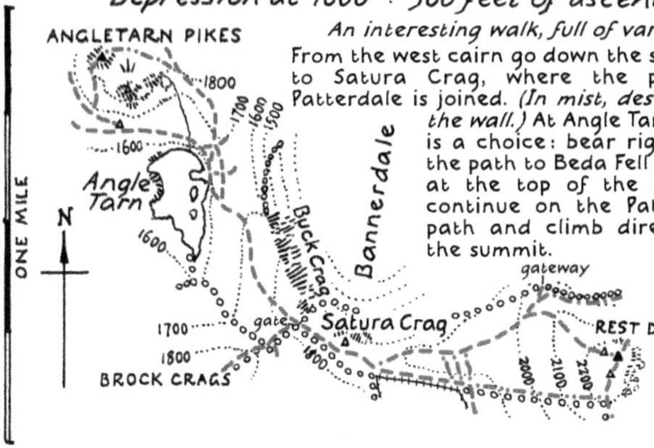

To THE KNOTT, 2423′: ¾ mile: SSE

Depression at 1925′: 500 feet of ascent

Merely a matter of following a wall.

From the south cairn the wall is soon reached. The depression is marshy. The High Street path is crossed at the remains of a gateway.

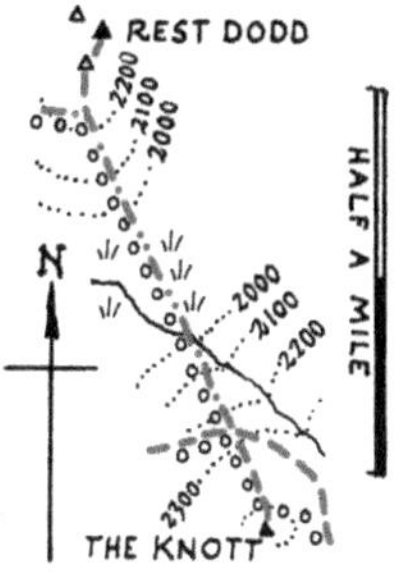

The Nab is completely within the Martindale Deer Forest.

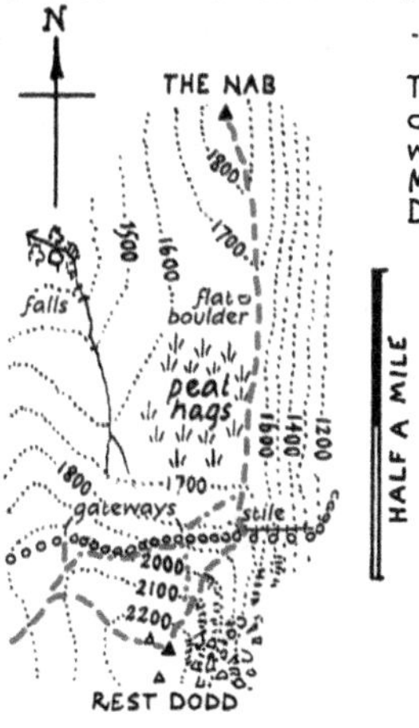

To THE NAB, 1887′: 1¼ miles NW, then E and N

Depression at 1650′ 250 feet of ascent

A clear path all the way.

Walkers are requested to keep to the preferred route, approaching The Nab along the ridge from Rest Dodd, which begins with a steep descent to a precarious looking stile, and returning the same way, without descending into the valley and thereby disturbing the deer (*see The Nab 2*). An alternative descent from Rest Dodd to a gap in the wall is possible, but not recommended.

Sallows

1691'

OS grid ref: NY437040

better known locally
as Kentmere Park

from Badger Rock

▲ YOKE

SALLOWS
▲   ● Kentmere

●   ▲ SOUR HOWES
Troutbeck

● Windermere

MILES

0   1   2   3   4

For most walkers, the fells
proper in this region start at
Garburn Pass and rise to
Yoke, Ill Bell and other fells
to the north, but there
are two hills, twins almost,
immediately to the south of
the Pass, worth a mention
although these are not
strictly walkers' territory.
The higher of the two is
named Sallows (on all maps),
bounding the Pass, and has
much merit as a viewpoint
and a scantier virtue as a
grouse sanctuary. The lower
is Sour Howes, for which
there is a separate chapter
in this book.

MAP

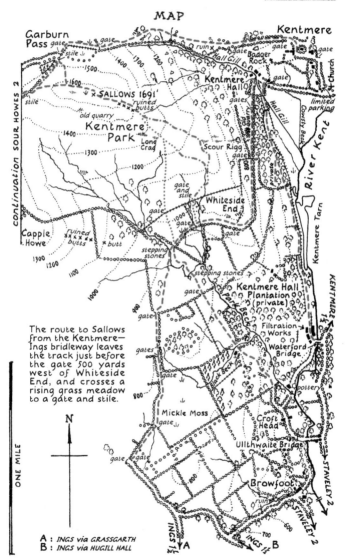

Garburn Pass

Kentmere

gate

gate

gate

stile

1500

1400

1700

ruin ✗

Hall Gill

gate

Badger Rock

Church

stile

1600

✗ SALLOWS 1691'
⤵ ✗ ruined butts

Kentmere Hall

gate

limited parking

stile

old quarry

Kentmere Park

1400

gates

River Kent

Cowsty Beck

Hall Gill

1300

Long Crag

Scour Rigg

gate

private

1200

gate and stile

Kentmere Tarn

Capple Howe

ruined butts ✗ ✗ ✗ ✗

✗ butt

gate

stepping stones

Whiteside End

gate

gate

1300

1200

1100

1000

stepping stones

gate

Kentmere Hall Plantation (private)

KENTMERE 1¼

900

gate

Filtration Works

The route to Sallows from the Kentmere— Ings bridleway leaves the track just before the gate 500 yards west of Whiteside End, and crosses a rising grass meadow to a gate and stile.

gates

Black Beck

gate

Park Beck

Waterford Bridge

pottery ?

N

800

gate

Mickle Moss

Croft Head

STAVELEY 2

ONE MILE

gate

Ullthwaite Bridge

gate

gate

800

Browfoot

ruin

INGS 1½

700

STAVELEY 2

INGS 1¼

700

600

A : INGS via GRASSGARTH
B : INGS via HUGILL HALL

INGS 1½ ↓A

INGS 1¼ ↓B

The southern boundary of Sallows is Park Beck. The map is extended to enable more detail of the routes from Staveley and Ings to be given. Private paths in Kentmere Park and Woods are omitted.

ASCENTS

FROM GARBURN PASS

The summit may be most easily and quickly visited from the top of Garburn Pass, where a stile in the wall gives access to the fell. There are two ways up: a direct path, or a more roundabout way beside a wall, turning sharp left where the good path from Sour Howes joins. Sallows is not, as it appears to be, a 'short cut' to Garburn Pass from the south; its tough heather slopes compel slow progress, and time will be lost. Garburn is best reached by orthodox routes.

FROM INGS—KENTMERE HALL BRIDLE PATH

An alternative way up, a mile-long ascent from the Ings—Kentmere Hall bridle path, offers an aspect of the fell seldom seen. The clearest path skirts the outcrop of Scour Rigg, with its four distinctive tops, before following the line of ruined shooting butts on a path that becomes more distinctive as height is gained.

THE SUMMIT

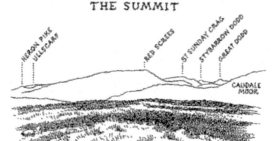

A curious curving mound of shale and grass, thirty feet long and narrow as a parapet, marks the highest part of the fell: it seems to be man-made, but is more probably a natural formation. It has no cairn. Heather and coarse grass cover the top of the fell, but there are small outcrops of rock west of the summit.

The summit mound

THE VIEW

The Lakeland scene occupies only half the panorama: it is outstandingly good to the west but unattractive northwards where Yoke fills much of the horizon. The rest of the view is exceedingly extensive, varied and interesting, covering a wide area from the Pennines across Morecambe Bay to Black Combe.

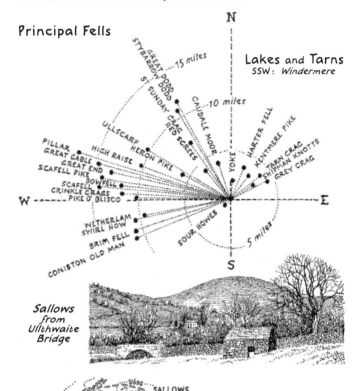

Principal Fells

N

Lakes and Tarns
SSW: *Windermere*

15 miles

10 miles

5 miles

STYBARROW DODD
GREAT DODD
S. SUNDAY CRAG
RED SCREES
CAUDALE MOOR
ULLSCARP
HERON PIKE
HIGH RAISE
PILLAR
GREAT GABLE
GREAT END
SCAFELL PIKE
SCAFELL
BOWFELL
CRINKLE CRAGS
PIKE O'BLISCO
WETHERLAM
SWIRL HOW
BRIM FELL
CONISTON OLD MAN
SOUR HOWES
YOKE
HARTER FELL
KENTMERE PIKE
TARN CRAG
SHIPMAN KNOTTS
GREY CRAG

W — — — — — — — — — — E

S

Sallows from Ullthwaite Bridge

SALLOWS
1600
stile
old quarry
ruined hut
SOUR HOWES
1500
1400
1587

RIDGE ROUTE

N

To SOUR HOWES, 1587' : 1¼ miles : W then SSW
Depression at 1450' : 230 feet of ascent

Easy, on a long, curving ridge.
A clear path can be followed all the way to the summit mound of Sour Howes. The route can be very damp after wet weather.

ONE MILE

Selside Pike

2149'

OS grid ref: NY491112

Haweswater Hotel
●

● Swindale Head

Mardale   ▲ SELSIDE PIKE
Head ●

▲ BRANSTREE

▲ HARTER FELL

MILES

0   1   2   3   4

from Mosedale Beck
near the waterfalls

NATURAL FEATURES

One of the lesser-known fells is Selside Pike on the eastern fringe of the district, commanding the head of the shy and beautiful little valley of Swindale. Its neglect is scarcely merited, for although the summit is a dull grass mound with little reward in views, the fell has an extremely rugged eastern face that closes the valley in dramatic fashion: here are dark crags, rarely visited waterfalls (The Forces), a curious dry tarn bed (Dodd Bottom) set amongst moraines and, above it, a perfect hanging valley, the two being connected by a very formidable gully. For countless ages Selside Pike has looked down upon Swindale and seen there a picture of unspoiled charm. In the 1950s engineers took over the valley with the idea of building a reservoir; now they have gone, mercifully leaving the valley as they found it. The little farmstead of Swindale Head remains totally unspoiled.

Selside Pike
from the Old
Corpse Road

Once upon a time, the Old Corpse Road was the route by which Mardale's dead were taken, by horseback, for burial at Shap; the last such journey was made in 1736 with subsequent local burials taking place at tiny Holy Trinity Church in Mardale Green. In 1936, after the plans to raise Haweswater and submerge Mardale were finalised, more than 100 bodies were disinterred and reburied at Shap.

MAP

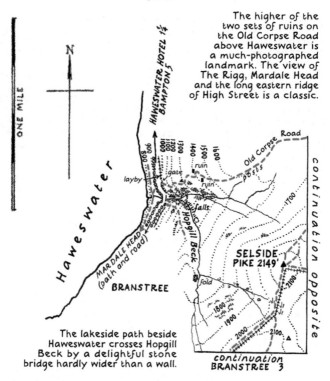

The higher of the two sets of ruins on the Old Corpse Road above Haweswater is a much-photographed landmark. The view of The Rigg, Mardale Head and the long eastern ridge of High Street is a classic.

The lakeside path beside Haweswater crosses Hopgill Beck by a delightful stone bridge hardly wider than a wall.

Swindale
with *Selside Pike at the head of the valley*

MAP

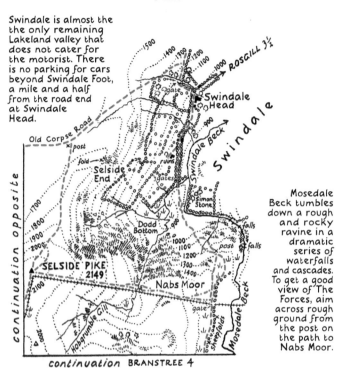

Swindale is almost the the only remaining Lakeland valley that does not cater for the motorist. There is no parking for cars beyond Swindale Foot, a mile and a half from the road end at Swindale Head.

Mosedale Beck tumbles down a rough and rocky ravine in a dramatic series of waterfalls and cascades. To get a good view of The Forces, aim across rough ground from the post on the path to Nabs Moor.

continuation opposite

continuation BRANSTREE 4

Swindale Head
from near the farm of the same name

ASCENT FROM SWINDALE HEAD
1200 feet of ascent : 1½ miles (via the north-east ridge)
1350 feet of ascent : 2¼ miles (via the Mosedale path)
NOTE : Add 1½ miles from Swindale Foot (the last place to park)

looking east-south-east

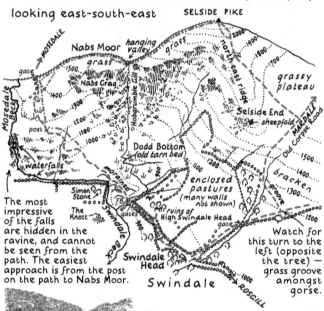

The most impressive of the falls are hidden in the ravine, and cannot be seen from the path. The easiest approach is from the post on the path to Nabs Moor.

Watch for this turn to the left (opposite the tree) — grass groove amongst gorse.

The scenery is excellent in the vicinity of Dodd Bottom but deteriorates when the tedious higher slopes are reached. If returning to Swindale, ascend by the ridge and descend by the wire fence, making a detour to see the waterfalls. There is no parking for non-residents beyond Swindale Foot, which entails an added mile and a half of road walking.

ASCENT FROM MARDALE
1400 feet of ascent : 2 miles
An attractive climb out of the valley *via* the Old Corpse Road is the start of an easy ascent with little more of interest.
See maps on pages 3 and 4.

The Forces:
the top waterfall

THE SUMMIT

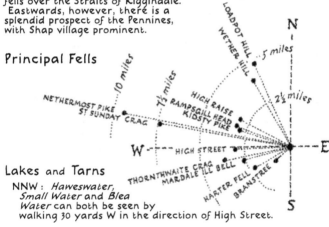

RAMPSGILL HEAD   HIGH RAISE

It is surprising to find a cairn of several tons of stones where all else is grass, and it seems likely that originally there was a rock outcrop here that has been broken up and formed into a cairn. Ten yards away is an angle in the fence, which is a guide, *in mist*, to Mosedale or Branstree.

THE VIEW

The view towards Lakeland is disappointing, being confined to the surroundings of Mardale except for a glimpse of distant fells over the Straits of Riggindale.

Eastwards, however, there is a splendid prospect of the Pennines, with Shap village prominent.

Principal Fells

LOADPOT HILL
WETHER HILL
5 miles
N
2½ miles
HIGH RAISE
RAMPSGILL HEAD
KIDSTY PIKE
10 miles
1½ miles
NETHERMOST PIKE
ST SUNDAY CRAG
W
HIGH STREET
E
THORNTHWAITE CRAG
MARDALE ILL BELL
HARTER FELL
BRANSTREE
S

Lakes and Tarns

NNW : *Haweswater, Small Water* and *Blea Water* can both be seen by walking 30 yards W in the direction of High Street.

RIDGE ROUTE

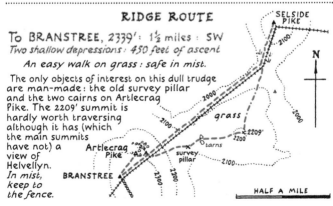

To BRANSTREE, 2339′ : 1½ miles : SW
Two shallow depressions : 450 feet of ascent

An easy walk on grass : safe in mist.

The only objects of interest on this dull trudge are man-made: the old survey pillar and the two cairns on Artlecrag Pike. The 2209′ summit is hardly worth traversing although it has (which the main summits have not) a view of Helvellyn. *In mist, keep to the fence.*

SELSIDE PIKE
2100
N
2000
grass
2100
×2209′
2200
tarns
Artlecrag Pike
survey pillar
2100
BRANSTREE
2300
2200
2000

HALF A MILE

Shipman Knotts

1926'

OS grid ref: NY472062

from Stockdale

Shipman Knotts is of moderate altitude and would have called for no more than the brief comment that it is a shoulder of Kentmere Pike had it not earned for itself a separate chapter by reason of the characteristic roughnesses of its surface. Rocky outcrops are everywhere on the steep slopes, persisting even in the woods of Sadgill, although these seldom attain the magnitude of crags. This fell is usually climbed on the way to Harter Fell from the south, and its rock should be welcomed for there is precious little beyond. The south slope carries an old cart track linking Stile End and Sadgill, which is the regular highway between Kentmere and Longsleddale. The highest point is 1120 feet.

▲ HARTER FELL

KENTMERE ▲ TARN
▲ PIKE   CRAG

ILL BELL ▲   ▲ GREY
                                CRAG
SHIPMAN KNOTTS ▲

• Kentmere

Longsleddale •

0   1   2   3   4

MAP

continuation KENTMERE PIKE 4

ASCENTS

from Kentmere (via Stile End):
1400 feet of ascent : 2 miles

Shipman Knotts is usually climbed as a
means of gaining access to the Harter Fell
ridge, but is an interesting short expedition in
itself. The ascent is most easily made alongside
the wall running up from the summit of the Stile
End—Sadgill 'pass', but walkers now seem to favour a
short cut that links grassy rakes on Wray Crag's flank.
Originally a quad bike track, this path continues to the top.
From Kentmere, the ridge north of the fell may be
reached by the path leaving Hallow Bank.

from Kentmere (via Green Quarter):
1250 feet of ascent : 2¼ miles

The summit of the pass can be reached from Green Quarter
via an easy path, sign-posted 'footpath to Longsleddale', that
crosses the flank of Green Quarter Fell, the 'outlying' fell to
south of Shipman Knotts. The views of the upper Kentmere
valley from this route are very fine.

from Sadgill : 1300 feet of ascent : 1½ miles

The former cart track from Sadgill has been extensively 'improved' in
recent years and you are as likely to meet a mountain bike or even
motorised transport as a fellow fellwalker. At the pass, follow the wall.

The summit from the south

THE SUMMIT

Three rocky knolls, on the eastern side of the wall, form the summit, and of these the middle one is highest. It is without a cairn. Reaching the summit is not easy as the path is on the western side of the wall, which is high and well built, and there is no stile or gate. Because of this a cairn was constructed

KENTMERE PIKE

on the western side of the wall opposite the highest point to at least give walkers a symbolic summit. The cairn has now vanished; ironically, the stones have most probably been used to repair the wall. *Wanted*: a stile or a gate.

There *is* one way to reach the summit without crossing the wall, however: from the north on the route from Goat Scar. But *in mist* this must not be attempted because of crags. See the ridge walk diagram on the facing page.

DESCENTS : *In mist*, the safest way is to follow the wall south to the pass, where turn left for Longsleddale, right for Kentmere. In clear weather the short cut past Wray Crag to Kentmere may safely be used although the start may be difficult to find; a faint path leaves the wall at a shallow grassy hollow. A longer alternative is to follow the wall northwards and descend *via* the route of ascent from Hallow Bank.

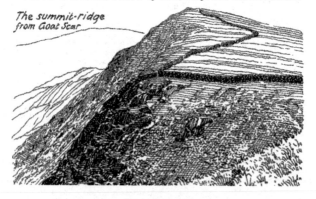

The summit-ridge from Goat Scar

THE VIEW

The northern half of the panorama is restricted to nearby heights of greater elevation; the southern is open, extensive and pleasing. There is a good view of Longsleddale.

Principal Fells

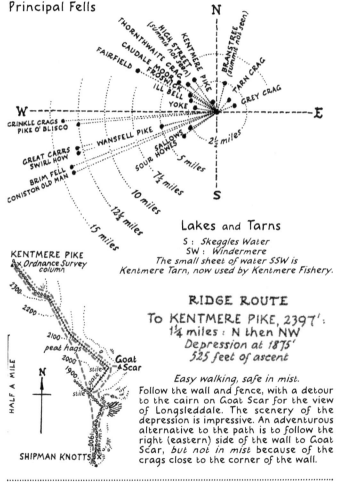

Lakes and Tarns

S : Skeggles Water
SW : Windermere
The small sheet of water SSW is
Kentmere Tarn, now used by Kentmere Fishery.

RIDGE ROUTE

To KENTMERE PIKE, 2397':
1¼ miles : N then NW
Depression at 1875'
525 feet of ascent

Easy walking, safe in mist.
Follow the wall and fence, with a detour to the cairn on Goat Scar for the view of Longsleddale. The scenery of the depression is impressive. An adventurous alternative to the path is to follow the right (eastern) side of the wall to Goat Scar, *but not in mist* because of the crags close to the corner of the wall.

....

A word about SADGILL (for artists) – A typical Lakeland scene of great charm is that of the picturesque hamlet of Sadgill in its bower of trees below the towering mass of Goat Scar with the arched bridge in front.

Sour Howes

1585'

OS grid ref: NY428032

better known locally as
Applethwaite Common

from Troutbeck

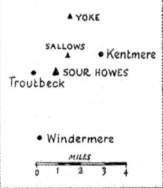

▲ YOKE

SALLOWS
▲   ● Kentmere

● ▲ SOUR HOWES
Troutbeck

● Windermere

MILES
0   1   2   3   4

Although all maps agree that the summit of this fell is named Sour Howes, its broadest flank, carrying the Garburn Pass Road down to Troutbeck, is far better known as Applethwaite Common; this flank is traversed also by the pleasant Dubbs Road. There is little about the fell to attract walkers, and nothing to justify a detour from the main Ill Bell ridge to the north, for although the views are really good they are better from the main ridge. There is heather on the eastern slopes, and therefore, inevitably, grouse; and therefore, inevitably, shooting butts: one may admire the construction of these butts but be glad they are now disused.

MAP

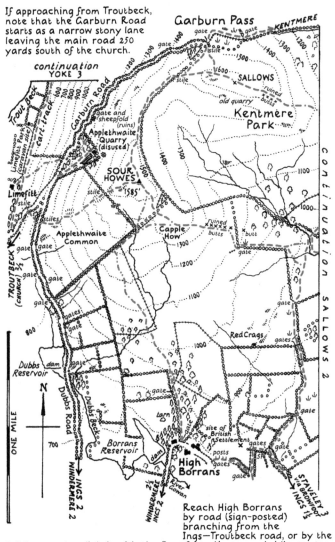

If approaching from Troutbeck, note that the Garburn Road starts as a narrow stony lane leaving the main road 250 yards south of the church.

Reach High Borrans by road (sign-posted) branching from the Ings—Troutbeck road, or by the bridleways that link it with the Browfoot—Kentmere bridleway two thirds of a mile to the east.

ASCENTS

Sour Howes is a fell with no obvious appeal to walkers, and few other than conscientious guidebook writers will visit its summit; nevertheless it makes a pleasant walk from Windermere, Ings or Staveley, especially on a clear day for the views are good.

FROM INGS, BROWFOOT and KENTMERE

Two lanes leave Ings (one *via* Grassgarth and one *via* Hugill Hall) and another leaves Browfoot (two miles up the Kentmere valley from Staveley) : these join, and at the terminus the old bridle path to Kentmere Hall may be followed for a mile, when it may be forsaken and a way made to the top by the shooting butts. This approach can be made from Kentmere Hall. The stile on Capple How has collapsed but it is easy enough to cross the wire fence.

FROM HIGH BORRANS

The path from High Borrans offers an enchanting approach, and this can be combined with a return *via* Capple How (see above) and the eastern bridleway for a good round trip.

FROM GARBURN PASS and THE GARBURN ROAD (to the west)

The summit is easily visited from the top of Garburn Pass, but an increasingly popular way up is by the path from the Garburn Road to the west, which is well provided with stiles and visits several delectable rocky outcrops. If the two routes are combined, the latter should be left for the descent, so that the wonderful view of Windermere is kept ahead.

THE SUMMIT

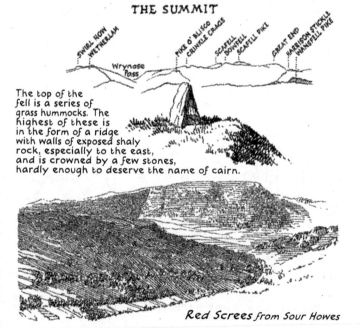

SWIRL HOW · WETHERLAM · Wrynose Pass · PIKE O' BLISCO · CRINKLE CRAGS · SCAFELL · SCAFELL PIKE · DOWFELL · GREAT END · HARRISON STICKLE · MANSFELL PIKE

The top of the fell is a series of grass hummocks. The highest of these is in the form of a ridge with walls of exposed shaly rock, especially to the east, and is crowned by a few stones, hardly enough to deserve the name of cairn.

Red Screes from Sour Howes

THE VIEW

The crowded skyline in the west arrests the attention, with the vertical profile of Scafell above Mickledore prominent in the scene. Langdale Pikes are well seen between and below Great End and Great Gable. There is a very extensive and beautiful prospect southwards from the far Pennines round to Morecambe Bay and Black Combe.

Principal Fells

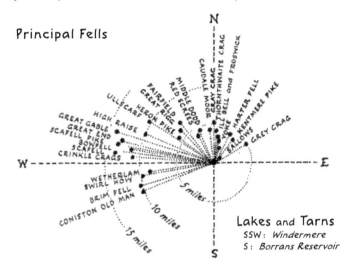

Lakes and Tarns
SSW: Windermere
S: Borrans Reservoir

Applethwaite Quarry

Most old and disused quarries are gloomy and repellant places but Applethwaite Quarry, near the Garburn Road, is relieved from desolation by a planting of conifers and a magnificent view. A favourite with foxes, this quarry!

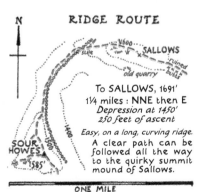

RIDGE ROUTE

SALLOWS
ruined
old quarry
wall
SOUR HOWES
1585'

To SALLOWS, 1691'
1¼ miles : NNE then E
Depression at 1450'
250 feet of ascent

Easy, on a long, curving ridge.

A clear path can be followed all the way to the quirky summit mound of Sallows.

ONE MILE

Steel Knotts

1414'

summit named Pikeawassa

OS grid ref: NY440181

from Howegrain Beck

Wether Hill's western flank swells into a bulge, Gowk Hill, which itself sends out a crooked bony arm northwards to form a lofty independent ridge running parallel to the main range and enclosing with it the short hidden valley of Fusedale. On the crest of this ridge, rock is never far from the surface and it breaks through in several places, notably at the highest point, which is a craggy tor that would worthily embelish the summit of many a higher fell. This freakish gnarled ridge is Steel Knotts; the summit tor is named on the best of authority (but not by many, one imagines) Pikeawassa (O.S. 1" and 2½" maps).

Howtown

STEEL KNOTTS

LOADPOT HILL

WETHER HILL

MILES

0   1   2   3

MAP

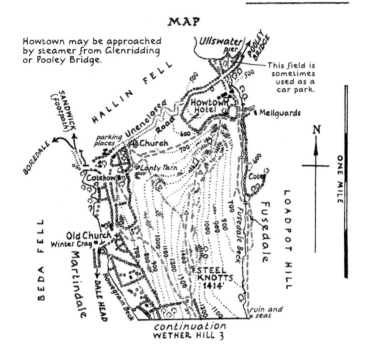

Howtown may be approached by steamer from Glenridding or Pooley Bridge.

This field is sometimes used as a car park.

ASCENTS

FROM HOWTOWN – *950 feet of ascent : 1 mile*

The natural route of ascent is by the craggy ridge above Howtown. It looks intimidating but is without perils and gives an exhilarating scramble. Leave the path at its base by a concrete post above and iron plate inscribed: and climb upwards between the rocks ; initially there is a track obscured by bracken. A cairn surmounts the steepest part of the ridge and the walking is then easy to the top of the fell.

AV 3·0

FROM LANTY TARN – *700 feet of ascent : ¼ mile*

The pronounced north-west shoulder of the fell, identified by two tiers of crag, begins near the tarn (a shallow pond). It offers a less satisfactory route than that from Howtown but, nevertheless, has become an established way to the top as evidenced by the thin path which climbs to the left (north) of the first crag then right (south) of the second crag, to a cairn above them. An easy slope then follows, with the path joining that from Howtown.

FROM MARTINDALE OLD CHURCH – *750 feet of ascent : ¼ mile*

This is the easiest way. Climb the fellside by the church to a good path slanting upwards (this is the Martindale path to the High Street range). Leave the path at a wall and turn up left to the ridge and again left to the top.

Although Steel Knotts is of small extent and modest elevation, it should not be climbed in mist. If caught by mist on the top, descend south to the wall and return by the path to Martindale Old Church.

THE SUMMIT

Steel Knotts may well claim to have the sharpest summit in Lakeland, for the rock tor (Pikeawassa) that crowns the top is so acute that only very agile walkers will be able to stand upon it, although, it will be noted, it is a popular perch for birds. There is no cairn. From the wall 400 yards south of the top, the summit structure assumes an almost perfect pyramid.

RIDGE ROUTE

To WETHER HILL, 2210'
1½ miles : S, then SSE, SE and NNE
Depression at 1200' : 1100 feet of ascent

An easy walk followed by a dull climb.
Follow the ridge south, joining a fair track to a ruined hut at the foot of the final slope. Of the two routes shown from here, the more southerly is the easier to follow. *This walk is safe in mist.*

Incidentally, this is the best way onto the High Street range from Martindale or Howtown, whether or not the summits of Steel Knotts and Wether Hill are visited. (The Keasgill groove is the usual one.)

THE VIEW

Principal Fells

This is the best viewpoint for the upper Martindale district, the highlight of a charming scene being the confluence of the remote Ramps Gill and Bannerdale valleys.

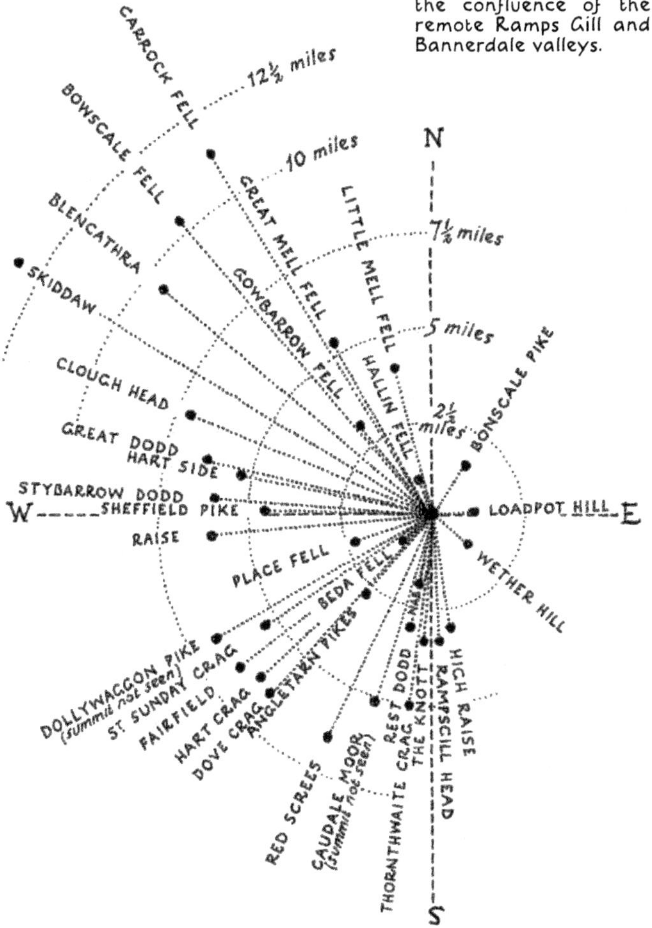

CARROCK FELL
BOWSCALE FELL
BLENCATHRA
SKIDDAW
CLOUGH HEAD
GREAT DODD
HART SIDE
STYBARROW DODD
SHEFFIELD PIKE
RAISE
W
GREAT MELL FELL
GOWBARROW FELL
LITTLE MELL FELL
HALLIN FELL
N
BONSCALE PIKE
LOADPOT HILL
E
PLACE FELL
BEDA FELL
WETHER HILL
DOLLYWAGGON PIKE
(summit not seen)
ST SUNDAY CRAG
FAIRFIELD
HART CRAG
DOVE CRAG
ANGLETARN PIKES
RED SCREES
CAUDALE MOOR
(summit not seen)
REST DODD
THE KNOTT
RAMPSGILL HEAD
HIGH RAISE
THORNTHWAITE CRAG
RAMPSGILL HEAD
S

12½ miles
10 miles
7½ miles
5 miles
2½ miles

Lakes and Tarns
NW and NNE: *Ullswater*
(two sections, divided by Hallin Fell)

Tarn Crag

2176'

OS grid ref: NY488079

Shap •

• Swindale Head

Mardale
Head •
▲ BRANSTREE • Wet
Sleddale

▲ HARTER FELL

▲ TARN CRAG

KENTMERE
PIKE
▲ GREY CRAG

• road
summit

Longsleddale •

MILES
0 1 2 3 4 5

from Sadgill Wood

NATURAL FEATURES

The gradually rising wall of fells bounding Longsleddale on the east reaches its greatest elevation, and its terminus, in Tarn Crag. To the valley this fell presents a bold front, with Buckbarrow Crag a conspicuous object, but on other sides it is uninteresting, especially eastwards where easy slopes merge into the desolate plateaux of Shap Fells. It is enclosed on the north by the wide, shallow depression of Mosedale, a natural pass linking Longsleddale with Swindale in wild and lonely surroundings: here a former shepherd's cottage, now a bothy, merely accentuates the utter dreariness of the scene. (Yet on rare occasions of soft evening light even Mosedale can look inexpressibly beautiful!) The walker hereabouts will be in no doubt, without reference to his map, that he has passed outside the verge of Lakeland.

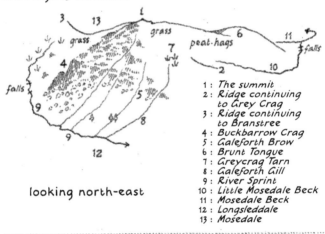

looking north-east

1 : The summit
2 : Ridge continuing to Grey Crag
3 : Ridge continuing to Branstree
4 : Buckbarrow Crag
5 : Galeforth Brow
6 : Brunt Tongue
7 : Greycrag Tarn
8 : Galeforth Gill
9 : River Sprint
10 : Little Mosedale Beck
11 : Mosedale Beck
12 : Longsleddale
13 : Mosedale

The head of Longsleddale

Tarn Crag 3

Mosedale Cottage
See note on facing page.

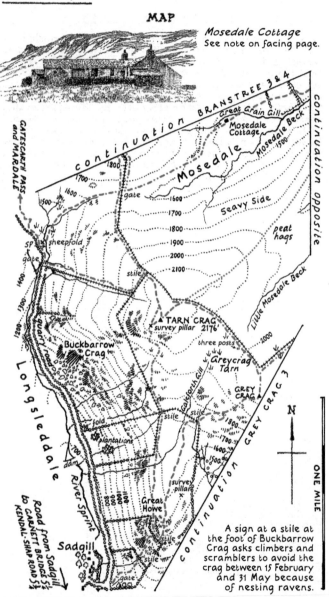

Longsleddale

GATESCARTH PASS and MARDALE

continuation BRANSTREE 3 & 4

continuation opposite

Mosedale

Great Grain Gill

Mosedale Cottage

Mosedale Beck

Seavy Side

peat hags

Little Mosedale Beck

gate

sheepfold

SP
gate

stile

TARN CRAG
survey pillar 2176'

Buckbarrow Crag

three posts

Greycrag Tarn

GREY CRAG

quarry road

fold

plantations

dam

River Sprint

Great Howe

survey pillar

stile

stile

stile

continuation GREY CRAG 3

stile
stile

gate

Sadgill

Road from Sadgill to GARNETT BRIDGE 5½ to KENDAL-SHAP ROAD 5½

N

ONE MILE

A sign at a stile at the foot of Buckbarrow Crag asks climbers and scramblers to avoid the crag between 15 February and 31 May because of nesting ravens.

MAP

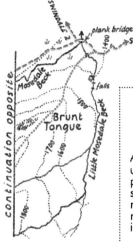

Mosedale Cottage has been maintained by the Mountain Bothy Association since 1999. Its primitive facilities are available, free of charge, to anyone able to reach this desolate spot.

ASCENT FROM LONGSLEDDALE
1600 feet of ascent
2 miles from Sadgill

An interesting walk, but not to be undertaken in mist because the path from Great Howe becomes sketchy below the summit. The route from the top of the quarry road beside the fence is best used in descent.

For fuller details of the Great Howe route, see Grey Crag 4.

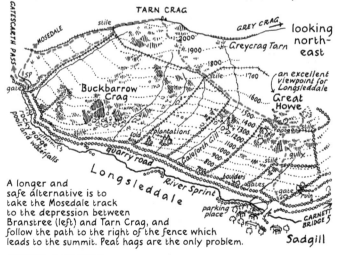

looking north-east

A longer and safe alternative is to take the Mosedale track to the depression between Branstree (left) and Tarn Crag, and follow the path to the right of the fence which leads to the summit. Peat hags are the only problem.

OTHER ASCENTS:
From Swindale or Shap, the obvious route of approach is by Brunt Tongue, an easy ascent. The summit fence needs to be scaled.

From the Kendal–Shap Road, the various routes pass first over Grey Crag (for details see Grey Crag 5 to 8). Clear, settled weather is essential on these unfrequented approaches.

THE SUMMIT

Not until Manchester Corporation's engineers climbed Tarn Crag, in the course of their duty, and departed from it for the last time, did its summit acquire distinction: the wide dreary top then found itself left with a curious structure — a high wooden platform with a core of stone and concrete, which served for a time as a survey pillar during the construction of the Longsleddale tunnel conveying the Haweswater Aqueduct south. Nowadays, the aqueduct is in place and the scars are gone from the valley — but the hoary survey pillar still stands, defying the weather and puzzling the few travellers who come this way and find no clue as to its purpose. No trace of the wooden platform remains, however.

The highest part of the fell, marked by an undistinguished cairn, larger than in the illustration above, is a hundred yards away, to the east.

DESCENTS: The routes of ascent should be used for descent. *In mist*, keep strictly to the fences. Crags obstruct the direct way down into Longsleddale. Eastwards, Shap Fells are a wilderness to avoid in bad weather.

The wooden structure has now gone

THE VIEW

Anyone who climbs Tarn Crag for a view of Lakeland will be very disappointed, for, excepting the Coniston fells, nothing is to be seen of the distant west because of the adjacent heights across the deep trench of Longsleddale. On a clear day there is ample recompense, however, in the excellent panorama from east round to south — where, for a hundred miles, the noble skyline of the Pennines and the wide seascape of Morecambe Bay present themselves to view without obstruction.

Principal Fells

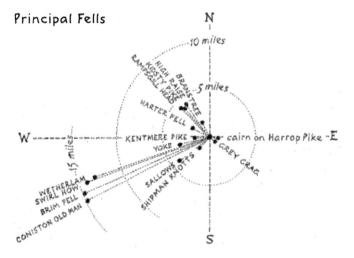

Lakes and Tarns : SW: Windermere

Kentmere Pike
across Longsleddale

RIDGE ROUTES

To BRANSTREE, 2339′ : 1¾ miles · N, then NW
Depression at 1650′ : 700 feet of ascent

Rough grass, but easy gradients; safe in mist.

This is a long featureless walk, marshy underfoot in places: interest is confined to the views of Longsleddale and Harter Fell. Traces of a cart track may indicate the route taken up the easy slope of Tarn Crag for the transport of material when the survey pillar was under construction. Keep to the left of the wall on Branstree for the best views, to the right of it for shelter from rain.

To GREY CRAG, 2093′
¾ mile · NE, then SE and S
Depression at 1940′: 170 feet of ascent

An easy walk, wet in places.

This walk is best accomplished by following the fence across the depression to avoid the marsh that masquerades as Greycrag Tarn. An unusual cluster of three fence posts is a landmark at the halfway point.

In mist, Grey Crag is better left alone.

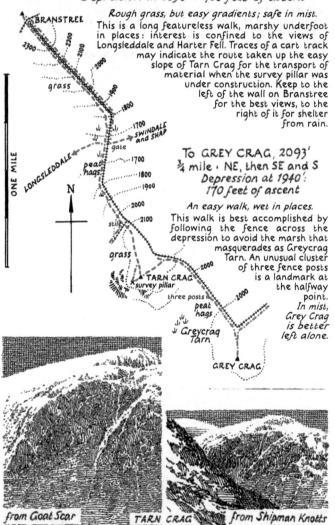

from Goat Scar

TARN CRAG

from Shipman Knotts

Buckbarrow Crag

Thornthwaite Crag 2569'

OS grid ref: NY432100

Hartsop

HIGH
STREET

CAUDALE
MOOR

THORNTHWAITE
CRAG

ILL BELL

Kentmere

Troutbeck

MILES
0 1 2 3 4

from Caudale Moor

NATURAL FEATURES

Occupying a commanding position overlooking four valleys, Thornthwaite Crag is one of the better-known fells east of Kirkstone, owing not a little of its fame to its tall pillar of stones, a landmark for miles around. Its name derives from the long shattered cliff facing west above the upper Troutbeck valley; there are also crags fringing the head of Hayeswater Gill and above the early meanderings of the River Kent. Apart from these roughnesses the fell is grassy, the ground to the east of the summit forming a wide plateau before rising gently to the parent height of High Street, of which Thornthwaite Crag is a subsidiary; it has, however, a ridge in its own right, this being a narrow steep-sided shoulder that ends in Gray Crag, northwards. Streams flow in three directions: north to Ullswater, south to Windermere and south-east along the Kentmere valley.

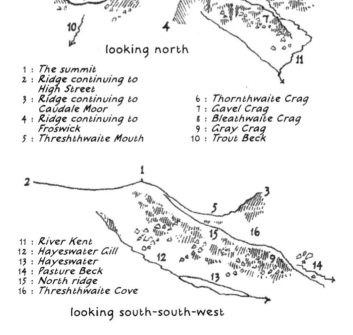

looking north

1 : The summit
2 : Ridge continuing to High Street
3 : Ridge continuing to Caudale Moor
4 : Ridge continuing to Froswick
5 : Threshthwaite Mouth
6 : Thornthwaite Crag
7 : Gavel Crag
8 : Bleathwaite Crag
9 : Gray Crag
10 : Trout Beck
11 : River Kent
12 : Hayeswater Gill
13 : Hayeswater
14 : Pasture Beck
15 : North ridge
16 : Threshthwaite Cove

looking south-south-west

Thornthwaite Crag 3

MAP

Hall Cove, the source of the River Kent, is hidden from view lower down the valley by the substantial buttress of Gavel Crag.

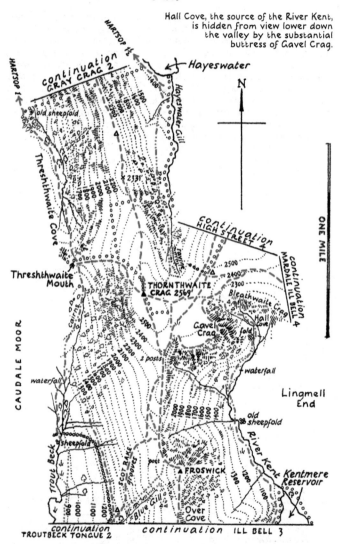

Threshthwaite Mouth, the narrow, well defined depression between Thornthwaite Crag and Caudale Moor, has an elevation of 1950'.

ASCENT FROM HARTSOP
2000 feet of ascent : 3¼ miles

Pronounce 'Threshthwaite' *Thresh'et*

THORNTHWAITE CRAG

HIGH STREET

CAUDALE MOOR

Threshthwaite Mouth

GRAY CRAG

Threshthwaite Cove

Raven Crag

There is shelter among the boulders below Raven Crag, an impressive object on the right.

Hayeswater Gill

Hayeswater

moraines

Threshthwaite Glen

sheepfold

kissing gate

former filter house

Wath Bridge

old mine

old mine

ruin

grid

gate

gate

gate

gate

car park

Hartsop

Between 1908 and 2014 Hayeswater was a reservoir serving Penrith. It has now reverted to a natural tarn. See *The Knott 2* for details.

If descending *via* Gray Crag, it is important to remember that the path makes a sharp right turn at the 1600' contour shortly before a crag.

In mist, use the Threshthwaite route only.

looking south-south-east

This is a very interesting and enjoyable expedition. Of the three routes illustrated, that *via* Hayeswater starts well but has a tame and tiring conclusion. If the return is to be made to Hartsop, Threshthwaite is the best approach, the descent being made along the north ridge over Gray Crag, which itself has an airy situation and good views.

ASCENT FROM TROUTBECK
2200 feet of ascent
5 miles via Scot Rake; 5½ via Threshthwaite Mouth

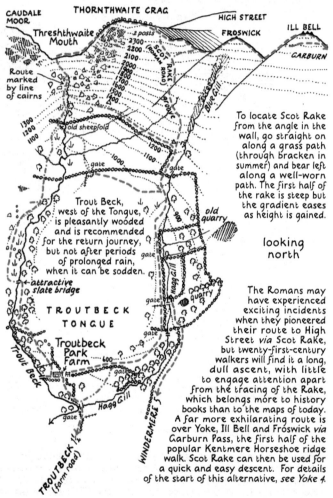

CAUDALE MOOR

THORNTHWAITE CRAG

HIGH STREET

FROSWICK

ILL BELL

Threshthwaite Mouth

GARBURN

2 posts
2300
2200
2100
2000
1900
1800
1700
1600
1500
1400

SCOT RAKE (ROMAN ROAD)

Blue Gill

Route marked by line of cairns

1300
1200
1100

old sheepfold

1200
1100

1000

gate

gate

1000

looking north

old quarry

gate

Ill Gill

gate

quarry

Trout Beck, west of the Tongue, is pleasantly wooded and is recommended for the return journey, but not after periods of prolonged rain, when it can be sodden.

attractive slate bridge

TROUTBECK TONGUE

Troutbeck Park Farm

gate

600

gate

Trout Beck

Hagg Gill

gate

WINDERMERE 5

TROUTBECK 1½ (farm road)

To locate Scot Rake from the angle in the wall, go straight on along a grass path (through bracken in summer) and bear left along a well-worn path. The first half of the rake is steep but the gradient eases as height is gained.

The Romans may have experienced exciting incidents when they pioneered their route to High Street *via* Scot Rake, but twenty-first-century walkers will find it a long, dull ascent, with little to engage attention apart from the tracing of the Rake, which belongs more to history books than to the maps of today. A far more exhilarating route is over Yoke, Ill Bell and Froswick *via* Garburn Pass, the first half of the popular Kentmere Horseshoe ridge walk. Scot Rake can then be used for a quick and easy descent. For details of the start of this alternative, see *Yoke 4*.

Scot Rake is the usual route, and the quickest, the Rake itself being visible from a distance slanting up the hillside ahead. The ascent is easy underfoot.

ASCENT FROM KENTMERE RESERVOIR
1650 feet of ascent : 2 miles

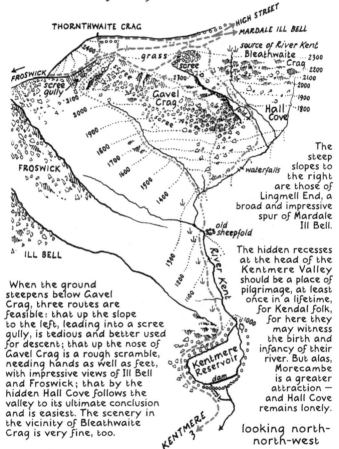

THORNTHWAITE CRAG

HIGH STREET

MARDALE ILL BELL

source of River Kent

grass

scree

Bleathwaite Crag

2400

FROSWICK

scree gully

2100

2000

1900

1800

1700

1600

1500

1400

Gavel Crag

scree

2300

2300
2200
2100
2000
1900
1800

Hall Cove

FROSWICK

ILL BELL

waterfalls

old sheepfold

River Kent

1300

1200

1100

1000

Kentmere Reservoir

dam

KENTMERE 3

The steep slopes to the right are those of Lingmell End, a broad and impressive spur of Mardale Ill Bell.

The hidden recesses at the head of the Kentmere Valley should be a place of pilgrimage, at least once in a lifetime, for Kendal folk, for here they may witness the birth and infancy of their river. But alas, Morecambe is a greater attraction — and Hall Cove remains lonely.

When the ground steepens below Gavel Crag, three routes are feasible: that up the slope to the left, leading into a scree gully, is tedious and better used for descent; that up the nose of Gavel Crag is a rough scramble, needing hands as well as feet, with impressive views of Ill Bell and Froswick; that by the hidden Hall Cove follows the valley to its ultimate conclusion and is easiest. The scenery in the vicinity of Bleathwaite Crag is very fine, too.

looking north-north-west

The summit of Thornthwaite Crag lies to the west of the line of the main ridge from Yoke—Ill Bell—Froswick to High Street and is out of sight during the ascent until the ridge is gained.

This approach leads into the unfrequented dalehead of Kentmere and abounds in interest and variety all the way from the village. Rainsborrow Crag, up on the left, is a tremendous object *en route*, and Ill Bell and Froswick reveal themselves most effectively.

THE SUMMIT

Thornthwaite Beacon

It is sometimes difficult to recall the details of familiar summits but surely all who have climbed Thornthwaite Crag will identify it in memory by its remarkable 14-foot column, one of the most distinctive cairns in Lakeland. It stands in the angle of a wall that traverses the summit. A few outcrops of flaky rock in the vicinity relieve the general grassiness of the top of the fell.

DESCENTS : In clear weather all the routes of ascent may be reversed, but that to Kentmere *via* Gavel Crag is not suggested nor should routes be 'invented' as there is rough ground about.

In bad conditions, descend to Troutbeck or Hartsop *via* Threshthwaite Mouth — to which the wall leads when followed north-west. For Kentmere, go to the end of the wall eastwards ; here turn right along a faint path for 200 yards to a scree gully on the left, which descend. A longer, but still safe descent for Kentmere or Troutbeck, is *via* Froswick, Ill Bell and Yoke to Garburn.

looking north to
Ullswater

Threshthwaite Mouth

looking south to
Windermere

THE VIEW

Principal Fells

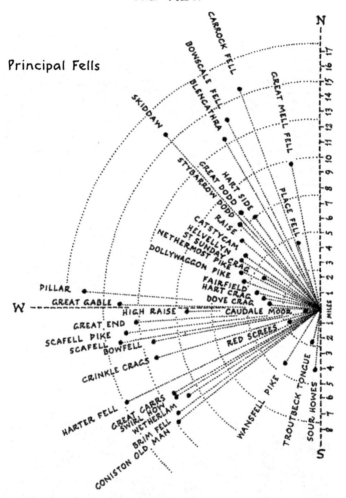

Lakes and Tarns

SSW: *Windermere* (two sections)
NNW: The upper reach of *Ullswater* may be seen by descending the
      west slope for 50 yards, or by following the wall north.
N: *Hayeswater* is brought into view by a short walk (130 yards) in the
    direction of High Street.

THE VIEW

The tall column, the wall, and adjacent high ground northwards between them interrupt the panorama — and various 'stations' must be visited to see all there is to see. The view is good, but not amongst the best; the northern prospect, in particular, is best surveyed from the slope going down to Threshthwaite Mouth.

The best feature in the scene is Windermere, to which the Troutbeck valley leads the eye with excellent effect.

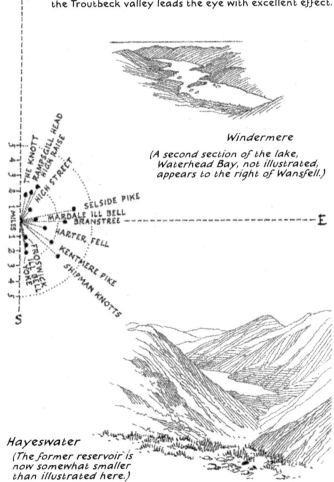

Windermere

(A second section of the lake, Waterhead Bay, not illustrated, appears to the right of Wansfell.)

Hayeswater
(The former reservoir is now somewhat smaller than illustrated here.)

RIDGE ROUTES

To CAUDALE MOOR, 2502': 1 mile: NW, W and WSW
Depression at 1950': 560 feet of ascent

A rough scramble, made safe in mist by walls.

There is more to this walk than appears at first sight, for the gap of Threshthwaite Mouth is deep and it links slopes that are steep and rough. Keep by the wall until the broken crag of Caudale is left behind. An easy but pathless alternative is to swing left from the thin path to Gray Crag and avoid the rough section on grass, *but not in mist.* The Caudale flank above the gap can be dangerous when the rocks are iced or under snow.

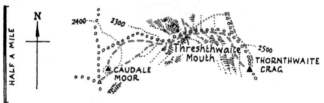

To GRAY CRAG, 2286': 1¼ miles: slightly W of N
Two minor depressions: 150 feet of ascent

An easy, interesting walk, better avoided in mist.

Straightforward walking along the descending and narrowing north ridge leads first to the nameless conical height of point 2331' then to the flat top of Gray Crag. Two broken walls are crossed *en route.* Both flanks are heavily scarped and *dangerous in mist.*

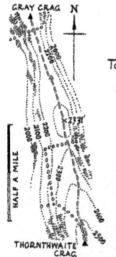

To FROSWICK, 2359'
1 mile
SSE then S and SE
Depression at 2100'
300 feet of ascent

A very easy walk. Follow the path by the broken wall to the south-south-east. When the wall bends left, continue straight on along the path to a junction marked by two posts. A long grassy descent leads to the final rise to the neat summit of Froswick.

RIDGE ROUTES

To HIGH STREET, 2718′ : 1¼ miles : SE, then E and NE
Depression at 2475′ : 250 feet of ascent

A very simple walk : safe in mist.

Take the prominent path east from Thornthwaite Crag and follow it as far as the wall corner. Then follow the broken wall to the top of High Street. All is grass.

To MARDALE ILL BELL, 2496′
1⅓ miles : SE, then E, ENE and ESE
Depressions at 2475′ and 2350′ : 200 feet of ascent

Easy walking, but a confusing area in mist.

Leave the corner of the High Street wall by a plain track trending eastwards and when this curves right go straight on over long grass in the same direction, descending slightly to the depression ahead. *In mist*, take care not to descend to the right into Hall Cove.

*Thornthwaite Crag
from the south ridge
of Caudale Moor*

Troutbeck Tongue   1191'

properly named
The Tongue, Troutbeck Park

OS grid ref: NY422064

from the Kirkstone-Windermere road

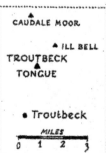

There are many Tongues in Lakeland, all of them wedges of high or rising ground between enclosing becks that join below at the tip, but none is more distinctive or aptly named than that in the middle of the Troutbeck Valley. Other Tongues usually have their roots high on a mountainside, but this one thrusts forward from the floor of the dalehead. Although of very modest altitude, it has an attraction for the gentle pedestrian as a viewpoint for the valley, and makes an admirable short excursion in pleasant scenery from Windermere or Troutbeck or, by Skelghyll Wood, from Ambleside.

MAP

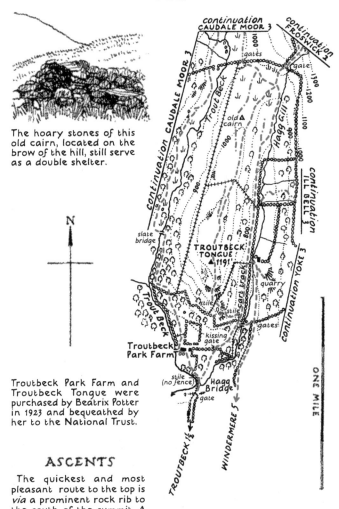

The hoary stones of this old cairn, located on the brow of the hill, still serve as a double shelter.

N

Troutbeck Park Farm and Troutbeck Tongue were purchased by Beatrix Potter in 1923 and bequeathed by her to the National Trust.

ASCENTS

The quickest and most pleasant route to the top is *via* a prominent rock rib to the south of the summit. A good path ascends from the cart track just beyond the angle of the wall south-east of the summit, avoiding crags.

The longer way, along the Tongue from the north, is the simplest of walks (visit the ancient cairn) but the pattern of the irrigation ditches here is a warning to expect much marshy ground.

THE SUMMIT

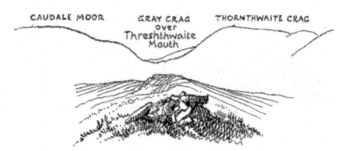

CAUDALE MOOR   GRAY CRAG over Threshthwaite Mouth   THORNTHWAITE CRAG

The rocky scramble up the south ridge from the cart track is entertaining enough to hold out the promise of a summit equally interesting, but the promise is not fulfilled by the reality, which is a grassy knoll a little higher than several more nearby, and graced by a small heap of stones. Apart from the view down the valley to Windermere, nothing here is worth comment.

DESCENTS : The quickest and easiest way down is *via* the ridge south to the cart track. *It is safe in mist.*

Slate bridge, Trout Beck

THE VIEW

Troutbeck Tongue is set deep
in the bottom of a great bowl
of hills, all of which overtop it
and limit the scene. Only to the
south is there an open view –
of Windermere – but there is
also a peep of distant fells
to the west.

Principal Fells

HART CRAG (Caudale Moor)
CAUDALE MOOR
GRAY CRAG
THORNTHWAITE CRAG
RED SCREES
FROSWICK
ILL BELL
N
YOKE
W
E
SCAFELL PIKE
BOW FELL
5 miles
20 miles
CRINKLE CRAGS
PIKE O' BLISCO
WANSFELL
SALLOWS
10 miles
Dodd Hill (Wansfell)
SOUR HOWES
S

Lakes and Tarns
SSW: *Windermere*
(middle and lower reaches)

Windermere and the Troutbeck Valley

Wansfell

1597'

OS grid ref: NY404053
(Wansfell Pike : OS grid ref: NY394042)

CAUDALE
▲ MOOR
▲
RED SCREES

▲ WANSFELL
● Ambleside

● Troutbeck

MILES
0   1   2   3

from High Grove

NATURAL FEATURES

Caudale Moor sends out three distinct ridges to the south, and the most westerly and longest of the three descends to a wide depression (crossed by the Kirkstone road) before rising and narrowing along an undulating spur that finally falls to the shores of Windermere. This spur is Wansfell, and although its summit ridge is fairly narrow and well defined, the slopes on most sides are extensive, the fell as a whole occupying a broad tract of territory between Ambleside and the Troutbeck valley. Except northwards, the lower slopes are attractively wooded ; the upper reaches are mainly grassy, but at the south-west extremity of the ridge there is a rocky bluff known as Wansfell Pike, which is commonly but incorrectly regarded as the top of the fell. It certainly receives more visitors than the true summit one mile to the north-east. Other crags masked by trees flank the Kirkstone road at Troutbeck, and Jenkins Crag in Skelghyll Wood is a very popular viewpoint. On the eastern flanks of the fell, in the village of Troutbeck, are three wells: St John's Well, St James' Well and Margaret's Well. Although no longer used as a source of water they can still be easily identified by their inscriptions.

MAP

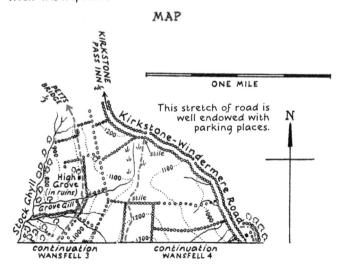

ONE MILE

This stretch of road is well endowed with parking places.

N

continuation
WANSFELL 3

continuation
WANSFELL 4

MAP

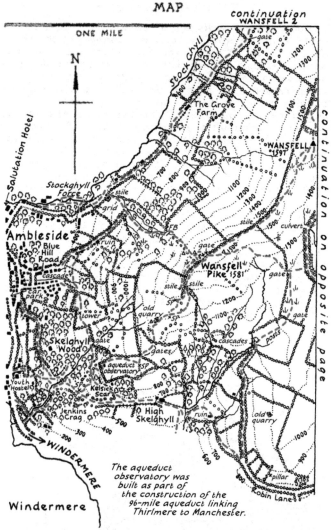

continuation
WANSFELL 2

ONE MILE

N

Salutation Hotel

Stock Gyll

continuation on opposite page

gate

1200

1300

1400

1500

The Grove Farm

WANSFELL 1597

Stockghyll Force

stile

grid

FB

1000

700

800

900

1100

1200

1300

1400

1500

stile

1500

culvert

1300

Ambleside

Blue Hill Road

cascade

ruin

gate

Wansfell Pike 1581

gate

stile   stile

SP

1200

stile

car park

tower

old quarry

×sp

1100

gate

Skelghyll Wood

gates

cascades

gate

posts

aqueduct observatory

SP

800

700

Kelsick Scar

Youth Hostel

Jenkins Crag

High Skelghyll

ruin

old quarry

1000

200   300   400   500

600

700

800

900

pillar

WINDERMERE

Robin Lane

The aqueduct observatory was built as part of the construction of the 96-mile aqueduct linking Thirlmere to Manchester.

Windermere

The rocky viewpoint of Jenkins Crag may be spelled 'Jenkyns', 'Jenkyn' or 'Jenkin.' The National Trust sign at the site states 'Jenkins', The Ordnance Survey 2½" map identifies it as 'Jenkin', while the Harveys equivalent opts for 'Jenkin's.' Periodically, trees at the site are lopped to maintain the view (see page 6).

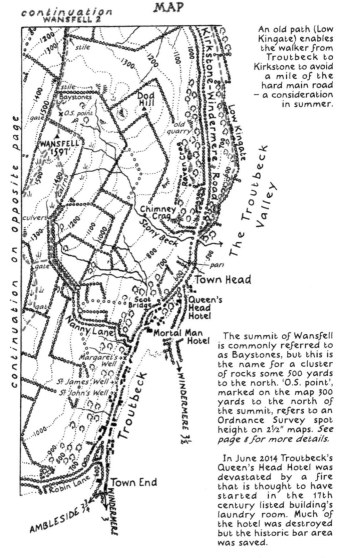

MAP

continuation WANSFELL 2

continuation on opposite page

An old path (Low Kingate) enables the walker from Troutbeck to Kirkstone to avoid a mile of the hard main road – a consideration in summer.

The summit of Wansfell is commonly referred to as Baystones, but this is the name for a cluster of rocks some 500 yards to the north. 'O.S. point', marked on the map 300 yards to the north of the summit, refers to an Ordnance Survey spot height on 2½″ maps. *See page 8 for more details.*

In June 2014 Troutbeck's Queen's Head Hotel was devastated by a fire that is thought to have started in the 17th century listed building's laundry room. Much of the hotel was destroyed but the historic bar area was saved.

Robin Lane and Nanny Lane are both wide tracks and are ideal for pedestrians ; they are not suitable for motor vehicles.

ASCENT FROM AMBLESIDE
1500 feet of ascent : 2½ miles

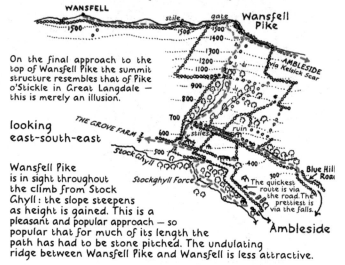

On the final approach to the top of Wansfell Pike the summit structure resembles that of Pike o'Stickle in Great Langdale — this is merely an illusion.

looking east-south-east

Wansfell Pike is in sight throughout the climb from Stock Ghyll: the slope steepens as height is gained. This is a pleasant and popular approach — so popular that for much of its length the path has had to be stone pitched. The undulating ridge between Wansfell Pike and Wansfell is less attractive.

ASCENT FROM TROUTBECK
1100 feet of ascent : 1¾ miles

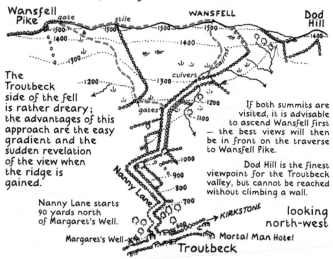

The Troutbeck side of the fell is rather dreary; the advantages of this approach are the easy gradient and the sudden revelation of the view when the ridge is gained.

Nanny Lane starts 90 yards north of Margaret's Well.

If both summits are visited, it is advisable to ascend Wansfell first — the best views will then be in front on the traverse to Wansfell Pike.

Dod Hill is the finest viewpoint for the Troutbeck valley, but cannot be reached without climbing a wall.

looking north-west

ASCENT FROM AMBLESIDE
1550 feet of ascent : 2¼ miles

There are three ways to reach the aqueduct observatory : *via* Blue Hill Road is the most interesting; *via* Old Lake Road the most commonly used; *via* Waterhead the quickest. A signpost, 15 yards before the path to Jenkins Crag, indicates the footpath to Kelsick Scar and Wansfell.

For beauty, seclusion and a seldom-seen side to Wansfell, this is the best approach. In autumn the trees of Skelghyll Wood are a joy, and the views from the path above the aqueduct observatory are charming throughout the year. Save it for a clear day.

looking east

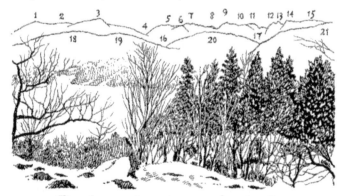

The view westwards from Jenkins Crag

1 : Coniston Old Man	8 : Scafell	15 : Pavey Ark
2 : Brim Fell	9 : Bowfell	16 : Little Langdale
3 : Wetherlam	10 : Esk Pike	17 : Great Langdale
4 : Wrynose Pass	11 : Great End	18 : Black Fell
5 : Cold Pike	12 : Loft Crag	19 : Park Fell
6 : Pike o'Blisco	13 : Pike o'Stickle	20 : Lingmoor Fell
7 : Crinkle Crags	14 : Harrison Stickle	21 : Loughrigg Fell

THE SUMMIT

CAUDALE MOOR   THORNTHWAITE CRAG

Kirkstone Pass

Threshthwaite Mouth

THE VIEW
FROM THE SUMMIT OF WANSFELL

As a viewpoint, the highest point of the summit is inferior to the lower Wansfell Pike, and, curiously, fewer fells can be seen. Nevertheless, the prospect westwards is very charming.

Principal Fells

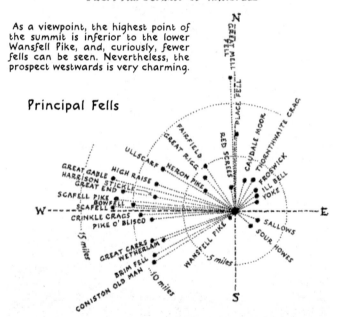

Lakes and Tarns
S: *Windermere*
WSW: *Little Langdale Tarn*
W: *Grasmere*
W: *Rydal Water*

Red Screes, from the summit

THE SUMMIT

The summit of Wansfell is marked by a well-built cairn about 4' high (not in the illustration on the facing page). However, the Ordnance Survey 2½" map shows a spot height, north beyond the fence and broken wall, of 487 metres (1597'). This is the same height as the summit, which is clearly higher, suggesting an error by O.S. A mile to the south-west is the lower Wansfell Pike; its accepted 'summit' is the rocky knoll with views of Ambleside.

....

THE VIEW
FROM WANSFELL PIKE

Wansfell Pike excels in its view of Windermere, the graceful curve of the lake showing to great advantage. Ambleside, below, is a splendid prospect. Westwards, the scene is especially beautiful. Red Screes is a fine object in the north; the east is dull.

Principal Fells

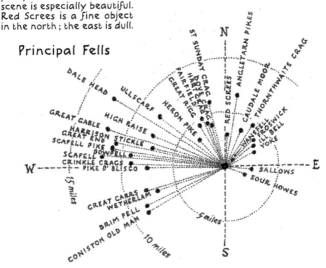

Lakes and Tarns

S: *Windermere*
SW: *Blelham Tarn*
W: *Little Langdale Tarn*
WNW: *Grasmere*
WNW: *Rydal Water*

The two sheets of water on the lower slopes of Sour Howes, south-east, are reservoirs.

Windermere, from Wansfell Pike

RIDGE ROUTE

To CAUDALE MOOR, 2502'
4½ miles : N, then NE and E
Depression at 1100'
1550 feet of ascent

A long, easy, uninteresting trudge
– the longest ridge walk between
two summits in Lakeland.

In May 2005, when the Countryside
and Rights of Way Act came into
effect, this route benefited from
the removal of PRIVATE notices
and the provision of stiles
between Wansfell and the
Windermere—Kirkstone Pass
road. This route is safe
in mist, but underfoot,
marshy patches may
prove unpleasant.
See *Caudale Moor 5*
for more details about
the route onwards from
St Raven's Edge.

Aqueduct
observatory
above
Kelsick Scar

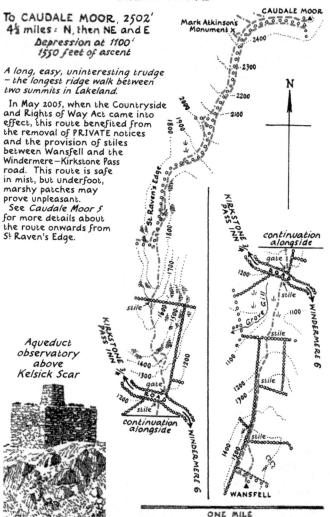

There are two such edifices, and a tower, above the line of the
Thirlmere aqueduct along the southern slopes of Wansfell Pike. Locating
them is a pleasant way of spending a halfday: an art lies in doing
this *sans* wallscaling.

Stockghyll Force

Wether Hill

OS grid ref: NY456168

2210'
approx

from Beda Fell

Howtown

LOADPOT
▲ HILL

Bampton

▲
WETHER HILL

▲ HIGH RAISE

MILES

0   1   2   3   4

NATURAL FEATURES

The High Street range has largely lost its appeal to the walker by the time he reaches the twin grassy mounds of Wether Hill on the long tramp along its spine northwards, and there is nothing here to call for a halt. The top, scarcely higher than the general level of the ridge, is quite without interest, while the eastern slopes are little better although traversed by two good routes from Bampton; but the western flank, characteristically steeper, has the peculiarity of Gowk Hill, a subsidiary height which itself develops into a parallel ridge running north to Steel Knotts: this encloses, with the main ridge, the little hidden valley of Fusedale. The best features of Wether Hill, paradoxically, are found in its valleys: eastwards, Cawdale Beck and Measand Beck have attractions rarely visited except by the lone shepherd; westwards, Fusedale Beck is fed from two wooded ravines, and here too is lovely Martindale.

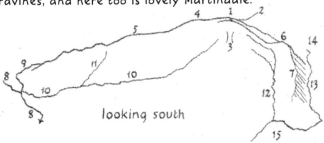

looking south

Haweswater
from the Standing Stones above Burnbanks

1 : The summit
2 : Ridge continuing to High Raise
3 : Ridge continuing to Loadpot Hill
4 : High Kop
5 : Low Kop
6 : Gowk Hill
7 : Steel Knotts
8 : River Lowther
9 : Haweswater Beck
10 : Cawdale Beck
11 : Willdale Beck
12 : Fusedale Beck
13 : Howe Grain
14 : Martindale
15 : Ullswater

Gowk Hill

Gowk Hill, at 1545', is 130' higher than Steel Knotts, but it is the shapely lower height that attracts fellwalkers, who tend to ignore its bigger sibling. However, the summit is worth visiting for its excellent views of upper Martindale.

MAP

Wether Hill's slopes sprawl extensively eastwards, descending gradually in easy ridges to a wide belt of cultivated land west of the Bampton—Burnbanks road — from which the ascent will generally be commenced on this side. No details of this cultivated area are depicted on the following maps (*on pages 5 and 6*) other than those necessary to get the walker to the open fell as quickly as possible.

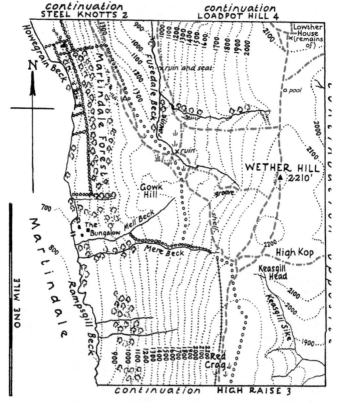

The good path into Fusedale starting from near Keasgill Head is the easiest way to descend from the main ridge to the west. Progress is swift down the easy grassy slope.

MAP

The eastern slopes of Wether Hill are bounded on the north by Cawdale Beck and on the south by Measand Beck, both attractive streams, but some detail of the adjacent fells is, in addition, given below because they carry routes that lead onto Wether Hill. The fell's territory reaches as far as the shores of Haweswater, *via* the broad ridge that extends past Low Kop to the east.

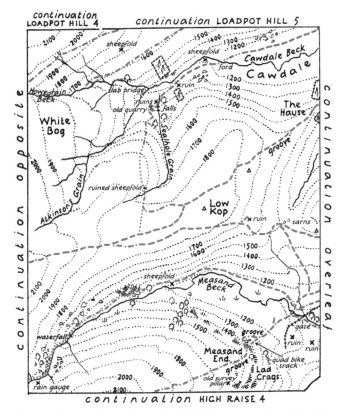

The subsidiary height of Low Kop (1876') appears to be a separate fell when viewed from The Hause, but is of little significance when reached — the path does not even make a detour to its grassy top.

MAP

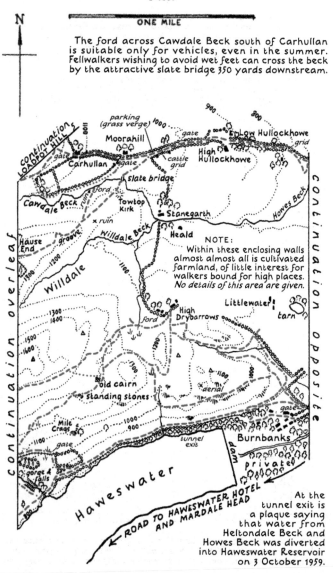

ONE MILE

The ford across Cawdale Beck south of Carhullan is suitable only for vehicles, even in the summer. Fellwalkers wishing to avoid wet feet can cross the beck by the attractive slate bridge 350 yards downstream.

N

parking (grass verge)

continuation LOADPOT HILL

Moorahill

gate

Low Hullockhowe

grid

High Hullockhowe

Carhullan

gate

cattle grid

slate bridge

Cawdale Beck

ruin   ford

Towtop Kirk

Stanegarth

Howes Beck

continuation opposite

x ruin

Hause End

groove

Willdale Beck

Heald

NOTE:
Within these enclosing walls almost almost all is cultivated farmland, of little interest for walkers bound for high places. No details of this area are given.

Willdale

continuation overleaf

ford

High Drybarrows

Littlewater tarn

aerial

old cairn
standing stones

Mile Crags

gate

gate

Burnbanks

private

gorge & falls

tunnel exit

dam

Haweswater

ROAD TO HAWESWATER HOTEL AND MARDALE HEAD

At the tunnel exit is a plaque saying that water from Heltondale Beck and Howes Beck was diverted into Haweswater Reservoir on 3 October 1959.

MAP

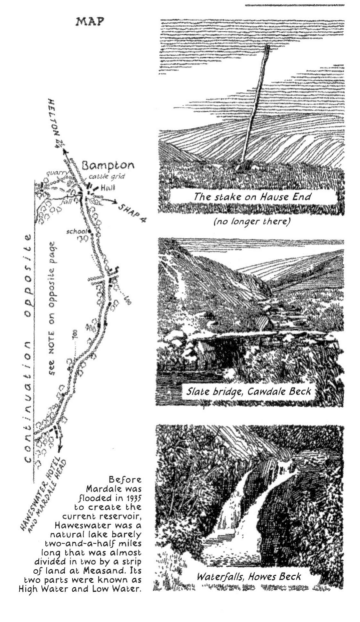

HELTON

Bampton

quarry

cattle grid
Hall

SHAP 4

fall

school

see NOTE on opposite page

continuation opposite

100

700

HAWESWATER HOTEL
AND MARDALE HEAD

Before Mardale was flooded in 1935 to create the current reservoir, Haweswater was a natural lake barely two-and-a-half miles long that was almost divided in two by a strip of land at Measand. Its two parts were known as High Water and Low Water.

The stake on Hause End

(no longer there)

Slate bridge, Cawdale Beck

Waterfalls, Howes Beck

ASCENTS from HOWTOWN and MARTINDALE
1750 feet of ascent, 3 miles, from Howtown
1550 feet of ascent, 2½ miles, from Martindale old church

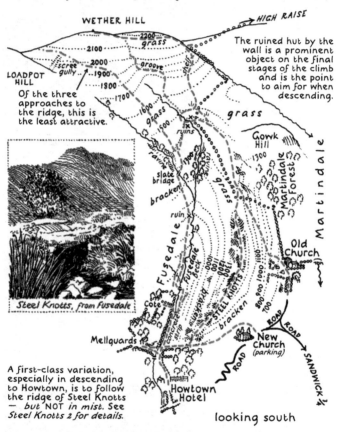

WETHER HILL

HIGH RAISE

2200 grass

2100

LOADPOT HILL

scree gully

2000

1900

1800

1700

groove

shelf

Of the three approaches to the ridge, this is the least attractive.

The ruined hut by the wall is a prominent object on the final stages of the climb and is the point to aim for when descending.

grass

grass

ruins

Gowk Hill

Martindale Forest

Martindale

Fusedale

Fusedale Beck

ruin

slate bridge

bracken

Old Church

ravine

grass

STEEL KNOTTS

bracken

Cote

concrete strip

Steel Knotts, from Fusedale

Mellguards

New Church (parking)

ROAD

ROAD

SANDWICK ¾

Howtown Hotel

A first-class variation, especially in descending to Howtown, is to follow the ridge of Steel Knotts — but NOT in mist. See Steel Knotts 2 for details.

looking south

Of the two routes from the ruined hut, that *via* the groove is the most direct, but is steeper. The shelf route to the main ridge near Keasgill Head is better used as a fast and easy way down.

There are many fells more worthy of climbing than Wether Hill, the final slope being very dull, but there are no more delightful starting points than Howtown and Martindale, the approach from the latter being especially good — until the last slope is reached.

ASCENTS FROM BURNBANKS AND BAMPTON
1550 feet of ascent from Burnbanks; 1750 from Bampton. 4½ miles from Burnbanks direct, 5 via Measand Beck; 5 miles from Bampton

The path over High Kop joins the path to the summit behind the ridge →

HIGH RAISE

WETHER HILL

LOADPOT HILL

High Kop

peat hags

White Bog

pool

2100
2000
1900

Black fell ponies graze on Wether Hill. Deer are often in sight on the top slopes.

HIGH RAISE

Knott Hill Sike

peat hags

ravine

Atkinson's Grain

ruined sheepfold

1900
1800

1700

rain gauge

waterfall

Sealhole Grain

grass

1600

1500

ruins and old quarry

Measand Beck has many falls and inviting pools.

Low Kop

groove

1700 1600 1500 1400 1300

old sheepfold

LOADPOT HILL

ruin (old quarry)

The Hause

Hause End.

1200

Cawdale Beck

HIGH RAISE

sheepfold

small tarns

1500

Willdale Beck

groove

1300

Measand Beck

grass

ruin

ruin

gate

standing stones

Willdale

ford

1200

1100

Carhullan

gate

falls

old cairn

Towtop Kirk →×
slate bridges

ford

Moorahill

parking on verge

cattle grid

Mile Crags

1200

1000

bracken

ford

High Drybarrows

1100

old aerial

High Hullockhowe

Low Hullockhowe

1000

900

dam

gate

box

900

800

cattle grid

HELTON 2½

Burnbanks

Howes Beck

700

looking west

HAWESWATER HOTEL AND MARDALE HEAD →

waterfalls

quarry

Bampton

cattle grid

SHAP 4

The good path on the fellside above Burnbanks is popular because of the fine views of the length of Haweswater in the valley below.

The Bampton route *via* Hause End is easy and interesting; the Burnbanks route across the open common is a little confusing in its early stages; on a hot day the Measand route, although pathless beyond the sheepfold, is attractive.

THE SUMMIT

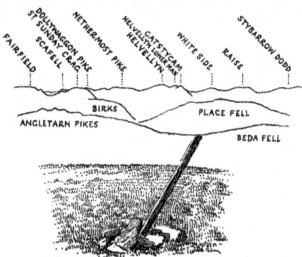

FAIRFIELD · SCAFELL · ST SUNDAY CRAG · DOLLYWAGGON PIKE · NETHERMOST PIKE · HELVELLYN LOWER MAN · HELVELLYN · CATSTYCAM · WHITE SIDE · RAISE · STYBARROW DODD

BIRKS · PLACE FELL

ANGLETARN PIKES

BEDA FELL

Two rounded grassy mounds of similar altitude, separated by a slight depression, form the summit. The more extensive of the two mounds, the southern, is quite featureless: the smaller northern mound, which is the recognised top, carries a small summit cairn in which the wooden stake shown in the illustration was formerly set; today the cairn remains but the stake has gone. The summit is popular with grazing animals of various species, but humans will find it a dreary and uninteresting place. The High Street crosses the top, but along here it is barely noticeable, being no more distinct than a sheep trod.

DESCENTS: All slopes are easy, and it is a waste of time to look for the few paths. For Bampton, pass over High Kop to join one of two good grooves. For Martindale and Howtown descend west to the ruin by a prominent broken crosswall below: leave the ruin on the right, passing through the gateway in the wall, for Martindale; but for Fusedale and Howtown leave the ruin well to the left.

In mist, there is little danger of accident, but keep out of stream beds which run in ravines.

Former boundary stone on High Kop, with High Raise in the background

THE VIEW

Principal Fells

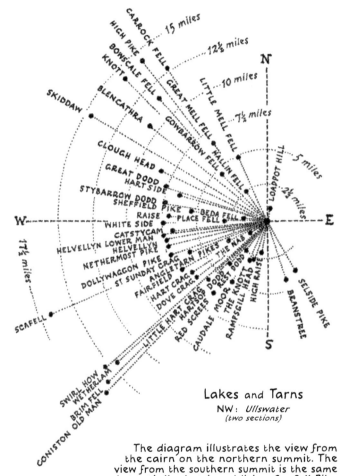

Lakes and Tarns
NW: *Ullswater*
(two sections)

The diagram illustrates the view from the cairn on the northern summit. The view from the southern summit is the same substantially, but in addition Scafell Pike can be seen. There is a wide prospect of the Pennines, but undoubtedly the best feature is the finely grouped Helvellyn and Fairfield fells across the rough, romantic Martindale country.

RIDGE ROUTES

To LOADPOT HILL, 2201' : 1 mile : N
Depression at 2025' : 180 feet of ascent

An easy walk, safe in mist.

Keep to the path on the left of the depression; all traces of the old path on the right side (the High Street) have vanished. The chimney stack of Lowther House, once a prominent landmark on this route, is now just a pile of stones — the summit (quartz cairn) is directly beyond.

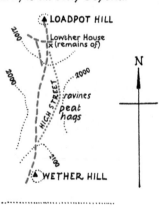

To HIGH RAISE, 2634'
2¼ miles : SSW
*Depression at 2150'
500 feet of ascent*

A long easy walk, safe in mist.

A clear path is to be found to the west of both summits of Wether Hill; it continues all the way to High Raise. The northern part of the wall is ruinous as far as Red Crag and beyond, its function having been taken over by the nearby fence. The southern part of the wall has been restored. When the wall ends, the path climbs across the open fell. The cairn is a hundred yards away to the left of the path at its highest point.

Measand Beck   The Forces of
Measand Beck
near its outlet into Haweswater, need
no introduction to frequenters of this
area, but the waterfalls illustrated, two
miles upstream, are rarely seen.

Yoke

2316'

OS grid ref: NY438067

▲ HIGH STREET

▲ ILL BELL
▲ YOKE

● Kentmere

● Troutbeck

MILES
0   1   2   3   4

from the Kirkstone-Windermere road

NATURAL FEATURES

Yoke is best known as the southern outpost of the Ill Bell ridge leading up to High Street from Garburn Pass, and is usually dismissed as a dull unattractive mound. As seen from Troutbeck, this seems a quite accurate assessment, but the Kentmere flank is very different, abounding in interest. On this side, below the summit, is the formidable thousand-foot precipice of Rainsborrow Crag (the safety of which is a subject of disagreement between rock climbers and foxes) and, rising above Kentmere village, is a knobbly spur that looks like the knuckles of a clenched fist — a place of rocky excrescences, craggy tors and tumbled boulders, and a fine playground for the mountaineering novice. Both flanks of Yoke carry the scars of old quarrying operations.

1 : The summit
2 : Garburn Pass
3 : Rainsborrow Crag
4 : Skeel Crags
5 : Buck Crag
6 : Castle Crag
7 : Piked Howes
8 : Ewe Crags
9 : Cowsty Knotts
10 : Raven Crag
11 : Badger Rock
12 : Lowther Brow
13 : Kentmere Reservoir
14 : Bryant's Gill
15 : River Kent
16 : Hall Gill
17 : Trout Beck
18 : Rainsborrow Tarn

looking north

Rainsborrow Tarn stands on the very edge of the crags, so much so that, from certain angles, it looks as if the water is flowing over the edge. *Do not search for this tarn in mist.*

MAP

A quirk of Garburn Pass is that neither of the two paths that lead north to Yoke start from the summit of the pass. The old path, following the wall north from the gate, is actually about 15 yards down the Kentmere flank from the highest point of the pass. The newer (western) path, which starts from a cairn at a point where the Garburn road makes a 90-degree turn, is about 250 yards from the summit of the pass. These days, very few walkers choose the path by the wall even if approaching from Kentmere: it is muddy and marshy, whereas the new path has been remade for much of its length and is generally dry underfoot.

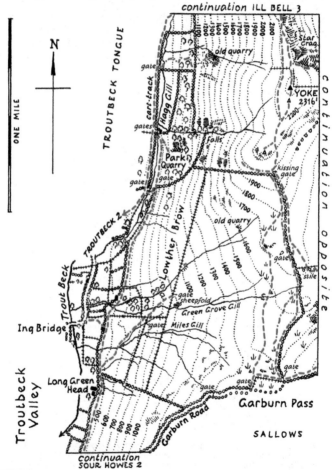

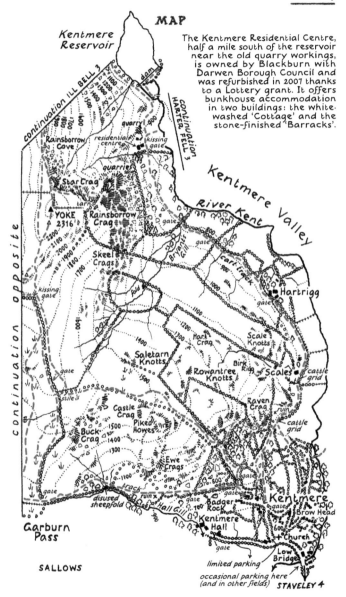

MAP

Kentmere
Reservoir

The Kentmere Residential Centre,
half a mile south of the reservoir
near the old quarry workings,
is owned by Blackburn with
Darwen Borough Council and
was refurbished in 2007 thanks
to a Lottery grant. It offers
bunkhouse accommodation
in two buildings: the whitewashed 'Cottage' and the
stone-finished 'Barracks'.

continuation ILL BELL 3

dam

continuation HARTER FELL 3

quarry

residential centre

kissing gate

Rainsborrow Cove

quarries

Star Crag

Kentmere Valley

River Kent

continuation opposite

YOKE
2316

Rainsborrow Crag

tarn

gate

Bryant Gill

gate

800

Skeel Crags

cart track

900

Hartrigg

kissing gate

ford

1000

gate

1100

1200

Hart Crag

Scale Knotts

gate

1400

1700

Soletarn Knotts

1500

Rowantree Knotts

Birk Rigg

Scales

cattle grid

gate

Castle Crag

Piked Howes

Raven Crag

ruin

cattle grid

Buck Crag

1500
1400
1300

stile

Ewe Crags

1100

spr.

track

gate

800

gate

Kentmere

gate

Brow Head

gate

disused sheepfold

Hall Gill

ruin x

700

Badger Rock

Kentmere Hall

gate

Church

Garburn
Pass

Low
Bridge

limited parking

occasional parking here
(and in other fields)

SALLOWS

STAVELEY 4

ASCENT FROM GARBURN PASS
850 feet of ascent : 1¼ miles

(3½ miles from Kentmere Church)
(4½ miles from Troutbeck Church)

A path bypasses the summit of Yoke to the west, but is seldom used by walkers: the fell top is established as a part of the popular Kentmere Horseshoe ridge walk. Fashions change; in 1955 the western path was the only path across the top of the fell, perhaps used by walkers on their way to (perceived) better things, in the shape of Ill Bell.

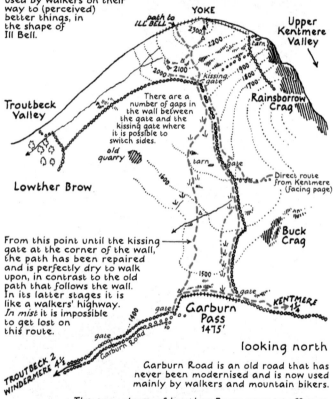

There are a number of gaps in the wall between the gate and the kissing gate where it is possible to switch sides.

From this point until the kissing gate at the corner of the wall, the path has been repaired and is perfectly dry to walk upon, in contrast to the old path that follows the wall. In its latter stages it is like a walkers' highway. *In mist it is impossible to get lost on this route.*

looking north

Garburn Road is an old road that has never been modernised and is now used mainly by walkers and mountain bikers.

The easy slopes of Lowther Brow seem to offer an alternative route from Troutbeck, but the promising tracks climbing through the bracken from the path behind Long Green Head (see map) do not continue far and the ascent becomes tiresome.

This is a dull, easy walk, but the dreary foreground is relieved by the splendid views to the west. It is the start (or end) of the popular Kentmere Horseshoe walk.

ASCENT FROM KENTMERE
1800 feet of ascent : 2½ miles (3 miles via Garburn Pass)

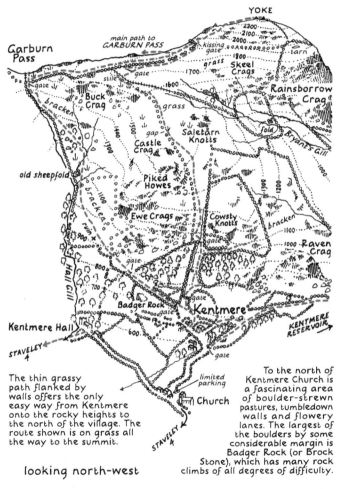

looking north-west

The thin grassy path flanked by walls offers the only easy way from Kentmere onto the rocky heights to the north of the village. The route shown is on grass all the way to the summit.

To the north of Kentmere Church is a fascinating area of boulder-strewn pastures, tumbledown walls and flowery lanes. The largest of the boulders by some considerable margin is Badger Rock (or Brock Stone), which has many rock climbs of all degrees of difficulty.

Although Garburn Pass offers the easiest route, the craggy screen rising steeply behind the village will tempt the more adventurous walker: the top of the spur is a maze worth exploring, but only the route depicted guarantees to avoid unclimbable walls.

THE SUMMIT

The highest point on the broad grassy top is a small rock-sided platform with a cairn, which is no longer as imposing as the one illustrated. Another cairn (a better viewpoint) stands 130 yards to the south.

DESCENTS : Either use the summit path or make a short descent down the western slope to the 'bypass' track skirting the summit : this, followed to the left (south), leads to the 'highway' path that goes down to Garburn Pass.

In mist, note that the north-east and east slopes are entirely dangerous, and that the lower western flank is very rough : it features, in a walled enclosure, the bracken-concealed, fearful abyss of Park Quarry, a fall into which would definitely end the day's walk. From the top cairn, descend west (170 yards only) to the track and turn left; alternatively, use the path to the south from the summit — both will lead to the good path (the westerly one) going down to Garburn Pass. When you reach the pass, at a prominent cairn, turn left for Kentmere or go straight on for Troutbeck.

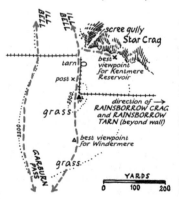

Park Quarry — in the sheltered depths of which flowers bloom and ferns flourish in December

THE VIEW

This is a good viewpoint, more particularly for the wide sweep of country and sea southwards. Of the Lakeland scene, the prospect due west is especially attractive.

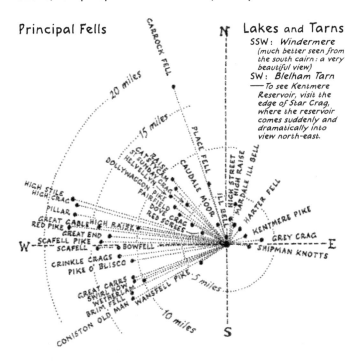

Principal Fells

CARROCK FELL
PLACE FELL
CAUDALE MOOR
20 miles
15 miles
CATSTYCAM
ST. SUNDAY CRAG
HELVELLYN
RAISE
DOLLYWAGGON PIKE
FAIRFIELD
DOVE CRAG
RED SCREES
HIGH STILE
HIGH CRAG
PILLAR
GREAT GABLE
RED PIKE
HIGH RAISE
GREAT END
SCAFELL PIKE
SCAFELL
BOWFELL
CRINKLE CRAGS
PIKE O' BLISCO
GREAT CARRS
SWIRL HOW
WETHERLAM
BRIM FELL
WANSFELL PIKE
CONISTON OLD MAN
5 miles
10 miles
ILL BELL
HIGH STREET
HIGH RAISE
MARDALE ILL BELL
HARTER FELL
KENTMERE PIKE
GREY CRAG
SHIPMAN KNOTTS

W — E
N
S

Lakes and Tarns

SSW: Windermere
(much better seen from the south cairn: a very beautiful view)

SW: Blelham Tarn
—To see Kentmere Reservoir, visit the edge of Star Crag, where the reservoir comes suddenly and dramatically into view north-east.

Raven Crag

Buck Crag

RIDGE ROUTE

To ILL BELL, 2484' : ⅔ mile : N
Depression at 2180' : 300 feet of ascent

An easy climb, safe in mist.

Pass a pair of old iron straining posts and cross the depression with the escarpment close by on the right. This is a simple walk in clear weather, but, although there is no difficulty in mist, it *may* then be not quite so easy to get safely off the top of Ill Bell.

HALF A MILE

To SALLOWS, 1691' : 2 miles : NE, then N

A simple walk, easy to follow in mist.

Sallows is the next fell south of Yoke, but to describe the way to it as a ridge walk is somewhat of a stretch; it is more like a route from one ridge to another. From Yoke's summit, take the path south where, at the kissing gate, it becomes a very well made track. Stay on this until Garburn Pass is reached at a cairn; go straight on in the direction of Troutbeck, going left over a stile immediately after a gate. There are two paths that lead to the distinctive summit; most walkers will choose the direct route.

Paths from Yoke

Badger Rock
(Brock Stone)

West face

East face

This isolated rock stands within fifty yards of the Garburn path, just beyond the last buildings of Kentmere. A well known local landmark, it has little fame outside the valley. Although the base of the rock is now silted up, there is little doubt that it is a boulder fallen from the fellside above, a theory supported by the cavities beneath (a refuge for foxes), and it may well be the biggest boulder in Lakeland. There are rock climbs on it of all degrees of difficulty.

Rainsborrow Crag

THE FAR EASTERN FELLS
Some Personal Notes in conclusion

It would be very remiss of me if I did not take this first opportunity publicly to acknowledge, with sincere gratitude, the many kind and encouraging letters that followed the publication of Book One. There have also been offers of hospitality, of transport (I have no car nor any wish for one), of company and of collaboration, and of financial help – all of which I have declined as gracefully as I could whilst feeling deeply appreciative, for I am stubbornly resolved that this must be a single-handed effort. I have set myself this task, and I am pigheaded enough to want to do it without help. So far, everything is all right. Sufficient copies of Book One were sold to pay the printer's bill, and here again I must thank all readers who recommended the book to others, for it is perfectly clear that, lacking full facilities for publicity and distribution, it could hardly have succeeded otherwise.

I have just completed the last page of Book Two, and feel like a man who has come home from a long and lonely journey. Rarely did I meet anyone on my explorations of the High Street fells. Usually I walked from morning till dusk without a sight of human beings. This is the way I like it, but what joys have been mine that other folk should share! Let me make a plea for the exhilarating hills that form the subject of this book. They should not remain neglected. To walk upon them, to tramp the ridges, to look from their tops across miles of glorious country, is constant delight. But the miles are long, and from one place of accommodation to another they are many. The Far Eastern Fells are for the strong walker and should please the solitary man of keen observation and imagination. Animal and bird life is much in evidence, and not the least of the especial charms of the area is the frequent sight of herds of ponies and deer that make these wild heights their home.

Perhaps I have been a little unkind to Manchester Corporation in referring to Mardale and Swindale in this book. If we can accept as absolutely necessary the conversion of Haweswater, then it must be conceded that Manchester have done the job as unobtrusively as possible. Mardale is still a noble valley. But man works with such clumsy hands! Gone for ever are the quiet wooded bays and shingly shores that Nature had fashioned so sweetly in the Haweswater of old; how aggressively ugly is the tidemark of the new Haweswater! A cardinal mistake has been made, from the walker's point of view, in choosing the site for the new hotel: much more convenient would have been a re-built Dun Bull at the head of the valley, or better still amongst the trees of The Rigg. For a walker who can call upon transport, however, the new road gives splendid access to the heart of the fells.

I leave this area to renew acquaintance with the more popular and frequented heights in the middle of Lakeland — the Langdale, Grasmere and Keswick triangle. This is a beautiful part of the district, and I shall enjoy it; but it is a weakness of mine to be for ever looking back, and often I shall reflect on the haunting loneliness of High Street and the supreme loveliness of Ullswater. It will please me then to think that this book may perhaps help to introduce to others the quiet delights that have been mine during the past two years.

Autumn, 1956   AW.

STARTING POINTS

AMBLESIDE
Wansfell 5, 6

ASKHAM
Arthur's Pike 3

BAMPTON
Loadpot Hill 9
Wether Hill 8

BURNBANKS
Wether Hill 8

CAUDALE BRIDGE
(BROTHERS WATER)
Caudale Moor 5
Hartsop Dodd 3

GARBURN PASS
(KENTMERE/TROUTBECK)
Froswick 2
Ill Bell 4
Sallows 3
Sour Howes 3
Yoke 5

HARTSOP
Brock Crags 2
Gray Crag 3
Hartsop Dodd 3
High Raise 5
High Street 5
The Knott 3
The Nab 3
Rampsgill Head 5
Rest Dodd 3
Thornthwaite
Crag 4

HELTON
Arthur's Pike 3
Loadpot Hill 9

HIGH BORRANS
Sour Howes 3

HOWTOWN
(INCL. THE HAUSE/
LANTY TARN)
Arthur's Pike 3
Bonscale Pike 3
Hallin Fell 2
Loadpot Hill 11
Steel Knotts 2
Wether Hill 7

INGS/BROWFOOT
Sour Howes 3

INGS–KENTMERE PATH
Sallows 3

KENDAL–SHAP ROAD
Grey Crag 5, 6, 7, 8

KENTMERE
(INCL. KENTMERE
RESERVOIR, GREEN
QUARTER & STILE END)
Froswick 2
Harter Fell 6
High Street 8
Ill Bell 5
Kentmere Pike 5
Mardale Ill Bell 4
Shipman Knotts 2
Sour Howes 3
Thornthwaite
Crag 6
Yoke 6

KIRKSTONE PASS
Caudale Moor 7

LONGSLEDDALE
(SADGILL)
Branstree 5
Grey Crag 4
Harter Fell 7
Kentmere Pike 6
Shipman Knotts 2
Tarn Crag 4

MARDALE
Branstree 5
Harter Fell 8
High Raise 7
High Street 6
Kidsty Pike 3
Mardale Ill Bell 5, 6
Selside Pike 5
Rampsgill Head 6

MARTINDALE
(INCL. BOREDALE
AND MARTINDALE
OLD CHURCH)
Angletarn Pikes 6
Beda Fell 3
High Raise 6
The Nab 3
Steel Knotts 2
Wether Hill 7

MOOR DIVOCK
Loadpot Hill 10

PATTERDALE
Angletarn Pikes 5
High Raise 5
High Street 5
The Knott 3
The Nab 3
Place Fell 5
Rampsgill Head 5
Rest Dodd 3

POOLEY BRIDGE
Arthur's Pike 3

SANDWICK
Hallin Fell 2
Place Fell 6

SWINDALE HEAD
Branstree 4
Selside Pike 5

TROUTBECK
Caudale Moor 8
Froswick 2
High Street 7
Ill Bell 6
Thornthwaite Crag 5
Troutbeck Tongue 2
Wansfell 5